# project 2: **Still-life with Gourds**



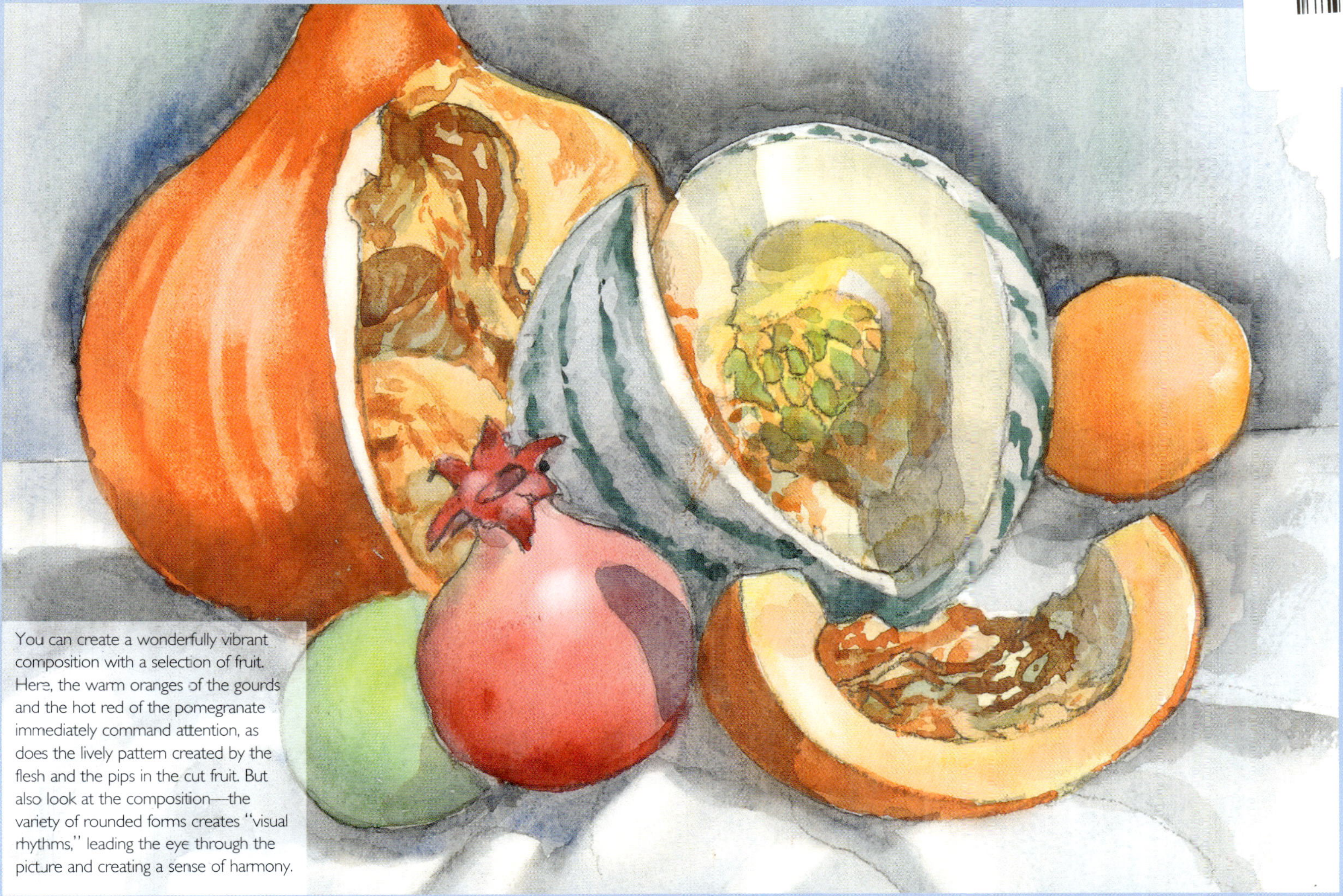

You can create a wonderfully vibrant composition with a selection of fruit. Here, the warm oranges of the gourds and the hot red of the pomegranate immediately command attention, as does the lively pattern created by the flesh and the pips in the cut fruit. But also look at the composition—the variety of rounded forms creates "visual rhythms," leading the eye through the picture and creating a sense of harmony.

- **Thick watercolor paper**
- **Watercolor palette**
- **Watercolors: ultramarine blue, burnt sienna, cadmium yellow, lemon yellow, cadmium orange, cadmium red, yellow ocher, neutral tint, viridian**
- **Brushes: No.12 round, 1-inch flat**
- **Jar of water**
- **2B pencil**
- **Eraser**
- **Kitchen towel**

**18** The painting would work better with something to draw the eye into the center, so add some rocks emerging in a diagonal line from the bottom right corner. Draw them on tracing paper first so that you can overlay them on the painting to check that they are in the right position. Make sure the rocks get smaller in size—this will help give the image an impression of depth. Then trace them onto the picture.

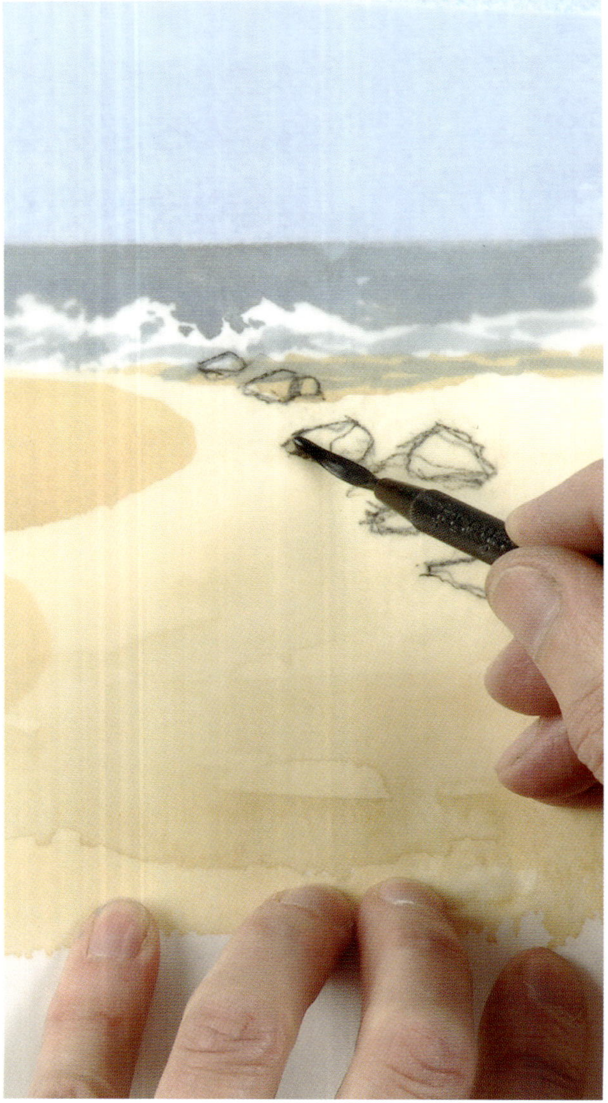

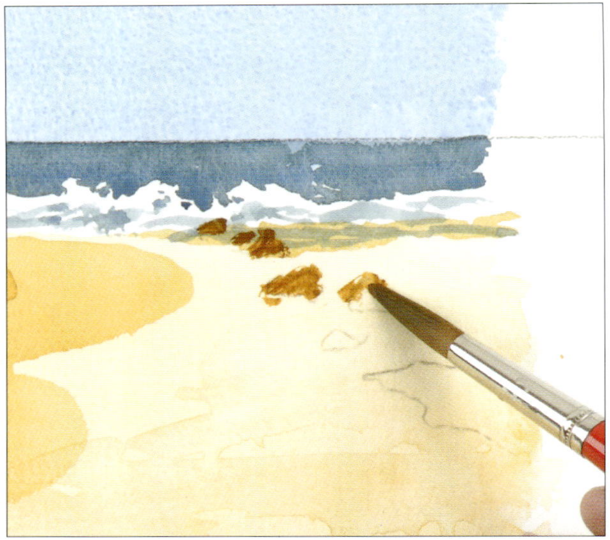

**19** Strengthen your beach wash with more raw sienna—and also add touches of raw umber and Payne's gray. Apply this mix to the rocks. Use loose brushwork to give the impression of the craggy texture of the rocks.

**20** Continue painting the rocks. Do not feel compelled to follow your outlines exactly. Rocks can be all kinds of shapes—and this variety will give the painting more life and visual interest.

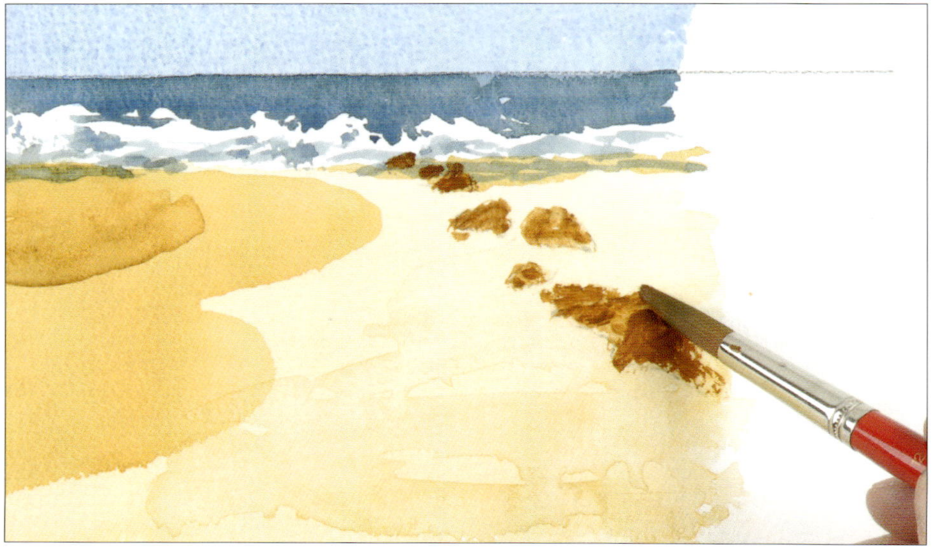

1 Begin by drawing the outlines of the fruit with a 2B pencil. Draw lightly at first, looking in particular at the exact positions where the outlines intersect with each other. Then, when you are happy with your drawing, firm up the lines, so that you can see them when you start applying the paint.

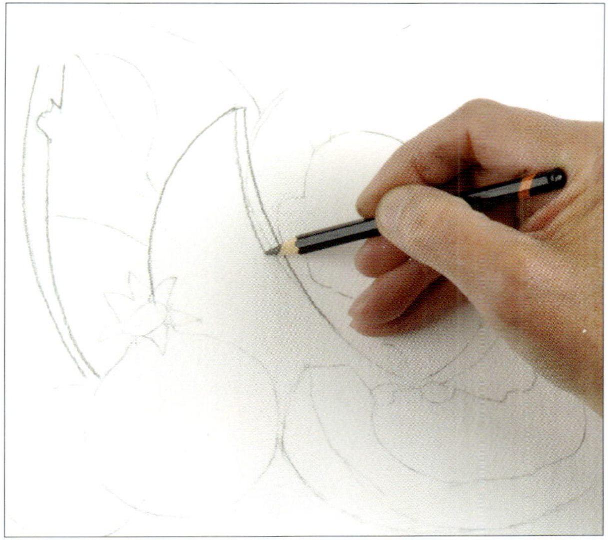

2 Continue working over the lines of your drawing. Correct any mistakes with an eraser.

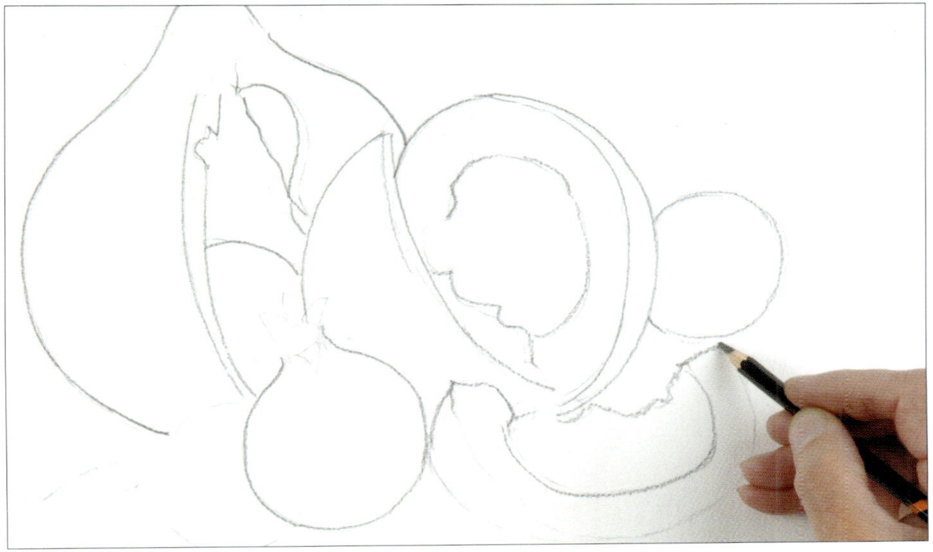

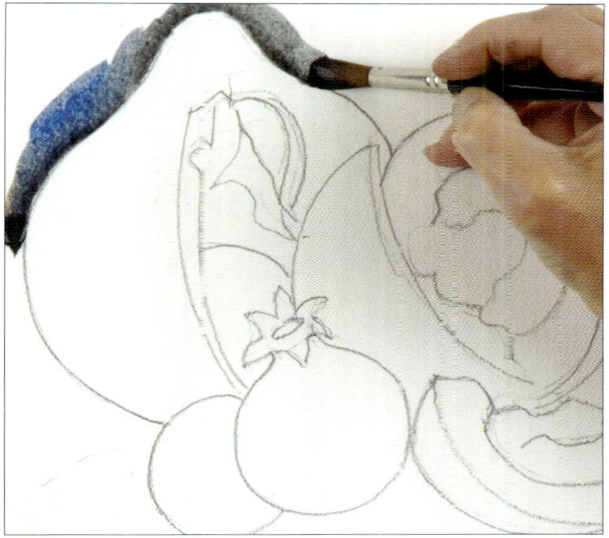

3 Now mix up a shadow tone with ultramarine and burnt sienna. Apply this to the background with the No.12 round brush. If the wash drips, touch the bead of paint with the tip of your brush and lift off the color.

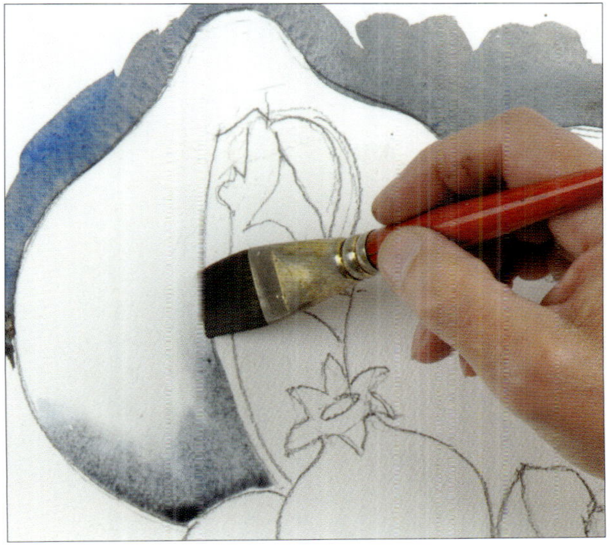

4 Finish putting in the background wash, making sure you work around the top edges of the fruit. Let the paint dry. Next, using the 1-inch flat brush, dampen the paper at the bottom of the big gourd with water. Then apply your shadow tone on top.

**15** Wash your brush in the jar of water and use it to dampen the beach in the foreground. Then float a little more of the beach mix onto the wet paper. This helps give some textural interest to the foreground.

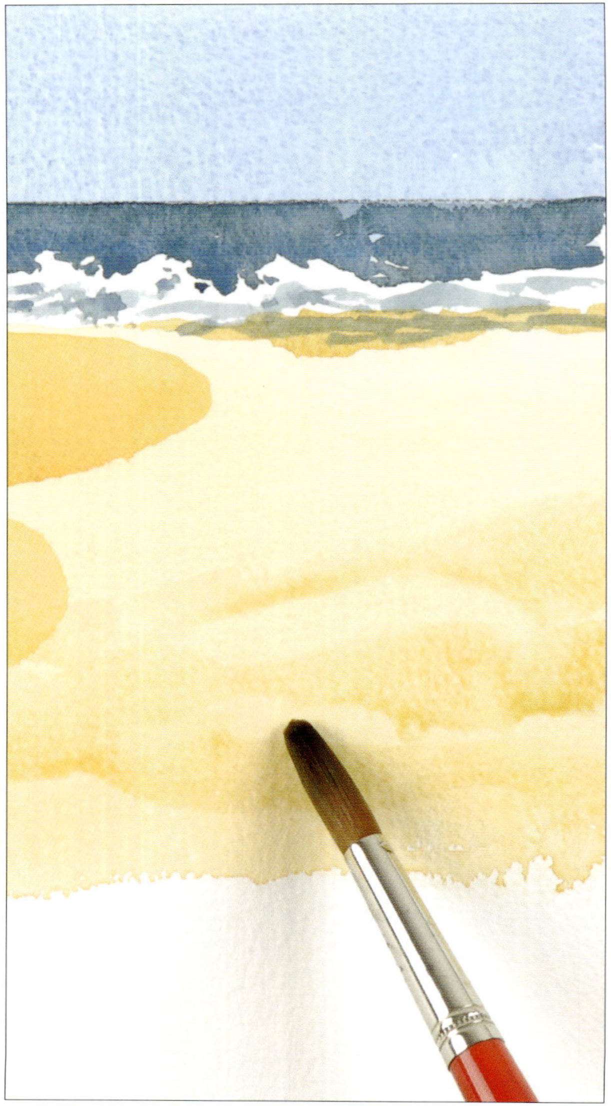

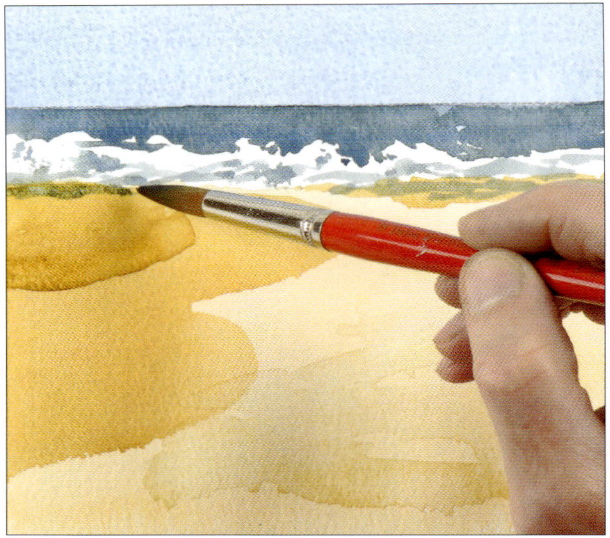

**16** Clean your brush again and add more of your wave mix over the sand. Try holding the brush toward the top of the handle—this will loosen up your painting style and help you capture the dynamic energy of the waves.

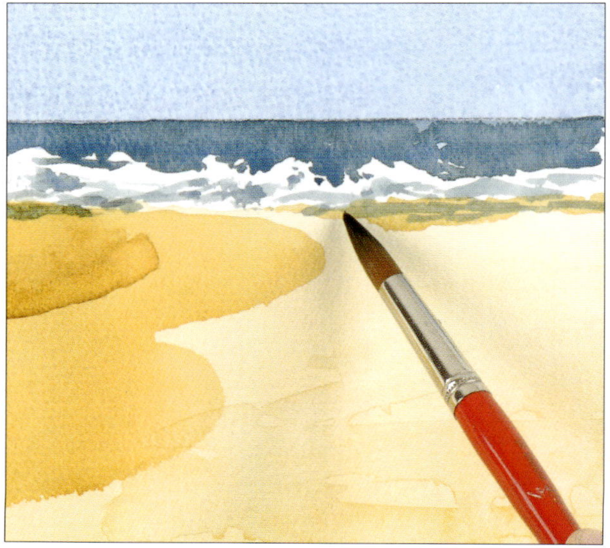

**17** Continue building up the waves with small dabs and strokes of color. Remember to leave lots of white paper showing for the spray. To add variety to your marks, hold the brush at an angle and just the graze the brush over the paper.

5 Continue to wet the shadow areas and then add your ultramarine and burnt sienna mix over the top. Note that the light is coming from the right, which means the left side of the each fruit will be in shadow.

6 Apply the shadow mix to the parts of the cut fruit that face away from the light—that is, to the left. Add the mix to the bottom and left sides of the apple, the pomegranate, and the orange.

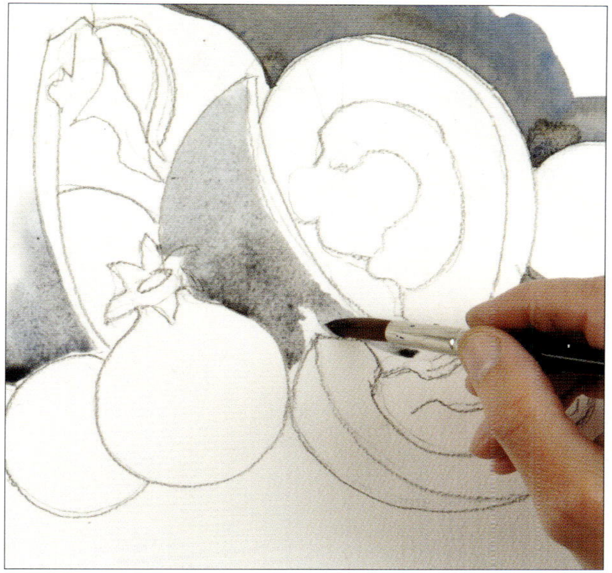

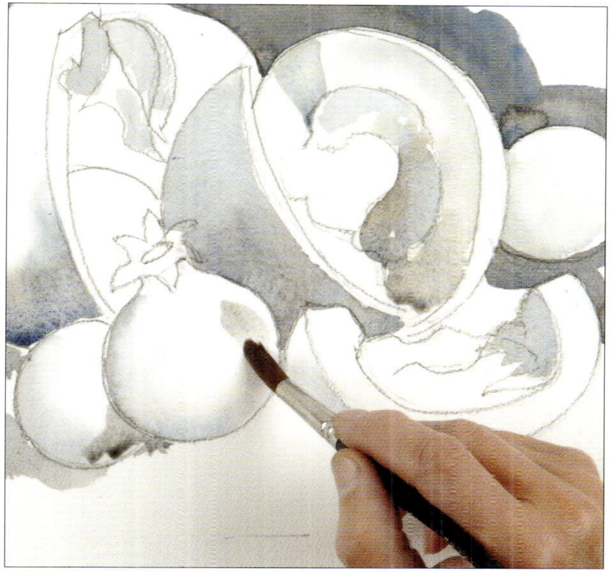

7 Now, with the same mix, add the shadows cast by the fruit. The apple and the large gourd cast shadows on the tablecloth, while the central gourd throws a shadow on the pomegranate.

8 When the shadow areas are established and dry, use an eraser to clean up any pencil lines that look too obtrusive. These lines will get trapped under the washes and be difficult to remove later. Don't remove all the pencil marks, but leave some for texture and detail.

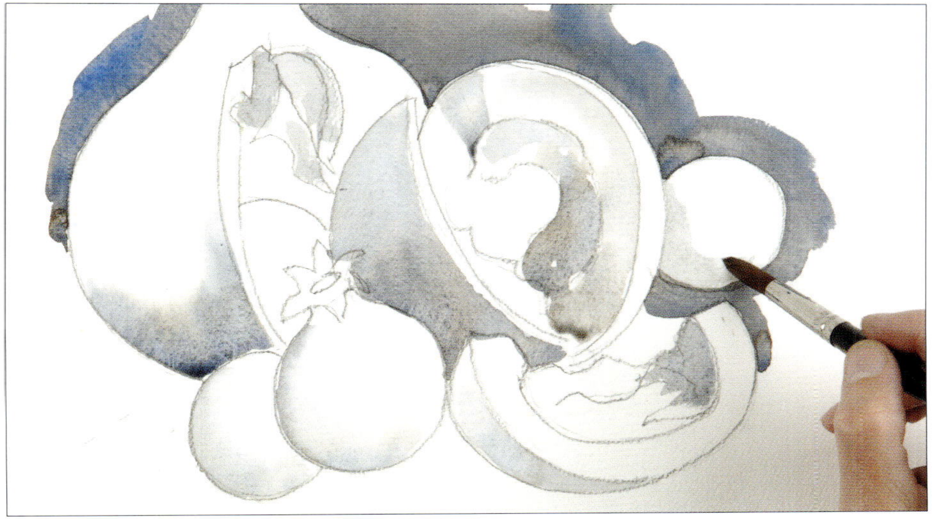

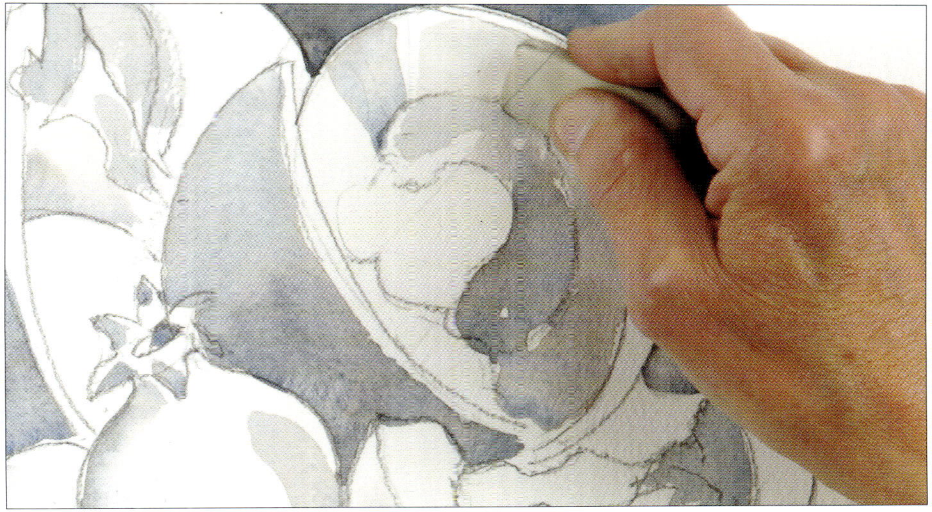

12 Let the washes dry, then add another semicircular wash for a very deep tone near the water on the left. Do not worry if a bead of paint collects at the bottom of the wash—this will dry with a definite edge and help suggest the crisp texture of wet sand.

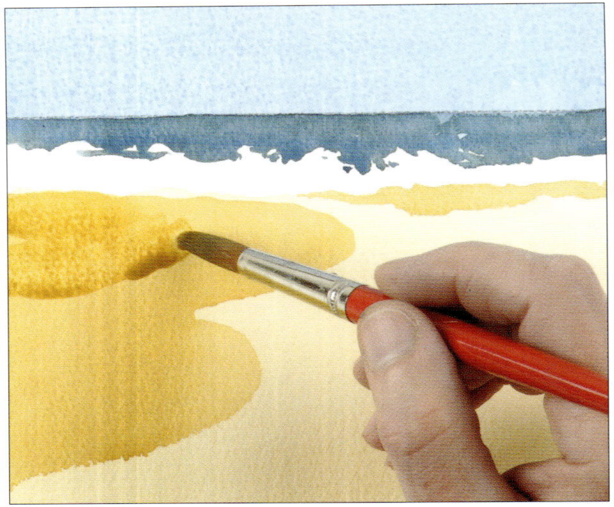

13 Now you need to give an impression of the water breaking on the shore. Clean and dry your brush in water and add a little of your sea mix to your cerulean sky wash. Begin to dab this color above the beach with the point of the brush. Do not completely fill the white paper—you want to suggest both blue water and white surf.

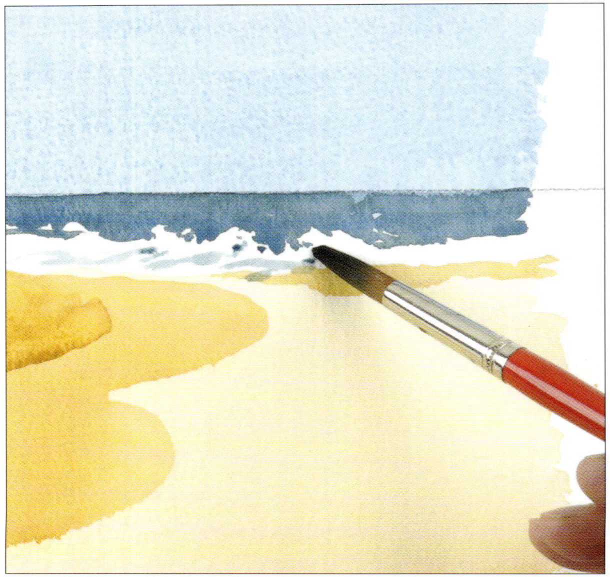

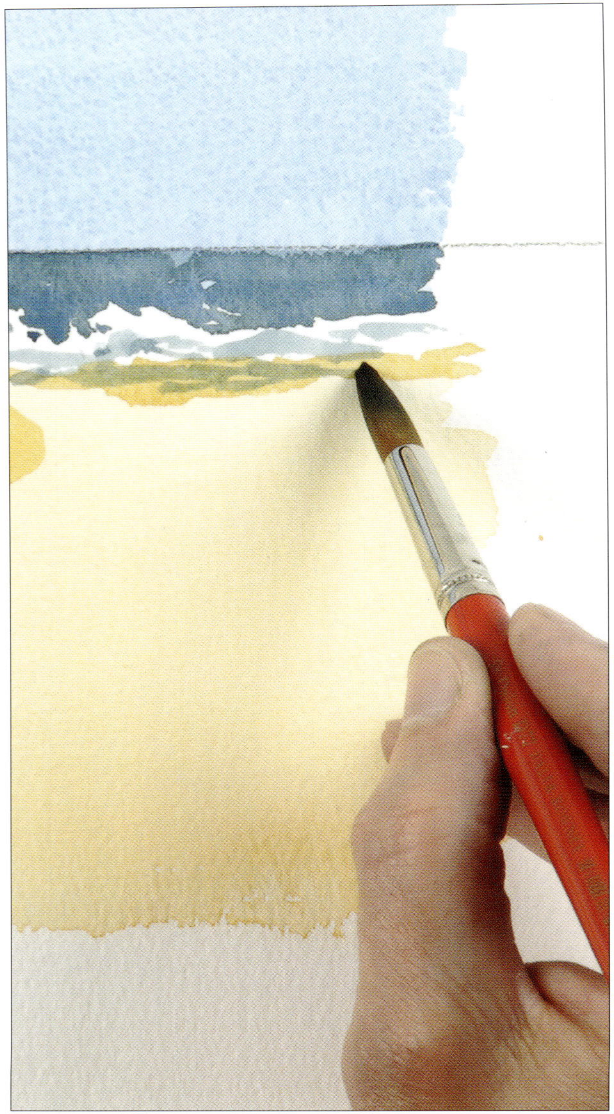

14 Add some of the wave mix over the darkened sand at the shoreline. This suggests water continually lapping over the wet sand. Note how this blue wash combines with the underlying yellow one to create a beautiful muted green.

9 Let the shadow washes dry completely, then start on the color. Do not worry about the texture or detail at this stage—just lay down flat areas of paint. Start by mixing up cadmium yellow with a touch of lemon yellow and apply this on the inside of the large gourd.

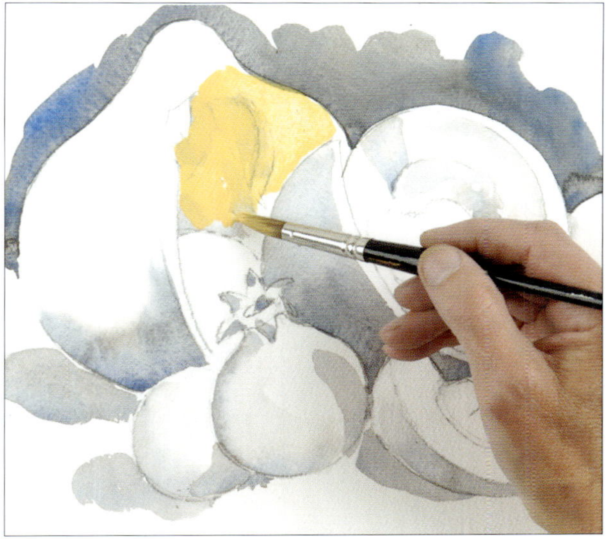

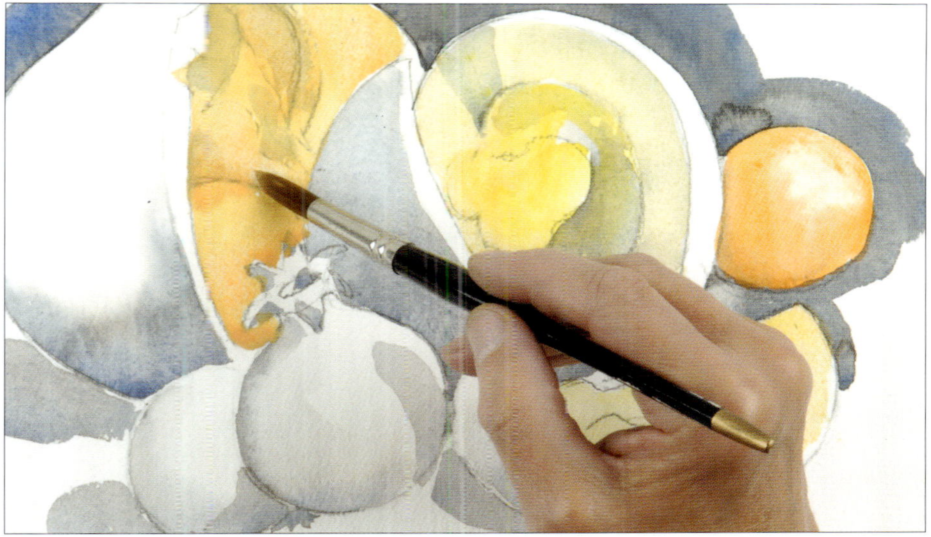

10 Use a wash of cadmium orange to paint the orange. While the paint is still wet, use a piece of kitchen towel to lift a little paint from the top of the orange. This provides an eye-catching highlight and helps convey the spherical form of the fruit.

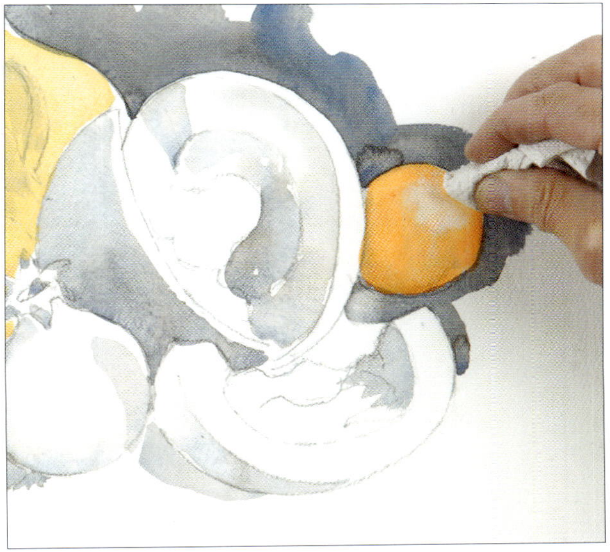

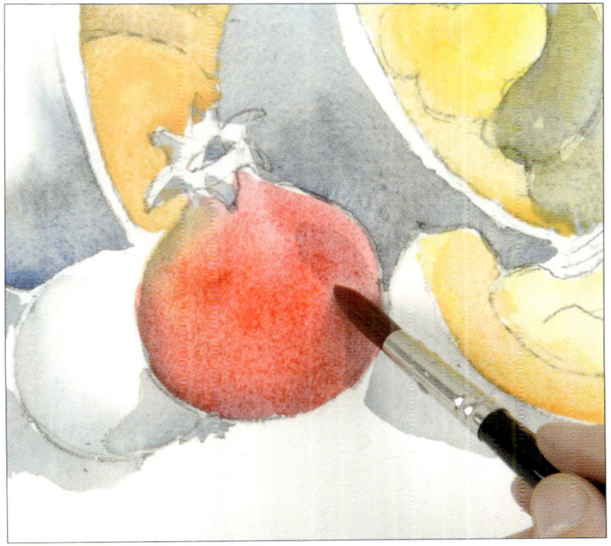

11 For the inside of the smaller gourd, apply a wash of lemon yellow. Note how the initial shadow tones turn the lemon yellow to a greenish-gray in places. Next, use cadmium orange to enhance and vary the color of the large gourd.

12 Apply a wash of cadmium red over the pomegranate. This hot red will make the pomegranate an important focal point in the picture.

9 Clean your brush in water and then mix a pale wash of raw sienna for the beach. Apply this color using a well-loaded brush and long, horizontal strokes. Make sure you leave some white paper showing between the beach and the sea for the crashing surf.

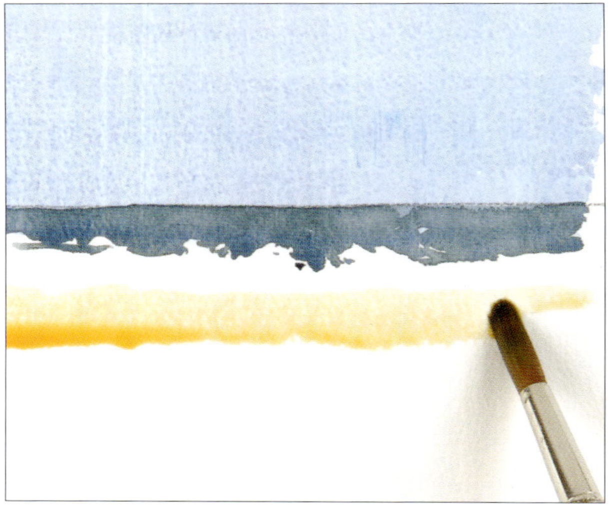

10 Continue laying in the beach wash, using long, bold horizontal strokes. Overlap the strokes slightly so the paint that collects at the bottom of one stroke is worked into the new stroke. This wash does not have to be absolutely flat like the sky —some imperfections can give interesting textural detail to the beach.

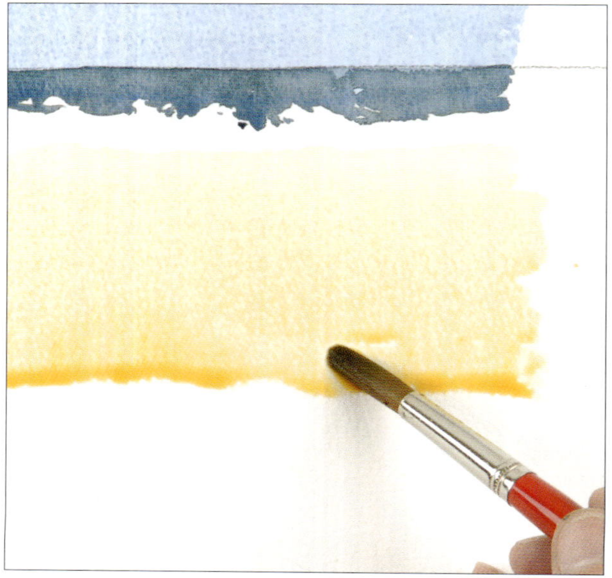

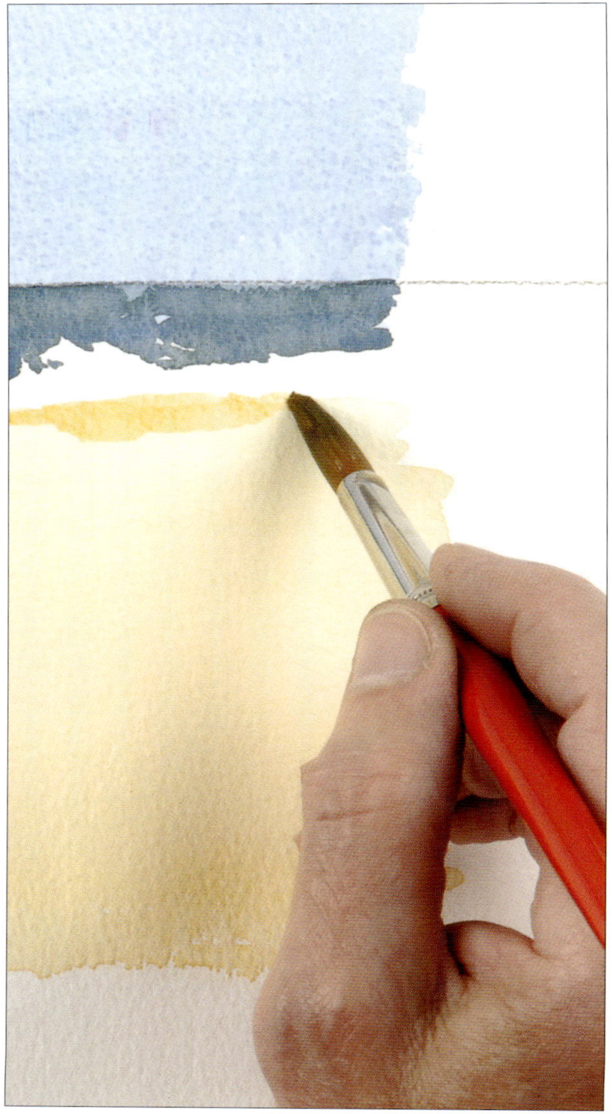

11 Finish the initial beach wash and let it dry. Now darken the mix by adding more raw sienna and a touch of Payne's gray. Use this mix to show areas on the beach where the waves have darkened the sand. Sweep the brush over the left side of the painting to create two semicircular washes. Also add smaller, gently curving strokes along the shoreline.

**13** While the paint is still wet, build up the shadowed underside of the pomegranate. This darker tone helps gives a sense of the curving form of the fruit. Let the red wash dry, then paint the apple with a green mixed from cadmium yellow and ultramarine. Add more ultramarine to the mix to paint the shadows.

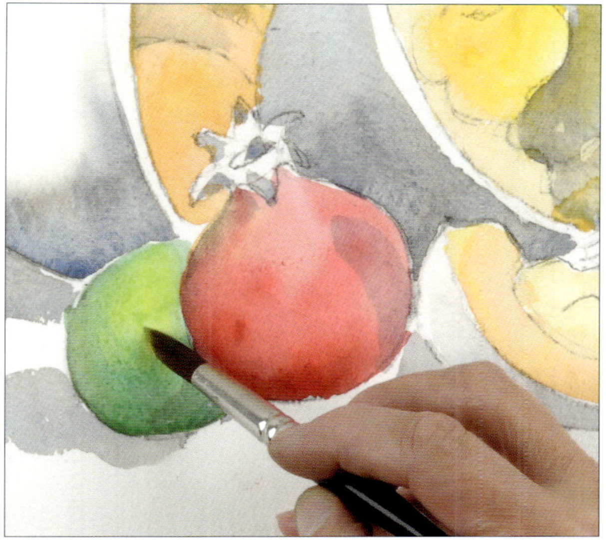

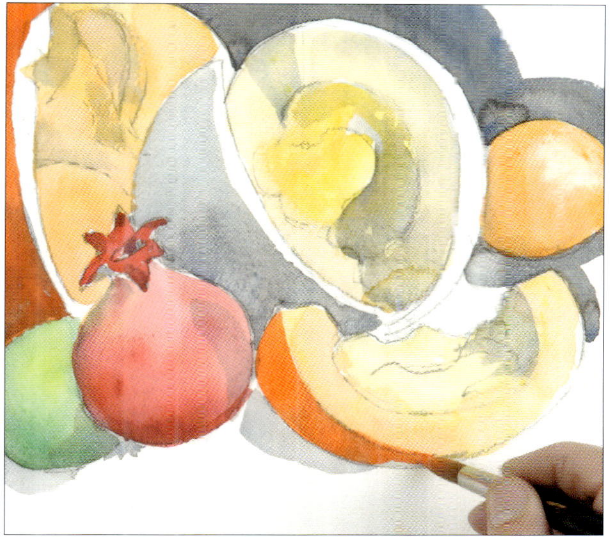

**15** For the outside of the big gourd, use cadmium orange, toned down with a touch of burnt sienna. Apply the mix with long, curving brushstrokes that follow the form of the fruit. Add a little more water to your wash, then paint the skin of the cut piece of gourd in the foreground.

**14** Now return to the cadmium red to paint the star-shaped top of the pomegranate. Use a less watered down mix of paint so you attain a deeper tone.

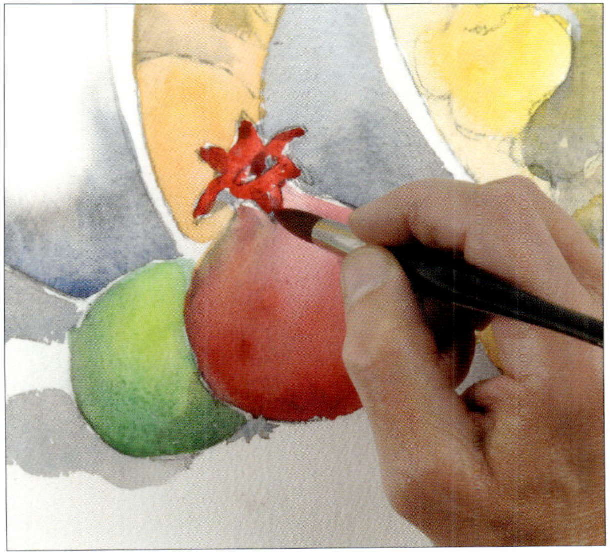

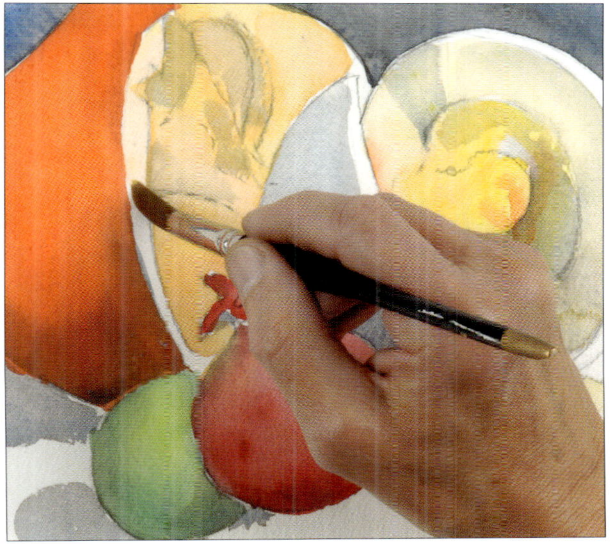

**16** Now apply a dilute mix of yellow ocher and lemon yellow to the edge of the cut section of the large gourd. Do not leave anything white—all parts of every fruit should have some color.

7 Work the sea wash down the paper an inch or so. Along the bottom of the edge of the wash, use the point of the brush to create a series of curved and jagged shapes. These shapes will form the tops of the waves crashing against the beach.

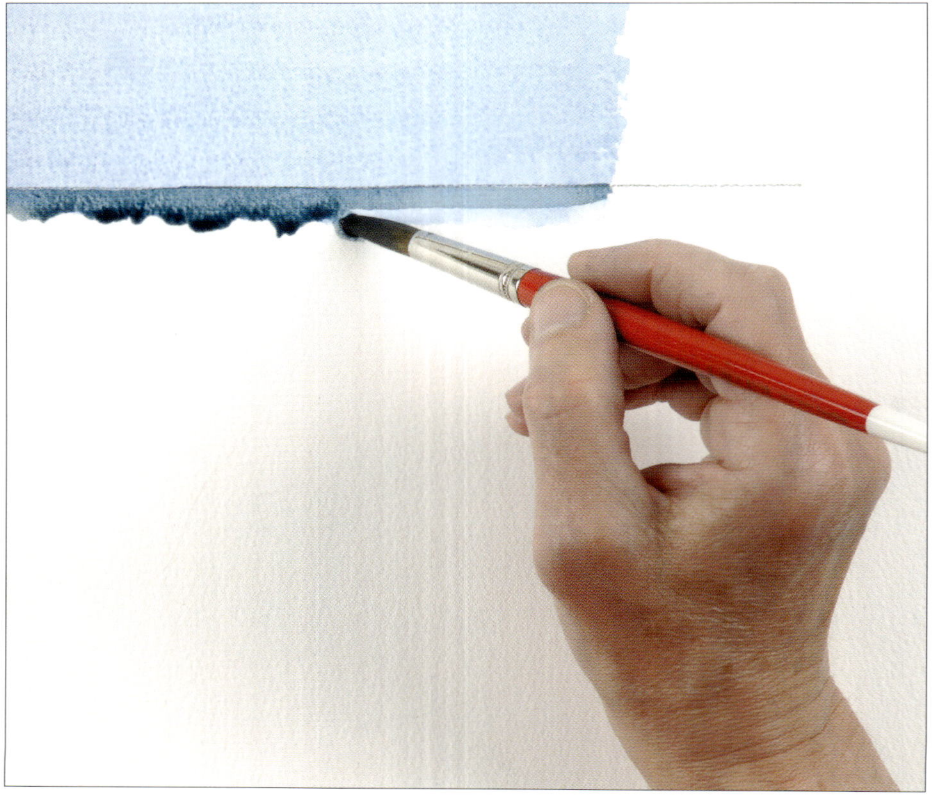

8 As the watercolor runs down to the bottom edge of the sea wash, continue to work it into a jagged wave shapes. Also add little dabs and dots of sea wash with the point of the brush—this will help give the impression of spray.

**17** Add more burnt sienna to your cadmium orange/burnt sienna mix and use this for the seeds inside the gourd. Don't try to register every detail. Instead give an indication of the seeds by drawing loose lines with the tip of the brush.

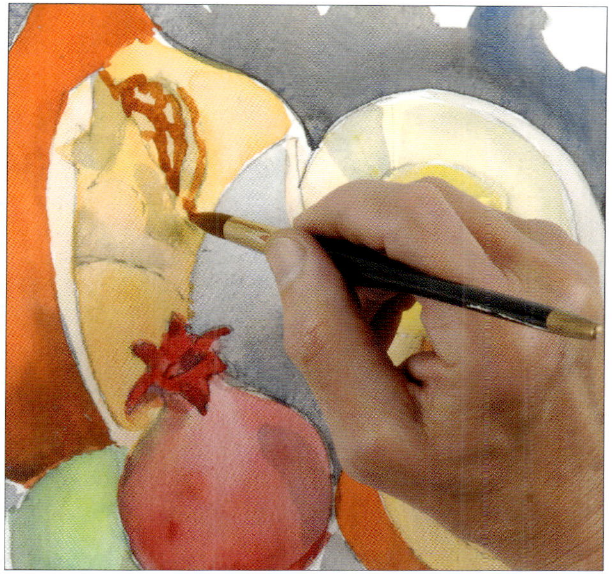

**18** Try to vary your marks when painting the seeds. Add more water to your mix to attain paler tones and use the side of your brush in places to create broader washes of paint.

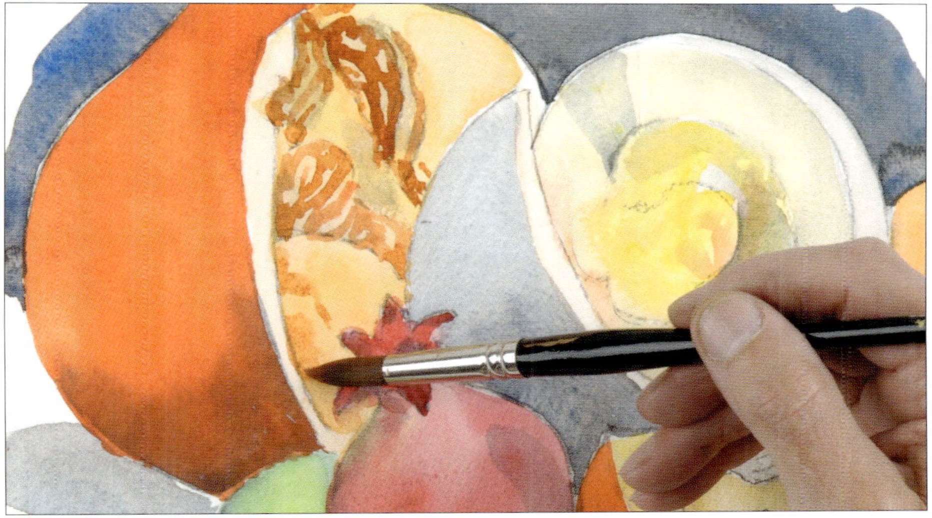

**19** Now add seeds in the cut piece of gourd. Again, make sure your brushstrokes follow the curved form of the gourd. Also, do not put in too much detail in the shadowed area on the right.

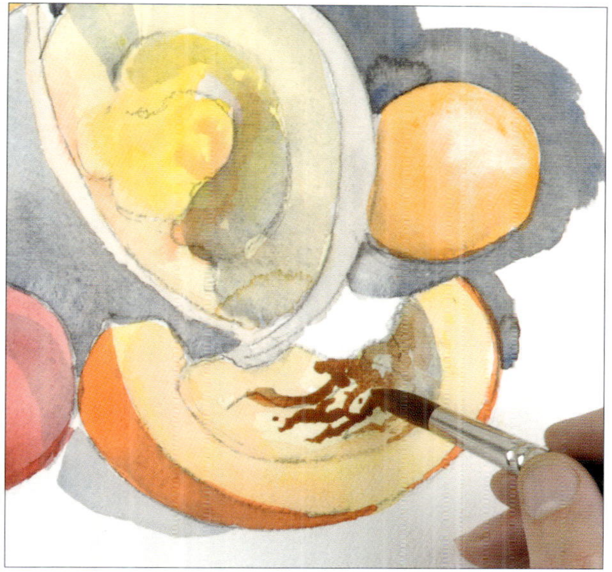

**20** Now mix up viridian with neutral tint to paint the stripes on the smaller gourd. Use the tip of the brush and again follow the curved form of the fruit. Do not worry if your lines vary in width; the markings should be neither precise nor symmetrical.

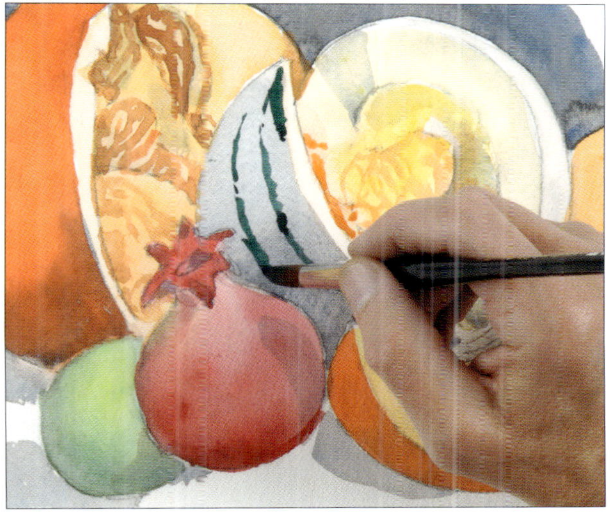

4 Continue applying horizontal strokes down the paper until you have covered the whole sky area. To make sure no white paper shows between sky and sea, allow the paint to run beneath the horizon line.

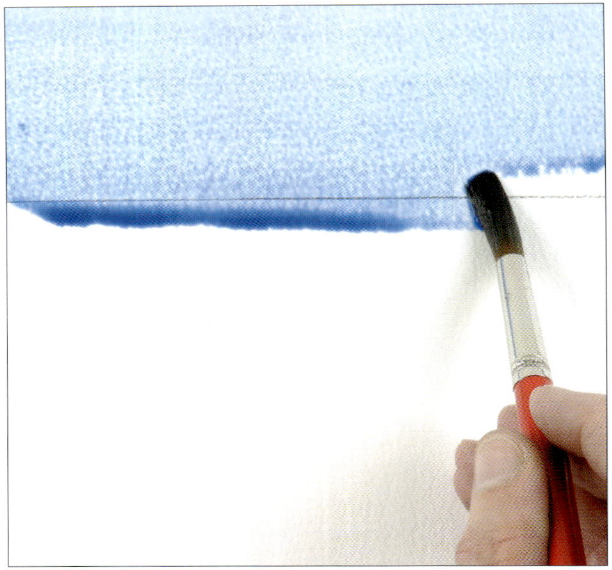

5 Now use a piece of kitchen towel to squeeze the paint out of the brush. Use the dry brush to soak up the bead of watercolor paint beneath the horizon. Now you have a flat wash of cerulean blue that perfectly suggests a cloud-free summer's sky.

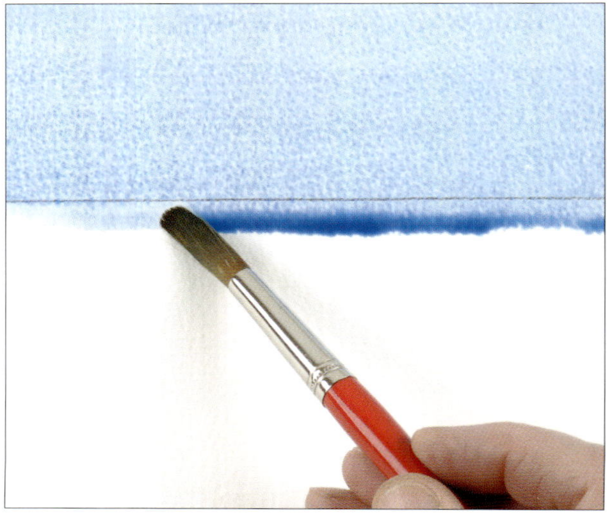

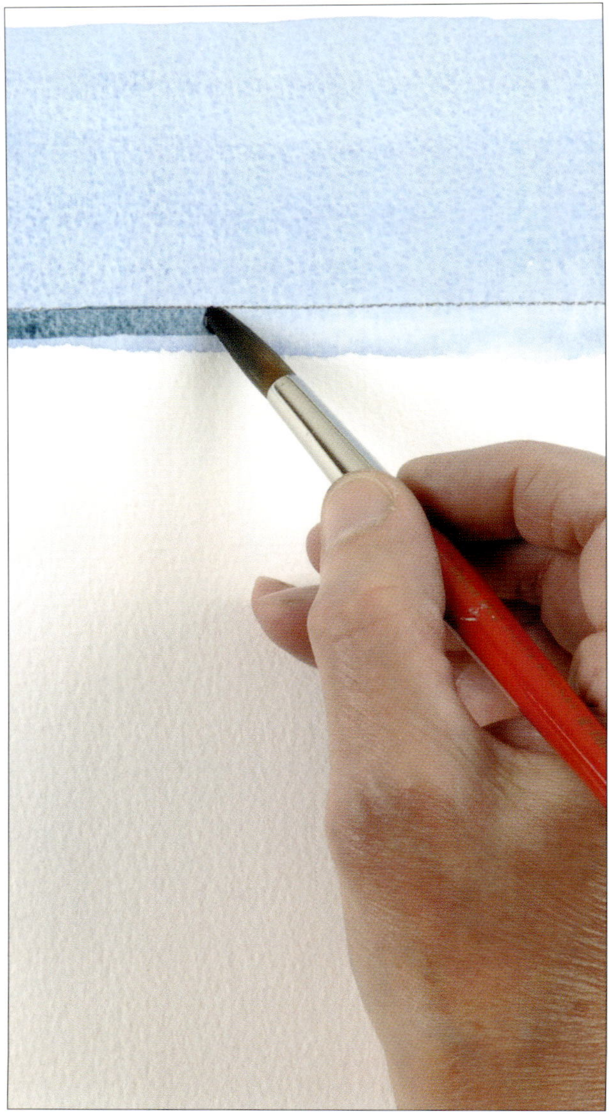

6 Mix a wash of ultramarine blue and add touches of viridian and Payne's gray. This creates a beautifully deep blue-green for the sea. When the sky wash is dry, apply this wash in a single stroke just below the horizon.

**21** Continue with your green mix to put in the lines on the outside of the large gourd. Then add the shadow tone on the underside of the gourd.

**22** Using your green mix of cadmium yellow and ultramarine, dab on some seeds on the center gourd. Note how this creates a lively, decorative pattern, full of contrast and bright color. This will help provide an important focal point in the picture.

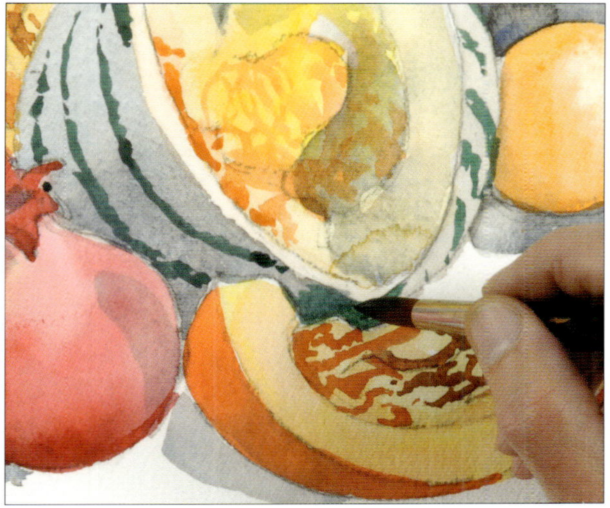

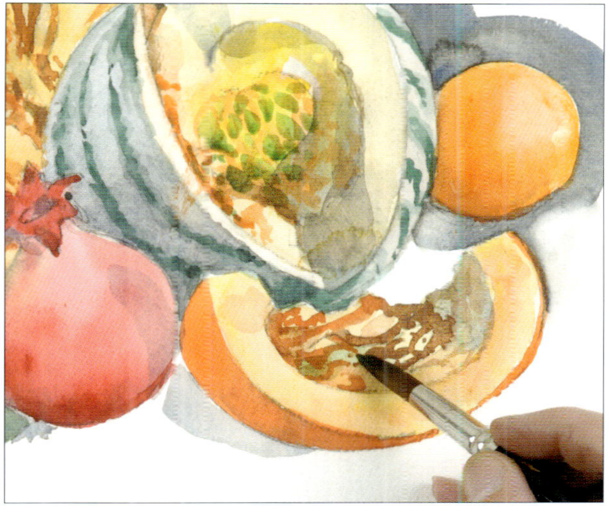

**23** Add more water to your green mix and gently brush this on the flesh of the cut piece of gourd in the foreground.

**24** Now we need to bring out the spherical form of the large gourd. Apply a brush dipped in water to the top half of the gourd. This will lighten the tone, helping to distinguish it from the shadowed lower half.

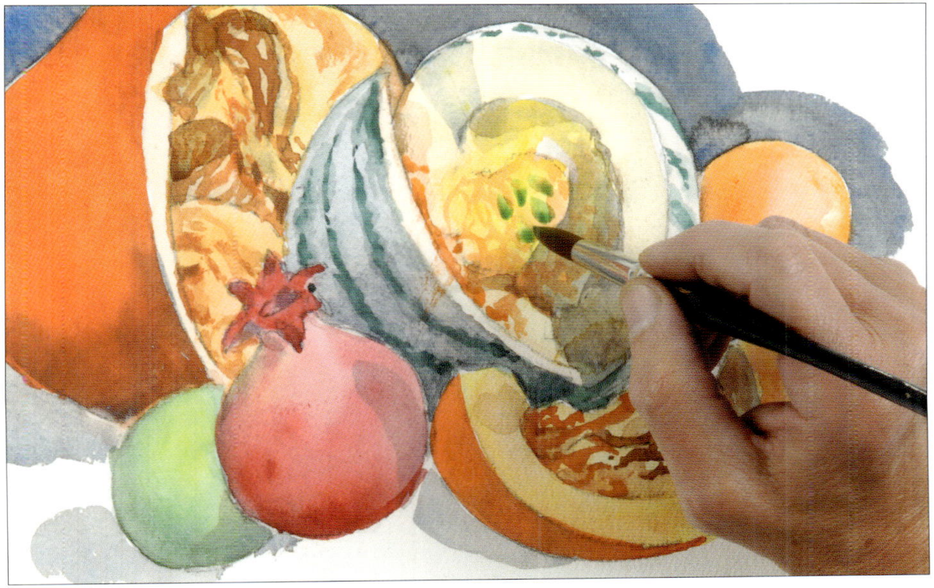

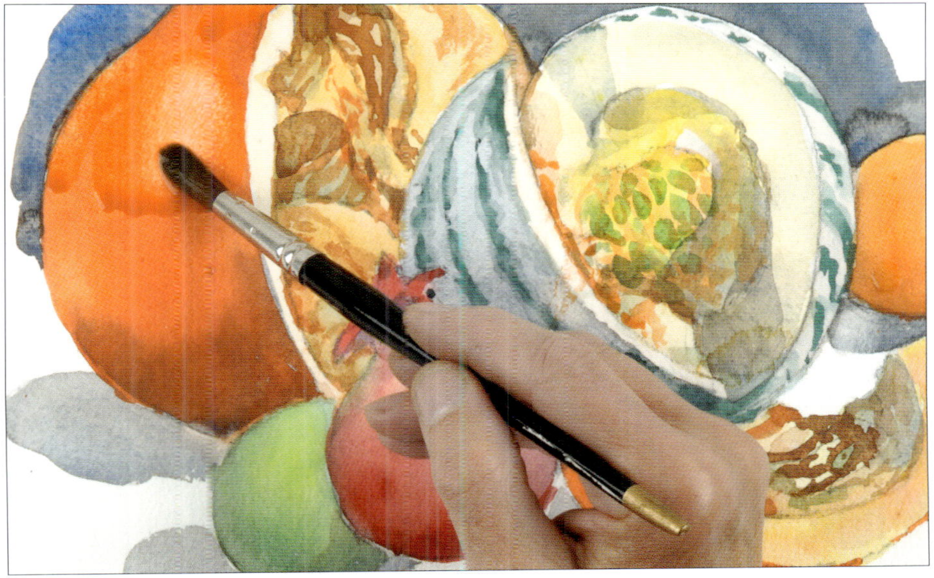

**1** Use a ruler and an HB pencil to draw the horizon line about two-thirds of the way up the paper. Make sure the line is parallel to the top and bottom of the paper. The line can be quite strong—you can always clean up any graphite smudges later with an eraser.

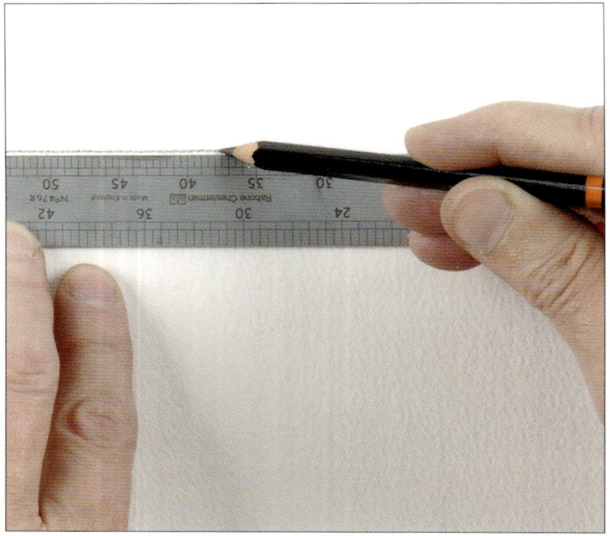

**2** Now tilt the drawing board toward you slightly so that you can lay a flat wash for the sky. Dip the No.10 round brush in the jar of water and dampen the sky area. Also dampen the area just below the horizon. Now mix a wash of cerulean blue in the palette. Fully load the brush and apply the color with a steady stroke across the top of the sky.

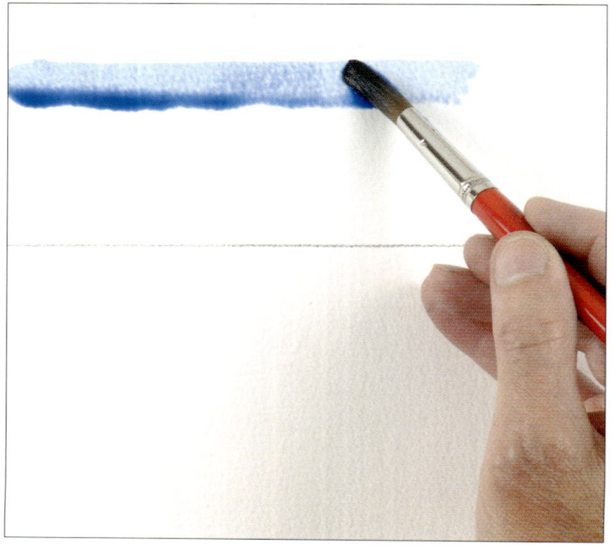

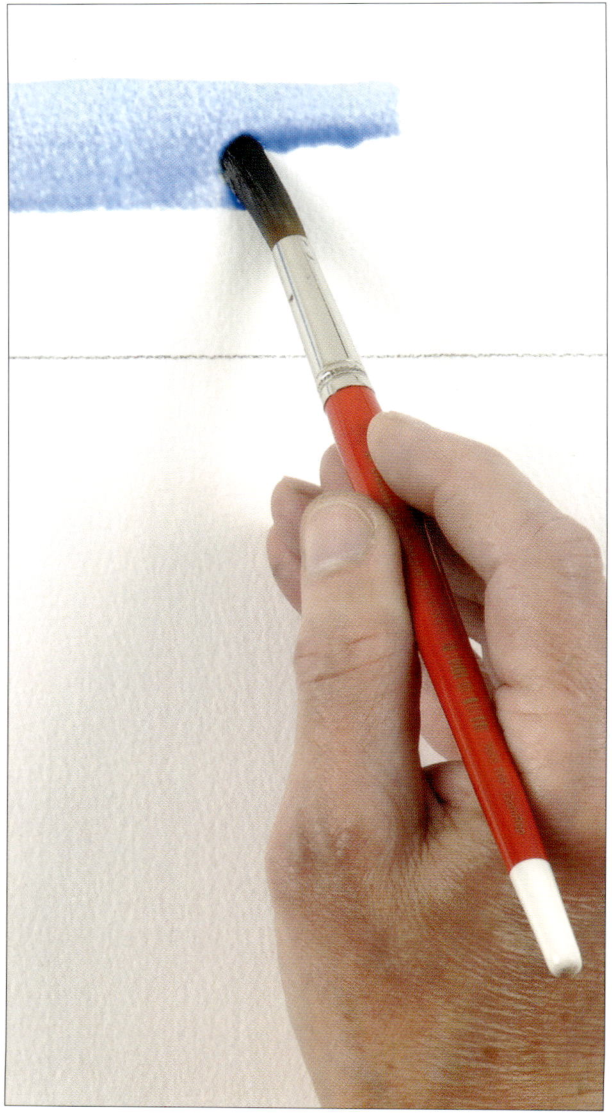

**3** Load the brush again and make another horizontal stroke underneath the first one. Slightly overlap the strokes so that the paint that collects in a bead at the bottom of the first brushstroke merges with the second one.

25 Using the edge of the flat brush and a dilute mix of cadmium orange with a touch of burnt sienna add thin strokes to the gourd. Always make sure your brushstrokes curve around the form of the gourd. These marks will give the gourd skin a realistic texture.

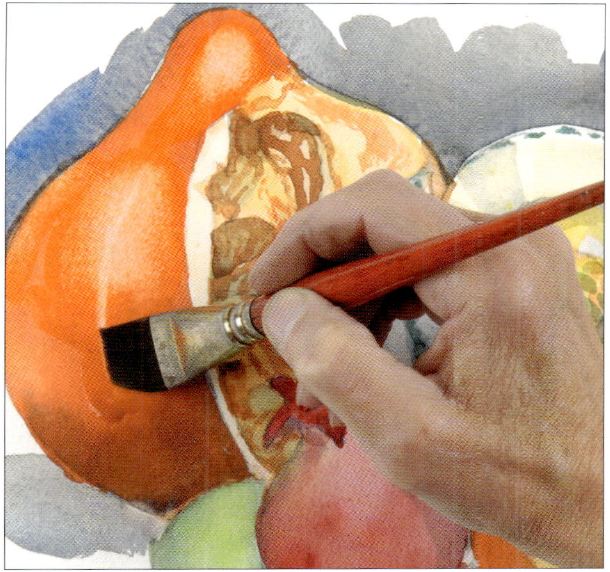

26 Continue with your orange mix to strengthen the shadowed underside of the cut segment of the gourd.

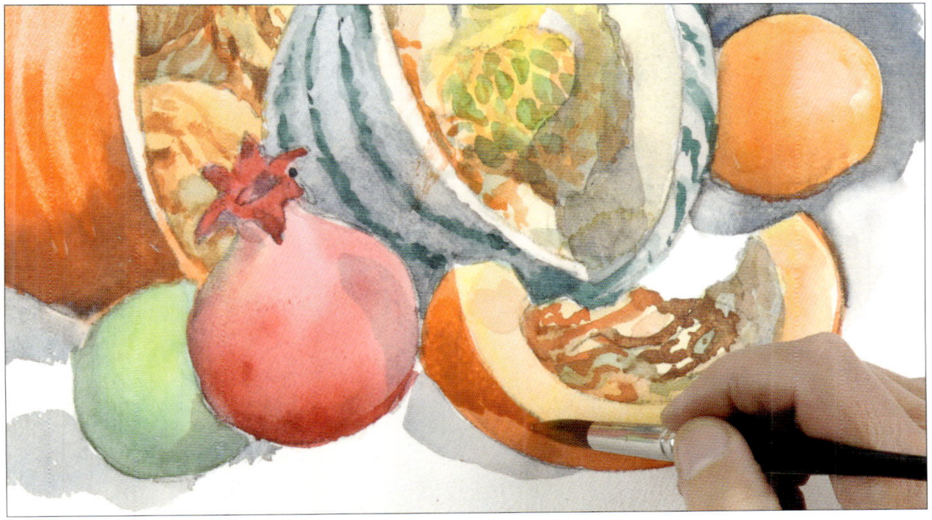

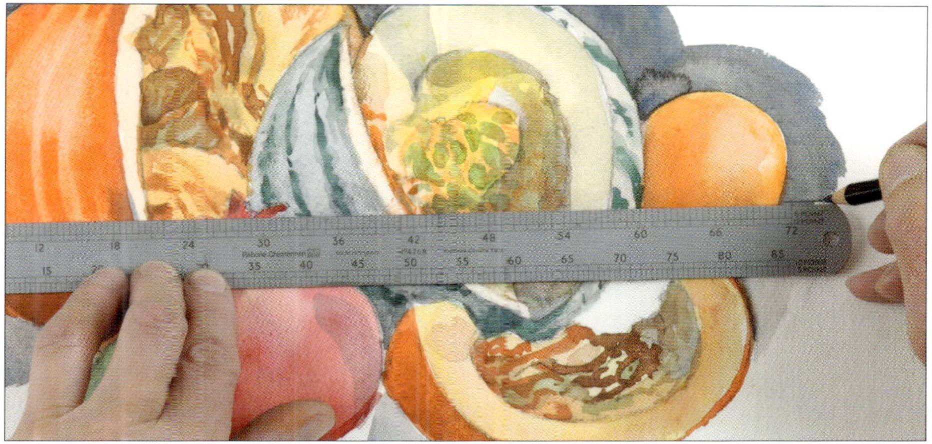

27 Now use a ruler and the 2B pencil to draw the back edge of the table. When you come to paint the tablecloth below this line, make sure it is lighter in tone than backdrop above the line.

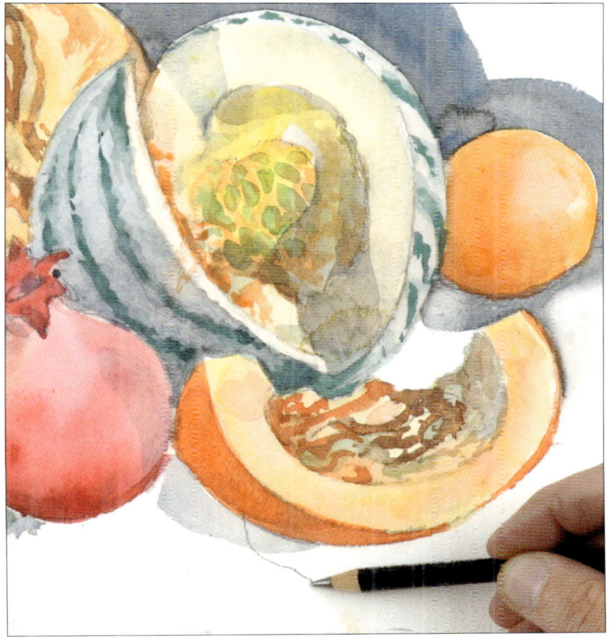

28 In the foreground, use your pencil to establish the position of some of the folds in the tablecloth.

# project 1: **Breaking Waves**

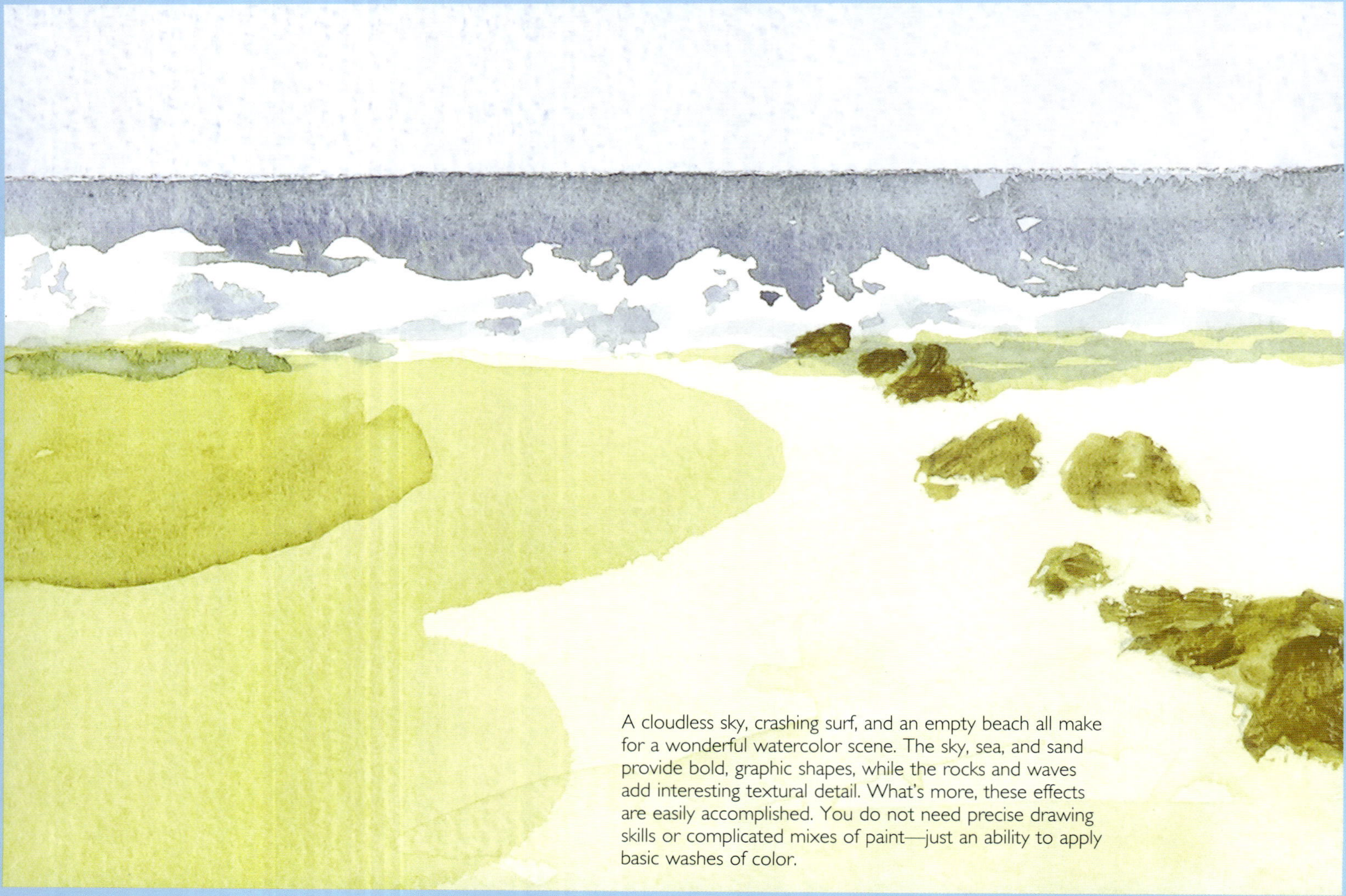

A cloudless sky, crashing surf, and an empty beach all make for a wonderful watercolor scene. The sky, sea, and sand provide bold, graphic shapes, while the rocks and waves add interesting textural detail. What's more, these effects are easily accomplished. You do not need precise drawing skills or complicated mixes of paint—just an ability to apply basic washes of color.

**MATERIALS**

**Drawing board**

**Watercolor paper**

**Watercolor palette**

**Watercolors: cerulean blue, ultramarine blue, viridian, Payne's gray, raw sienna, and raw umber**

**No.10 round brush**

**Jar of water**

**HB pencil**

**Ruler**

**Eraser**

**Kitchen towel**

**Tracing paper**

29 Now give some indication of the tablecloth by adding your shadow mix of ultramarine and burnt sienna. Be selective—do not paint the whole tablecloth or it will dominate the painting and detract from the fruit.

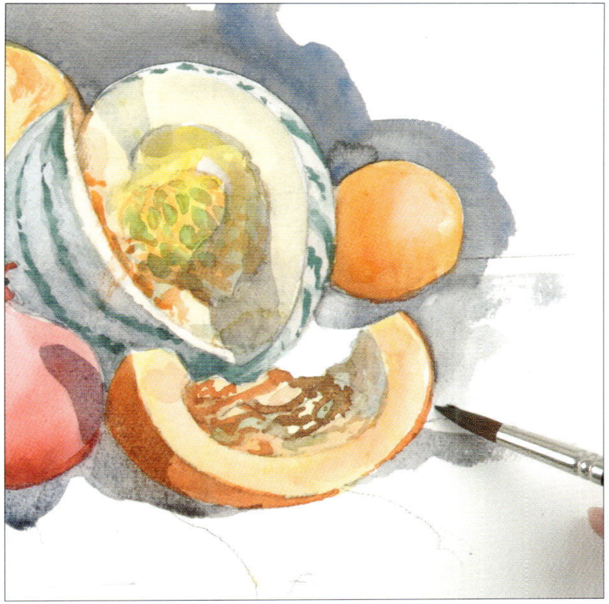

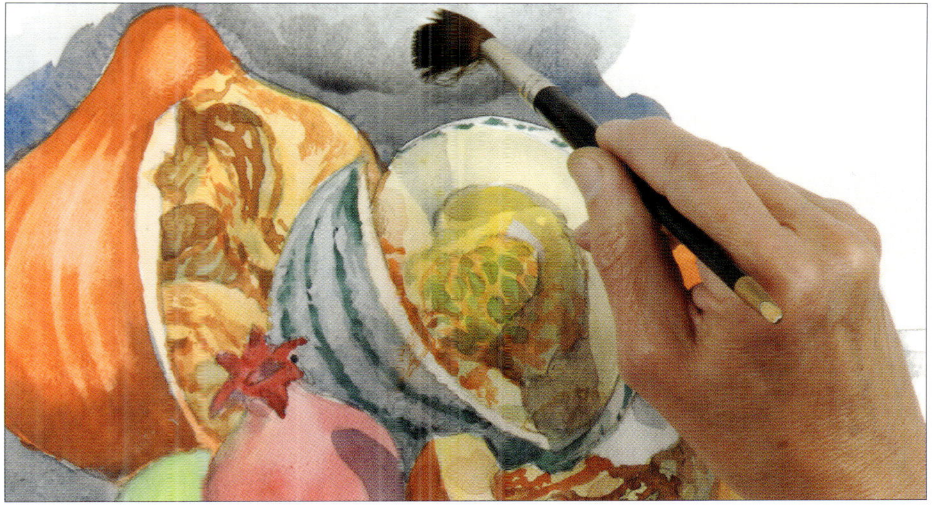

30 In the foreground, indicate the folds of the tablecloth. The white of the paper can stand for the lit side of each fold, so just paint the shadowed sides. If the contrast appears too bold, use a piece of kitchen paper gently to apply the shadow mix to the lit sides of each fold.

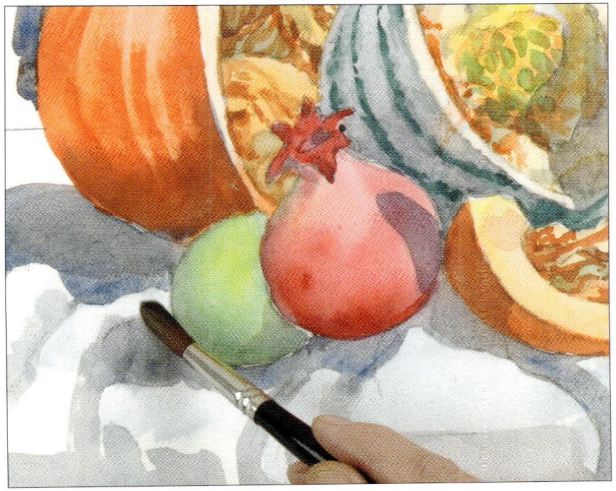

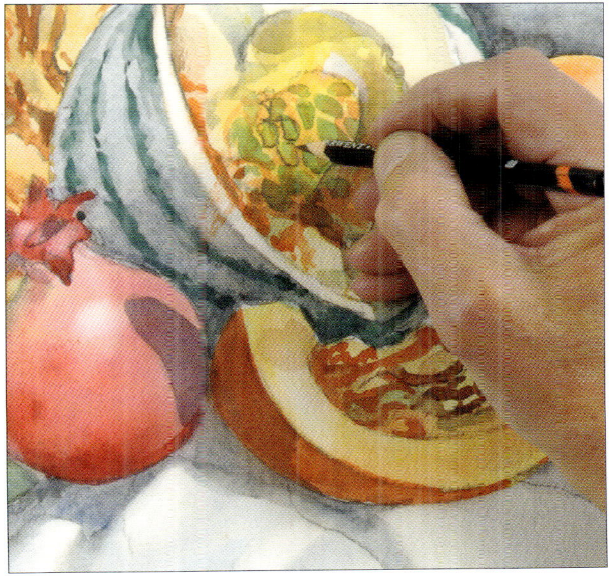

31 Strengthen the background by applying more of your shadow mix. To vary the color, add a touch of viridian to your mix. This dark background will make the fruit leap forward toward the viewer.

32 Now put in the final touches. You can create a few highlights in the fruit by lifting out color with a clean wet brush. Also, use a pencil to clarify and define the seeds in the center gourd.

5 Add shadows under the protruding top of the building, using the tip of the brush to create thin horizontal strokes. Still working with the tip of the brush, define the shadows around and under the capitals at the top of the columns.

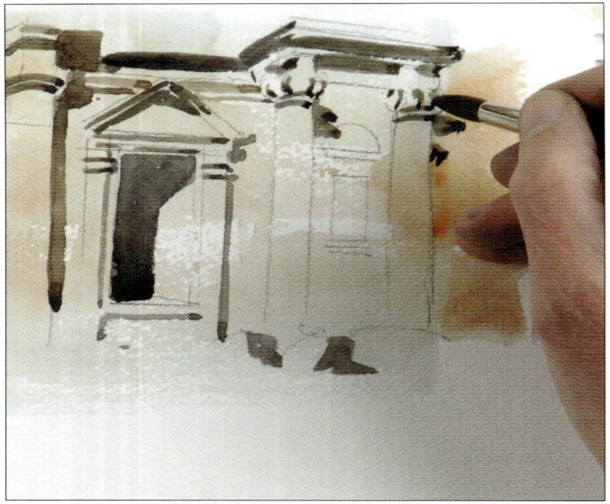

6 Fill in the shadow in the window—and the thin shadows around the semicircular feature above it.

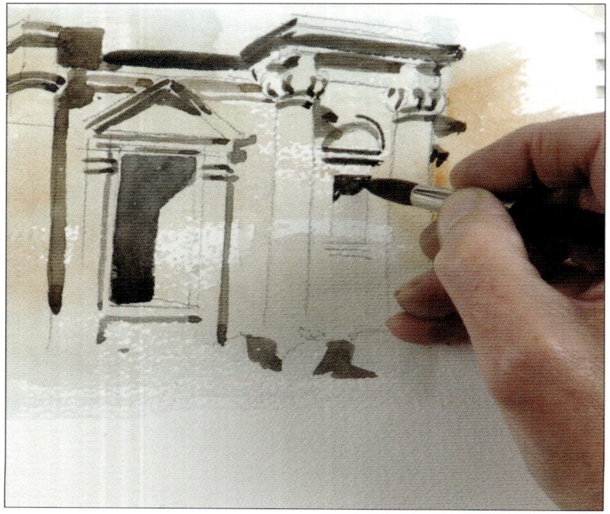

7 Then with long, thin vertical lines, add the shadows along the sides of the two columns on the right. The picture now has a series of cast shadows—they not only enhance the solidity of the building, but also add tonal contrasts that excite and entertain the eye.

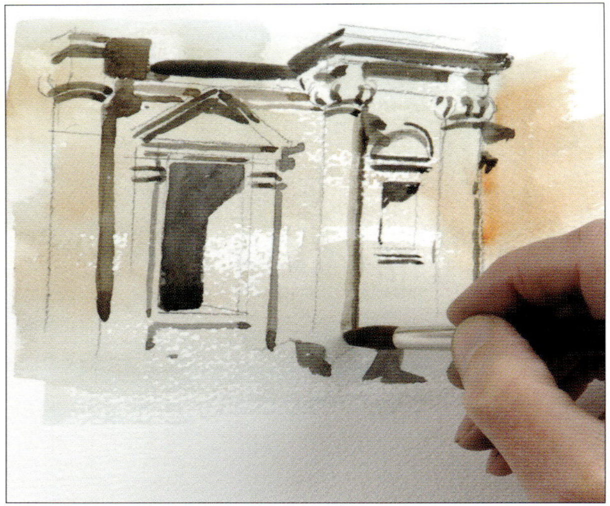

8 Finally, dilute your burnt umber mix, and add a few brushstrokes to define the front and bottom of the building. With the addition of shadows, you can now perceive the three-dimensional space the building occupies—the way a ledge or a capital protrudes, the way a window or a doorway recedes.

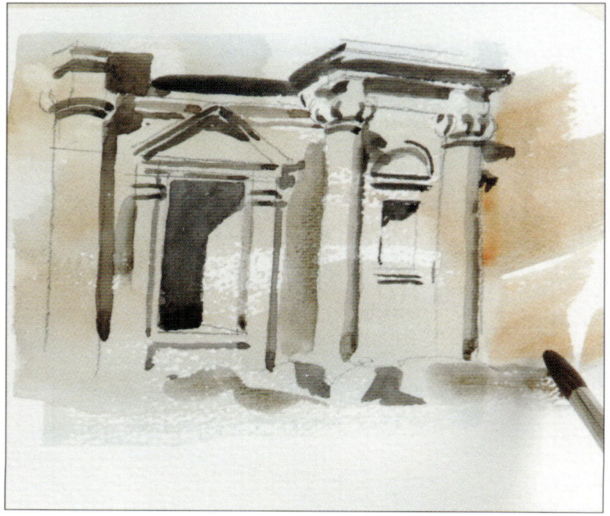

# project 3: **Woodland Sun**

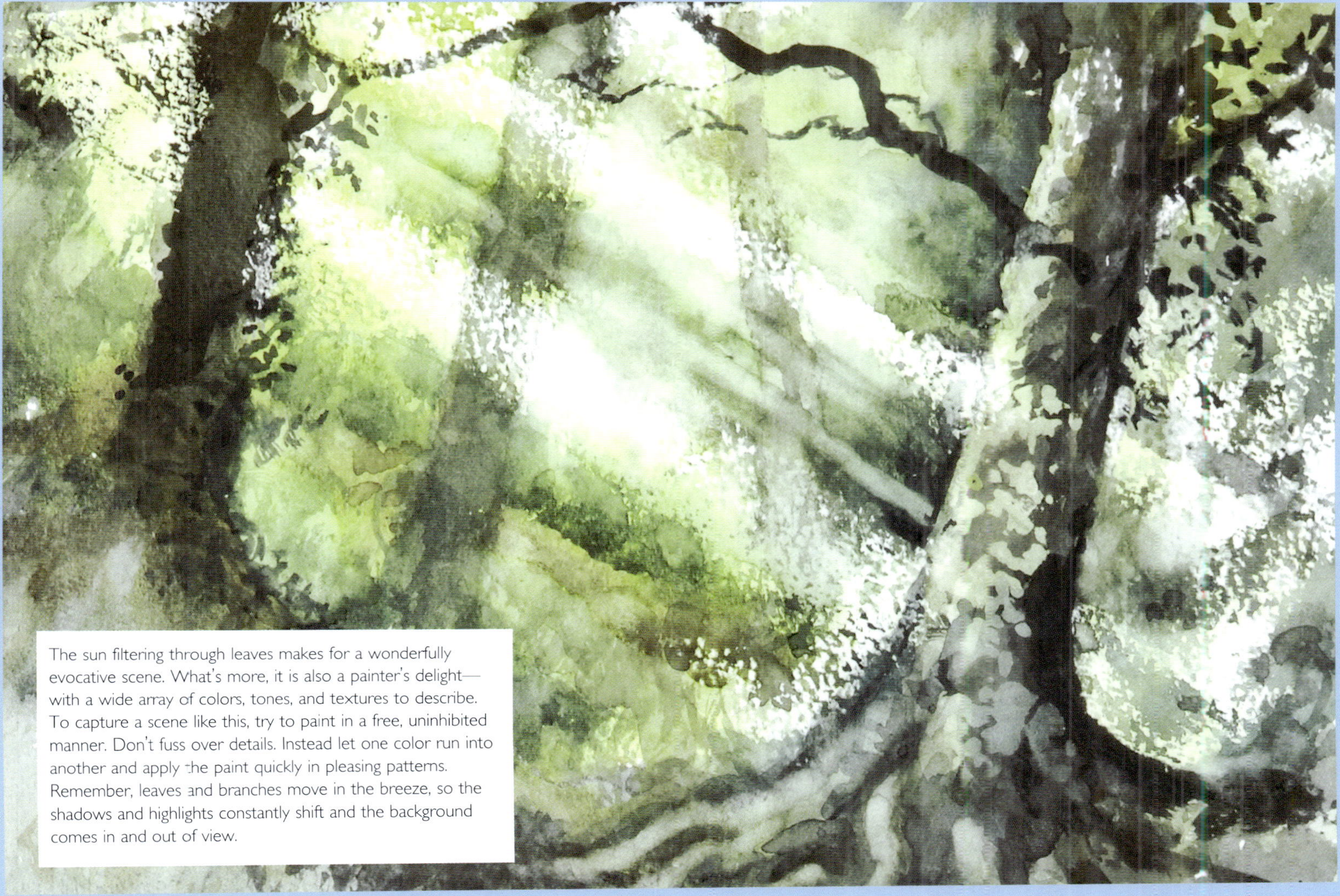

The sun filtering through leaves makes for a wonderfully evocative scene. What's more, it is also a painter's delight—with a wide array of colors, tones, and textures to describe. To capture a scene like this, try to paint in a free, uninhibited manner. Don't fuss over details. Instead let one color run into another and apply the paint quickly in pleasing patterns. Remember, leaves and branches move in the breeze, so the shadows and highlights constantly shift and the background comes in and out of view.

## MATERIALS

- Drawing board
- Thick rough or semi-rough watercolor paper
- Watercolor palette
- Watercolors: cadmium yellow light, ultramarine blue, viridian, burnt sienna
- Brushes: No. 8, No.12, No. 1
- Jar of water
- 2B pencil
- White candle
- Craft knife

1 By accurately registering cast shadows, you can create a real sense of the solidity of your subject matter. What's more, shadows can add great drama and vitality to a picture. In this exercise, start by drawing the outline of a building in pencil. Then mix a very watery wash of burnt sienna and raw sienna. Apply this with a household, or decorator's, brush over the drawing.

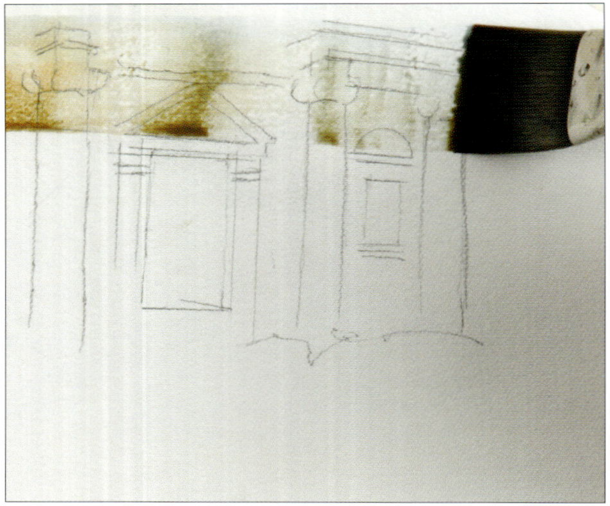

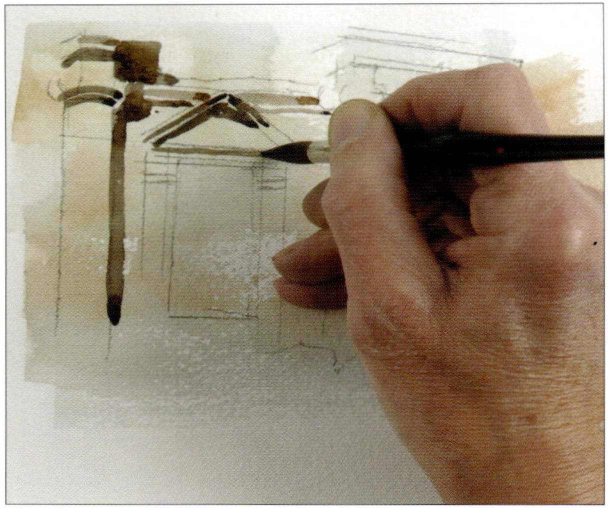

3 Now mix up a strong wash of burnt umber and, with a medium round brush, begin registering the shadow areas. As the sunlight is coming from the left, the bottom and the right sides of every architectural feature will cast a shadow. Start by putting a shadow along the right side of the pillar and the bottom edges of the pediment.

2 Continue adding the watery wash over the building. Do not cover the building entirely—leave white areas showing through in places. The idea is simply to give some indication of the local color of the architecture.

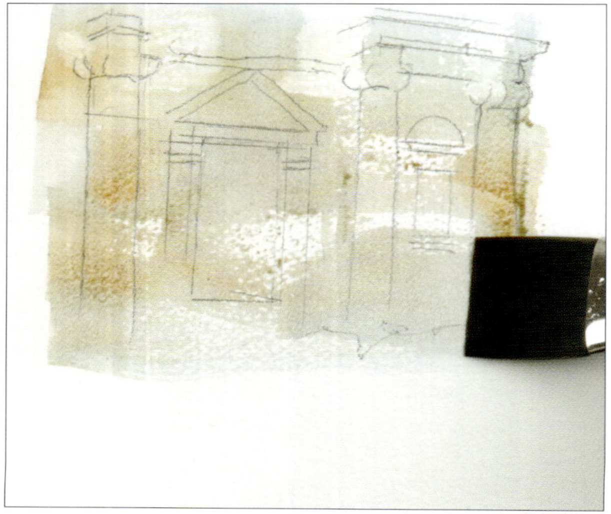

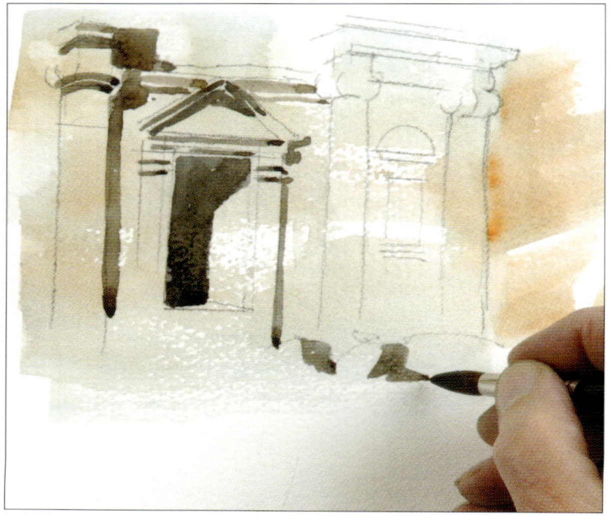

4 Add the cast shadow thrown into the doorway—note, how the viewer can now perceive depth beyond the door. Also, add to two small shadows, with slightly weaker paint, to help define the bottom of the right side of the building.

1 Start by outlining the trees with a 2B pencil. Make sure the trunks slant in different directions and are spaced unevenly. Also, to attain a sense of depth, make sure the foreground trunks are wider than those in the background. Add the branches at the top and the roots that have forced themselves above ground. Note how the eye is pulled through the two trees in the foreground into the distance.

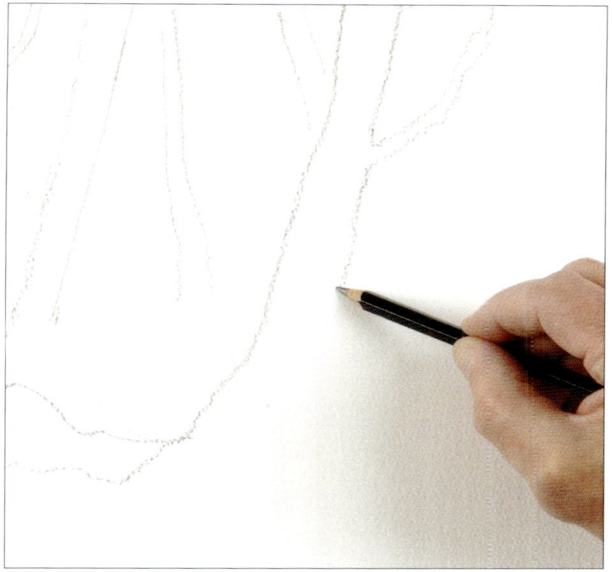

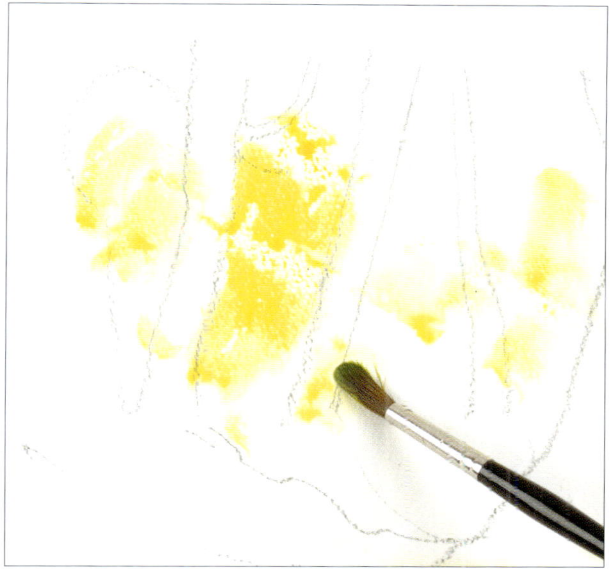

3 Now you are ready to paint. Tape the paper to a drawing board and tip it slightly toward you—so the paint always runs down the paper. With the No.8 brush, wet the paper with clean water. Then add a bright sunshiney mix of cadmium yellow light and the merest touch of ultramarine. The paint will be absorbed by the damp paper and establish an overall tone for the painting. Now you will be able to see exactly where you have applied your wax!

2 Now establish the highlight areas by using the edge of a sharpened white candle. Wherever you apply the candle wax, the picture will remain white, as the paint will not be able to reach the paper. Press the candle firmly in two diagonals across the picture to create the two shafts of light. Also skim it over the far right of the picture. (You can look at the paper at an angle to see exactly where you have applied the wax.)

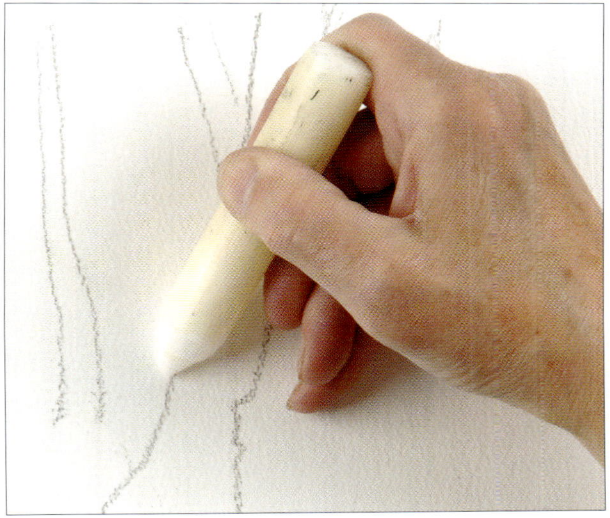

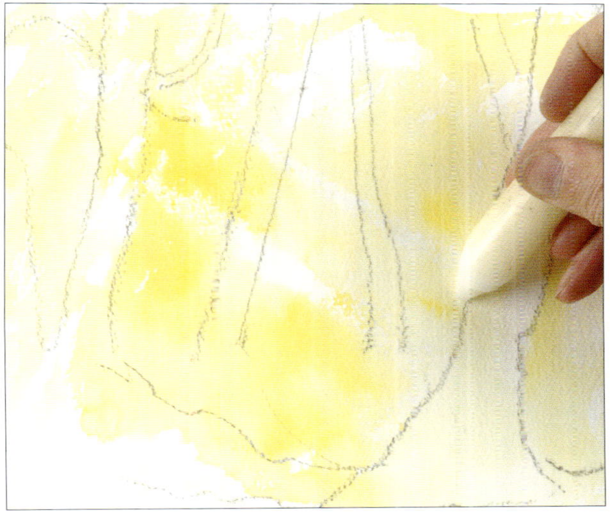

4 Let your initial wash dry completely. You can use a hair dryer to speed up this process. Then reapply the candle to the two shafts of light cutting across the picture. Feel free to work over the initial wash of yellow paint. In this way, you will attain a broken color effect in the final painting—perfect for the effect of light filtering through the trees.

**5** Make sure your gray hill is darker than the blue one behind it. If not, add another wash of gray. If you have difficulty in judging the tone of different colors, half-close your eyes—color becomes less important and the lightness and darkness of washes more apparent.

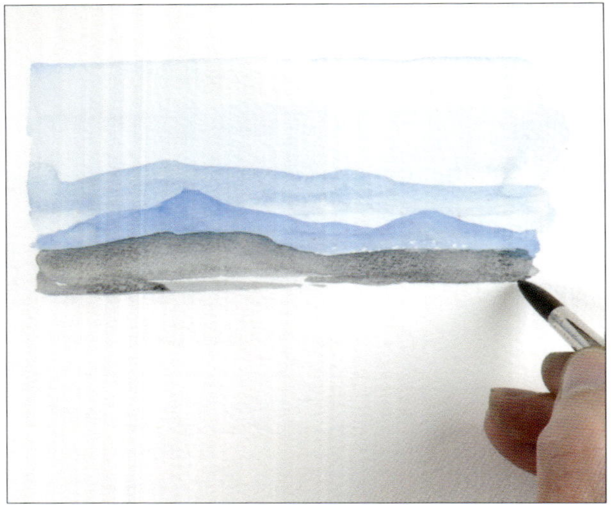

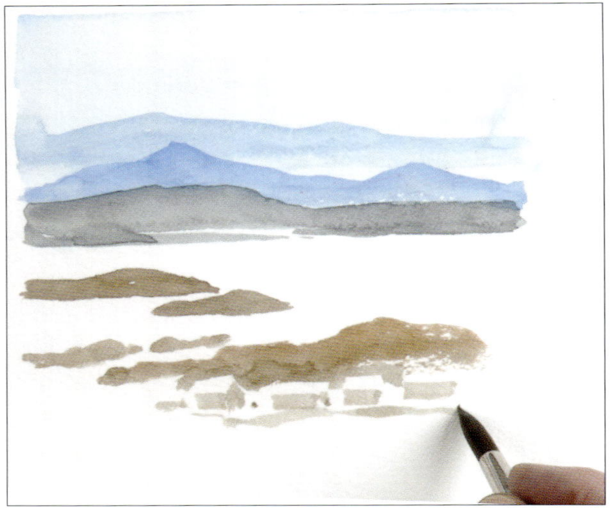

**7** Continue adding rocks to the foreground. Then water down the mix and add a few small horizontal strokes to indicate reflections in the water. Adding detail to the foreground helps to aid further, the sense of recession in the picture.

**6** Now make up a brown mix and use this to paint long, thin rocks peeping up above the surface of a lake. Think of these rocks as visual stepping-stones into the picture.

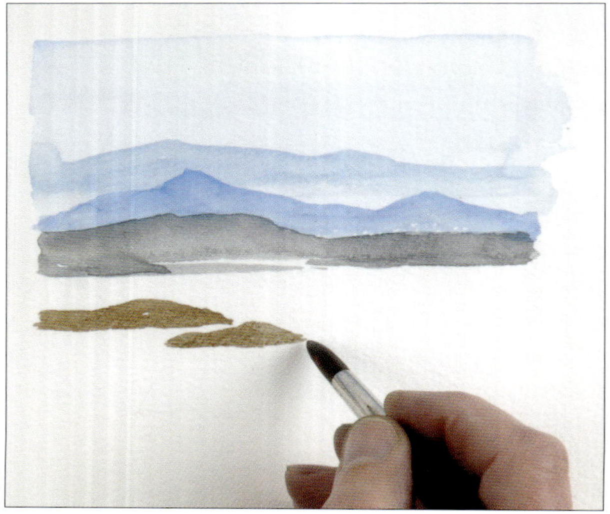

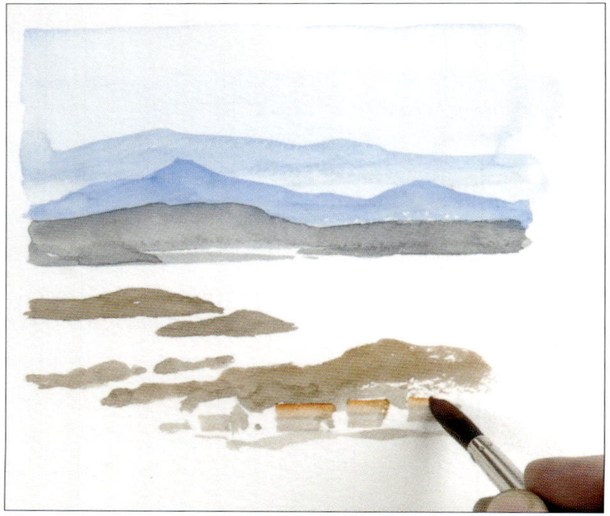

**8** As a final touch, mix a warm orange wash to add a few more rocks. Warm colors, like orange, leap forward—while cool colors, like blue, tend to "sit back." The final picture has wonderful sense of depth. In the foreground, there are strong tonal contrasts, warm colors, and lots of rock detail. The background, by contrast, is made up of misty, cool colors.

5 Now add a touch of viridian to your yellow mix and apply this with the No.12 brush in between the trees. Look at the way the paint collects at the top of each area of wax. This creates a sharp edge for well-defined shafts of light.

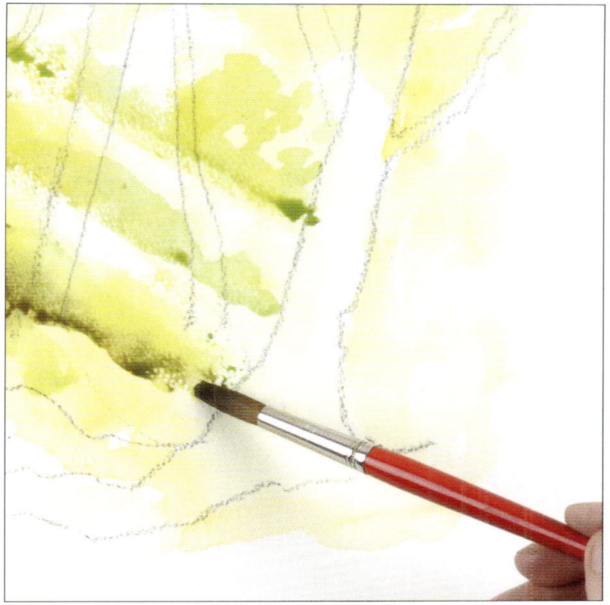

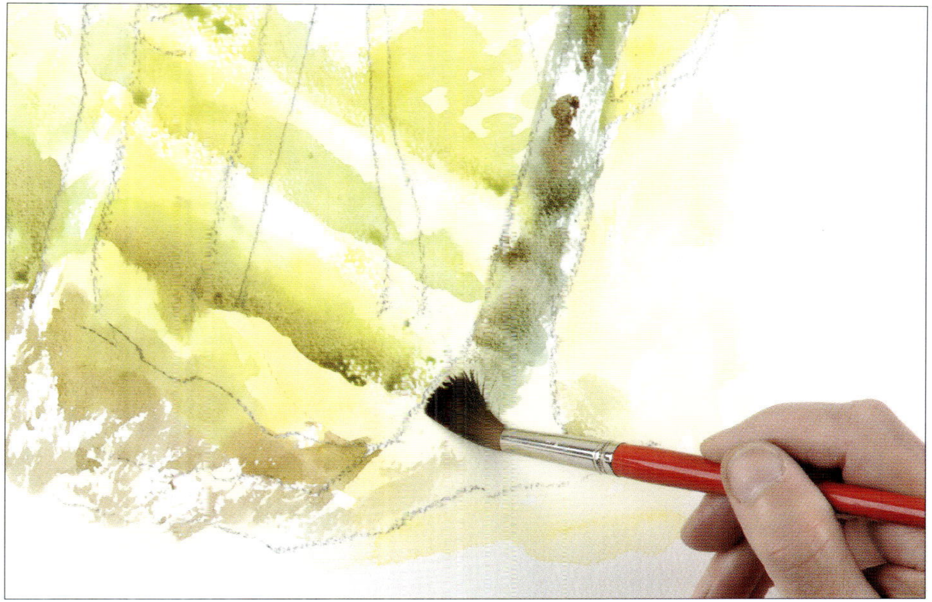

6 Now in a new well in your palette, add a touch of your green mix to some burnt sienna to give a darker, earthier color. Apply it to the foreground with the side of the brush to attain an impression of the texture of the woodland floor.

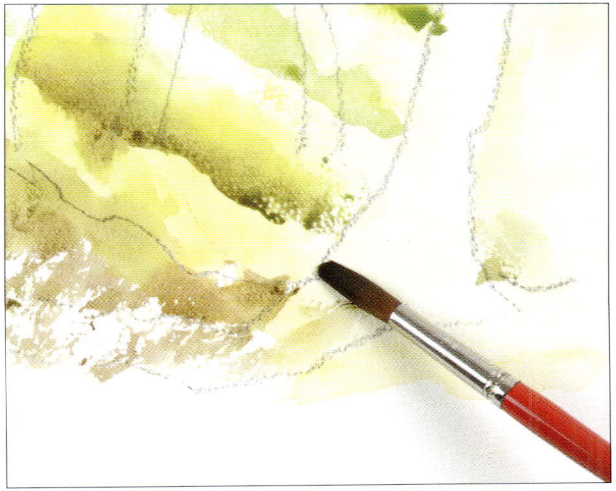

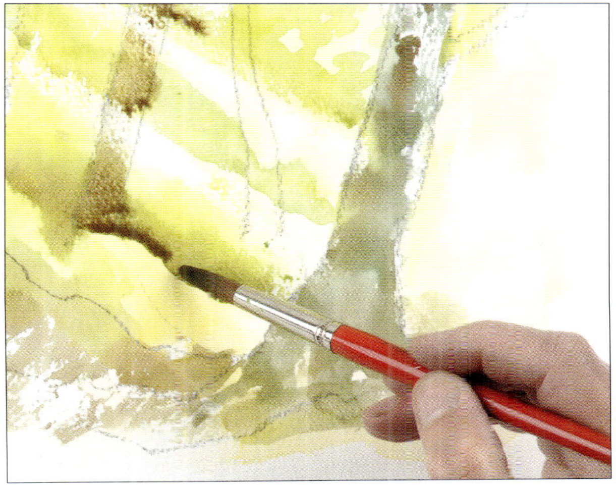

7 Dab your brown mix on the main tree trunk on the right. Then return to your green mix and run this over the trunk.

8 Switch back to the brown mix to paint the second to left tree trunk. Let the paint run down the paper until it forms a sharp edge against the wax. This will help establish the ground.

1 It is essential to create a sense of recession in a landscape—so the viewers actually believe they are looking at a three-dimensional world rather than a flat arrangement of colors. To do this, subject matter in the distance should be paler, less contrasty and contain more blue than subject matter in the foreground. For this landscape, first mix a watery blue wash and apply this with a large flat brush to the top of your paper.

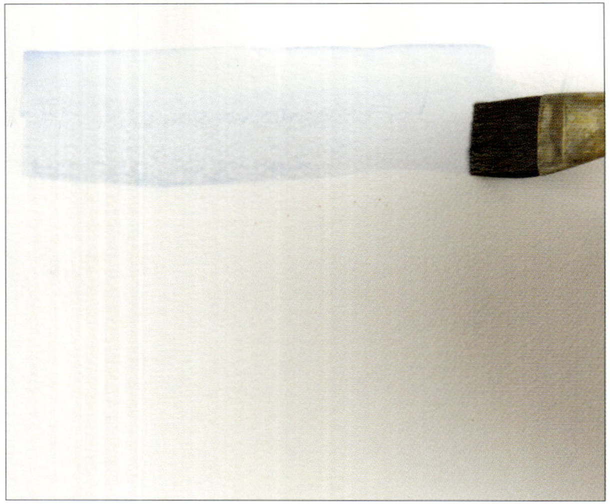

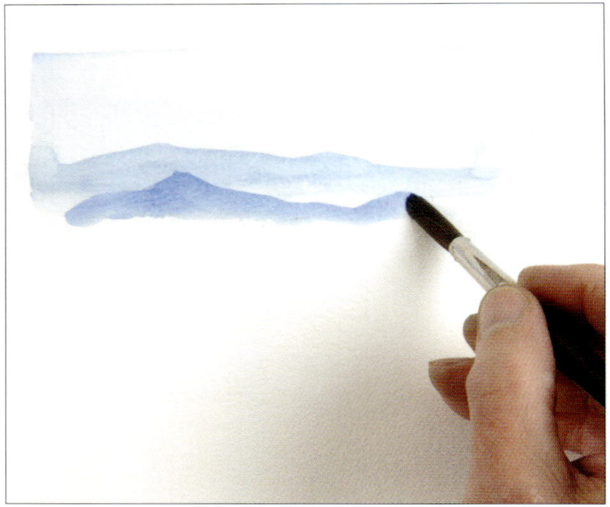

3 Strengthen your blue mix and, when the first hill is dry, add a second one. Make sure the shape of this hill differs from the first one. Let this wash dry.

2 Let the sky wash dry—use a hair dryer, if necessary, to speed up the process. Then add more pigment to your blue mix and, using a medium round brush, paint in a distant hill over the bottom of your sky wash. As the sky wash is dry, you will attain a pleasing crisp hilltop.

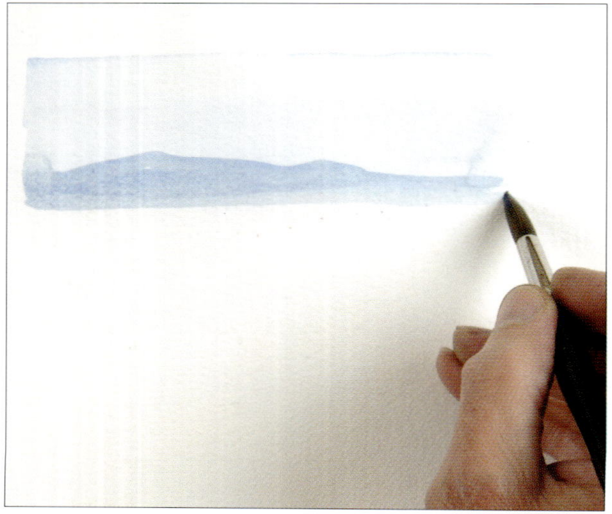

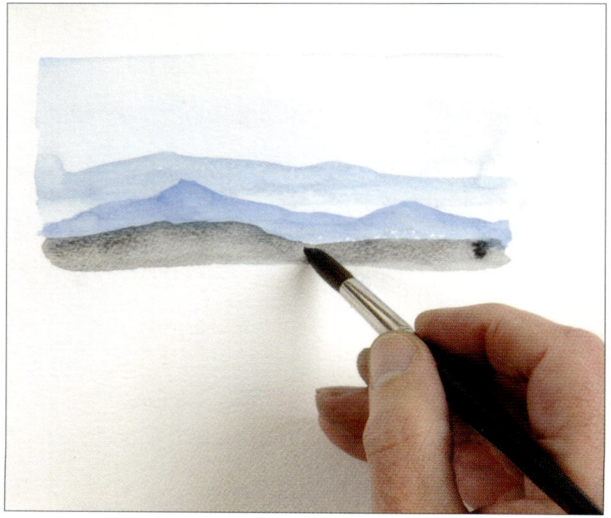

4 Now make up a dark gray mix. When the blue hill is dry, paint a gray hill in front of it. Do not worry if you overlap the colors—the blue will show through the gray hill, intensifying its tone and enhancing its color.

**9** Now add more burnt sienna to your brown mix and use this to paint the trunk on the far left. This trunk is in the foreground so it needs a strong tone to bring it forward.

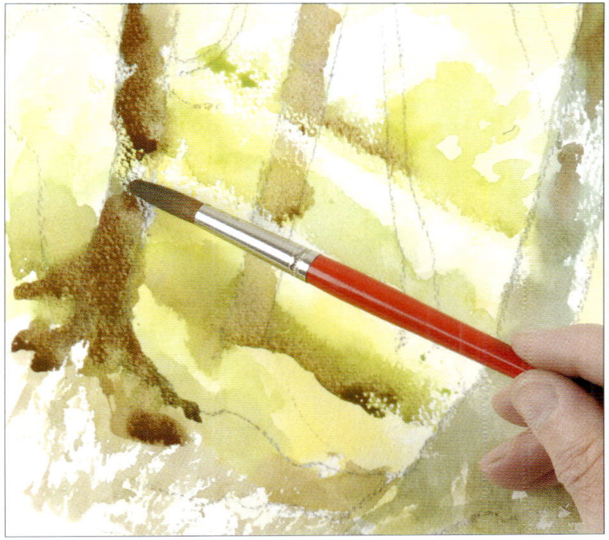

**10** Return to your green mix to paint the tree in the background. As this tree is the farthest away, use a light touch, dabbing the paint on tentatively. (The wax resists this green in places.)

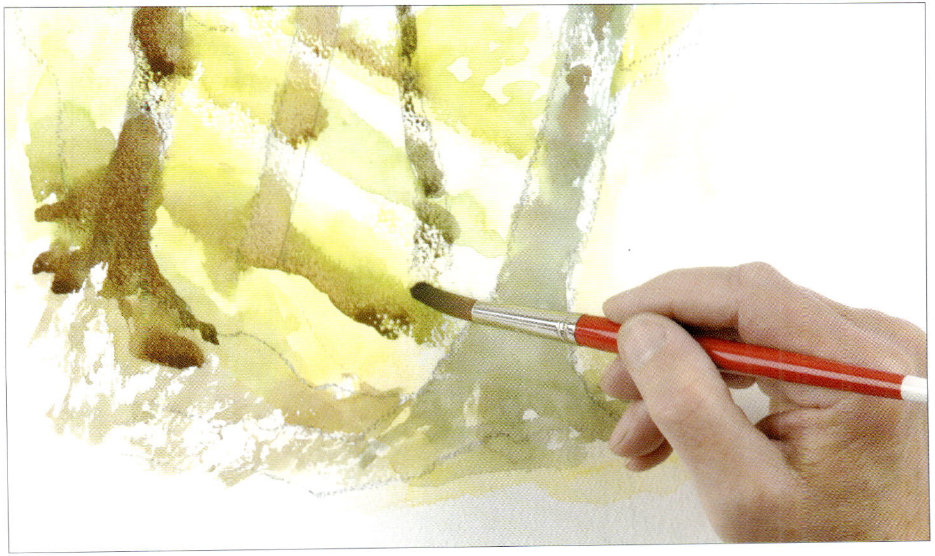

**11** Now, for the deep green of the foliage, mix up a wash of ultramarine, cadmium yellow, and a little burnt sienna. Dab this around—and, in places, over—the tree trunks.

**12** Continue adding the foliage mix across the picture. Do not continually reload your brush with paint, but let the paint run out, so you get weaker brushstrokes. The paper will show through these brushstrokes, adding interesting textures.

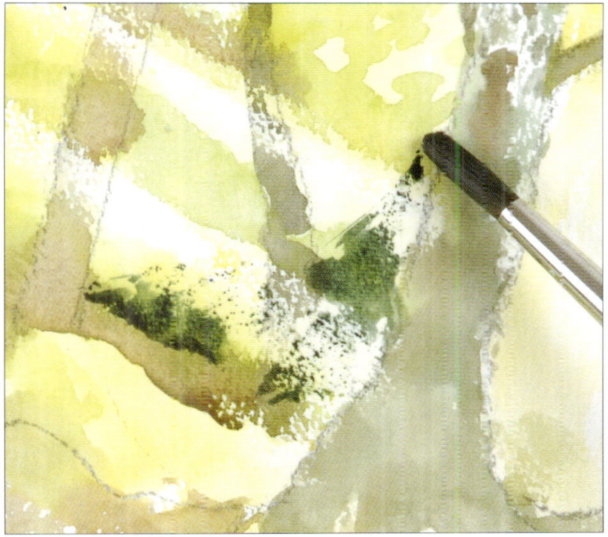

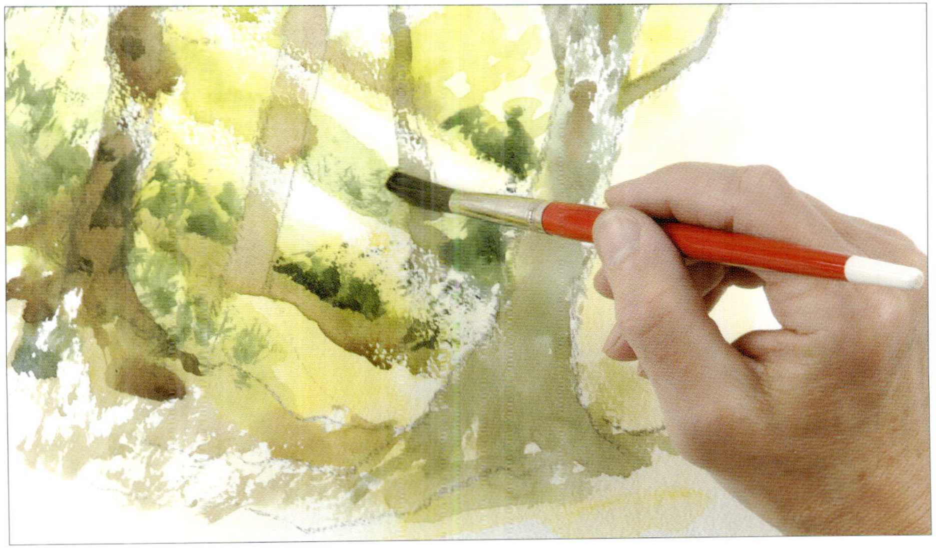

 **recession: monochrome**

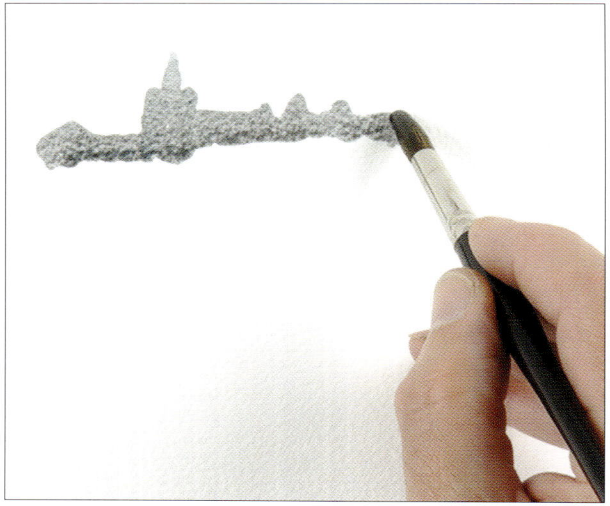

1 This technique involves imposing one wash over another, allowing each to dry before applying the next. The counterchange from light to dark suggests that the land is receding into the distance. Start by painting the outline of a skyline. Here, the wash is a mix of Payne's gray with some burnt sienna. How elaborate you make your skyline is up to you.

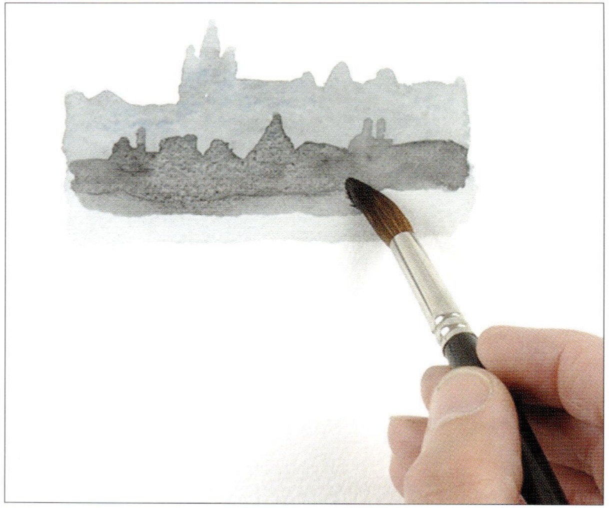

3 Now paint in the outline of the mid-distant skyline, using the same mix. Notice how the wash appears darker. This is because, in applying the paint over the previous wash, it is now effectively double strength.

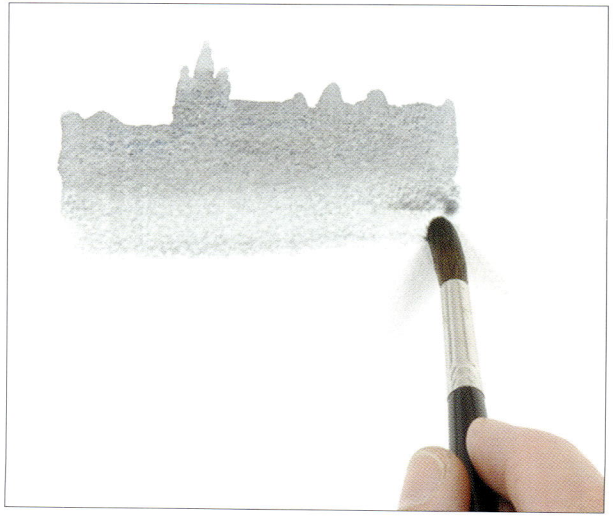

2 With the main shapes in place, use the same color to apply a flat wash below your skyline. Allow it to fade gradually as you come farther down the paper. Leave the paint to dry.

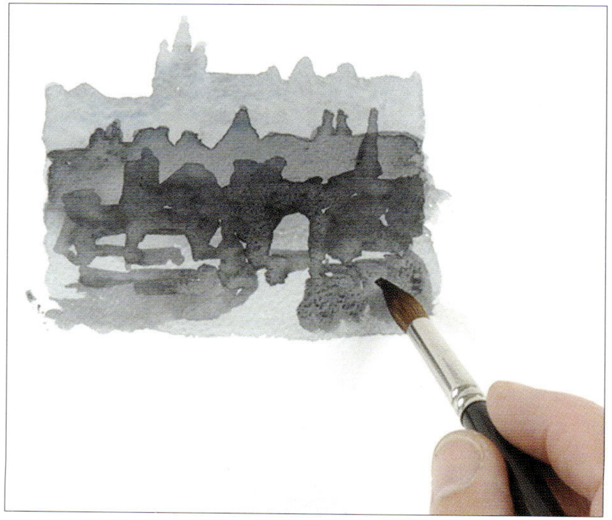

4 Now paint in the foreground skyline. Leave some of the background color showing through; this implies areas of light, and adds depth. Add a few shadows to complete the effect.

**13** Return to your initial muted green mix (cadmium yellow light, viridian, plus touches of burnt sienna and ultramarine) to paint the big block of foliage at the top of picture. Dab on some tiny leaf shapes with the tip of the brush.

**14** Continue with this muted green mix to strengthen the tone on the second-to-left tree trunk. Note how the paint does not adhere to the areas where wax has been applied, helping to create the effect of diagonal beams of sunlight.

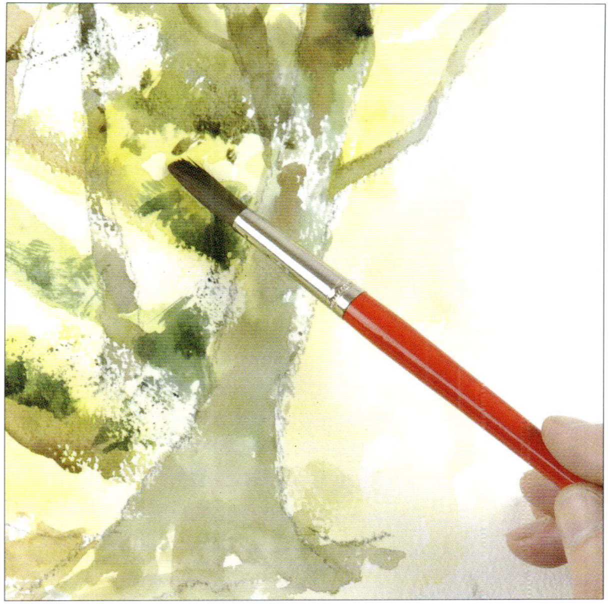

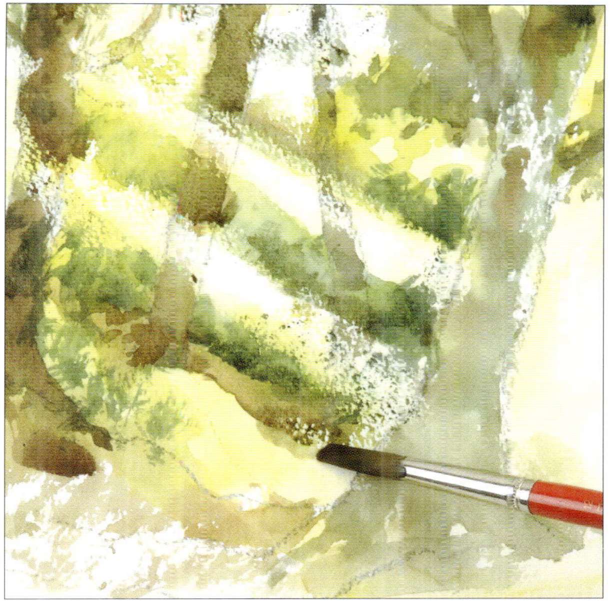

**15** Add small washes of the green mix over the browns to build up the tone and color. Keep everything loose by holding the brush lightly at the top of the handle.

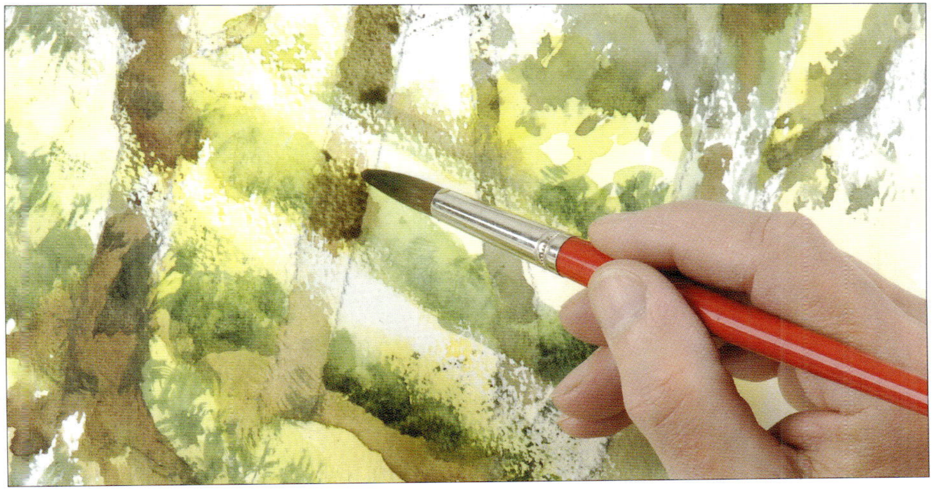

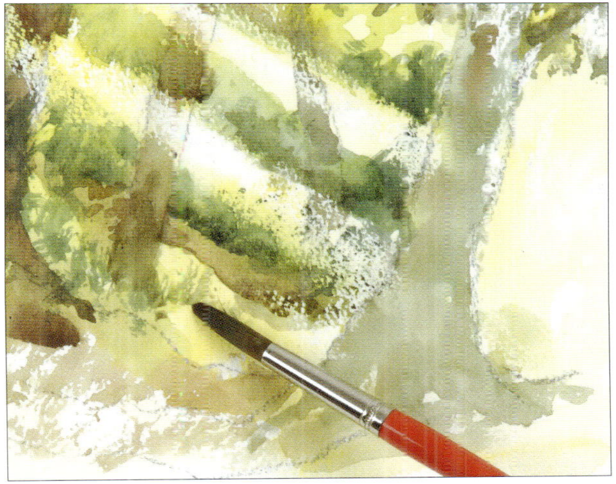

**16** To create tufts of grass in the foreground, first wipe your brush or dab it on a spare piece of paper to get rid of excess paint. Then, with small movements of the wrist, flick the brush up and outward.

5 Stipple your dark mix at the top of the orange to describe the hollow that once held the stalk. Then dip your brush in water and use it to take back some color below the line that runs around the shadowed side. Use the tip of your brush and carefully lift off color with small, precise strokes.

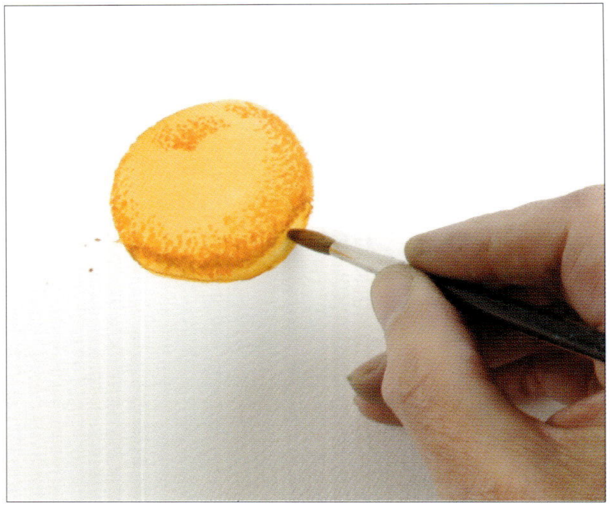

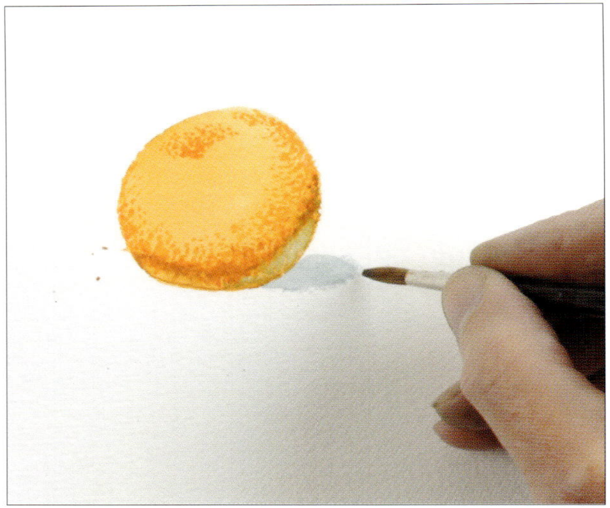

7 Now mix a blue pigment and use it to add the cast shadow of the orange. Note that blue is the complementary color to orange—that is, on the opposite side of the color wheel. Often, you find the complementary color of an object in its cast shadow. So a red apple might have a greenish shadow and a yellow banana might have some purple in its shadow.

6 In a separate well in your palette, mix a little of your orange wash with a green pigment. Use this color to indicate the light thrown up onto the orange from the white table.

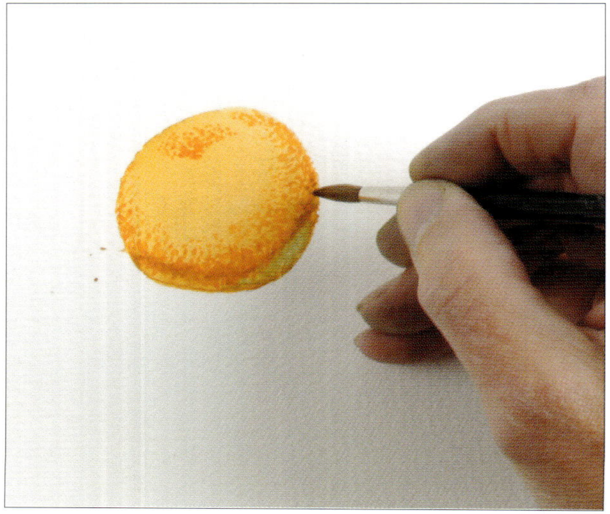

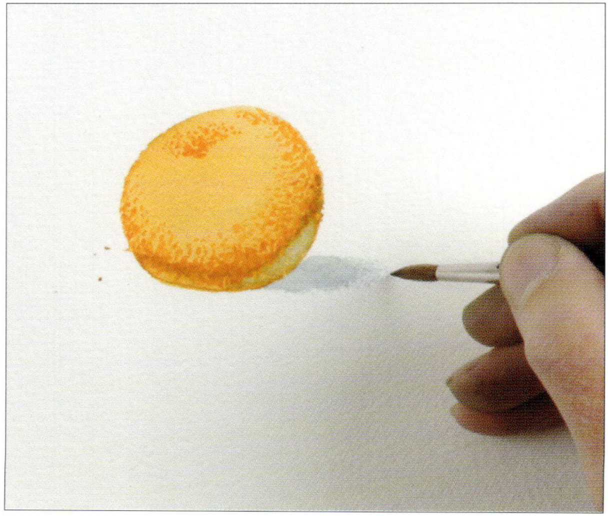

8 Now dip the brush in clean water and lift off tone at the outer edge of the cast shadow. The cast shadow should be darkest immediately under the object and gradually become paler as it stretches outward. The final picture is enlivened by the pattern of dots created by the stippling technique.

**17** Now you want to start giving a stronger impression of depth in the picture. Clean your brush in water, and apply water to the edges of the washes in the background. This will make them paler and softer, so that they "sit back" in the picture. Keep a fairly relaxed grip on the brush and stop when you see a pleasing effect emerging.

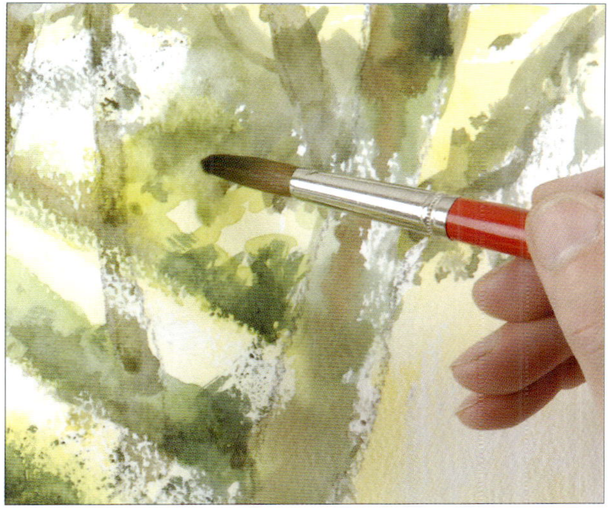

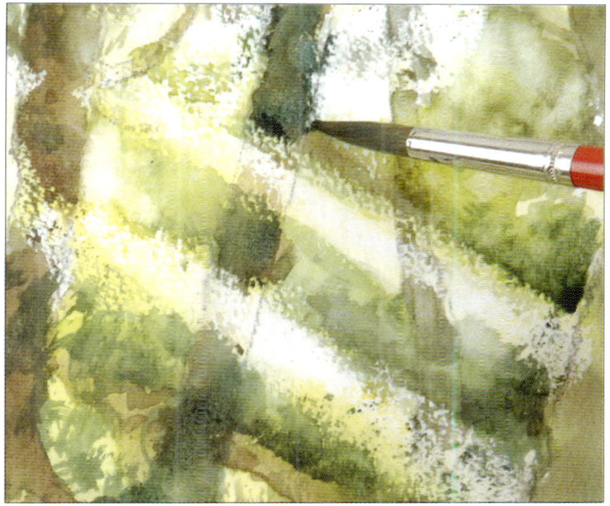

**19** Now return to your deep green mix of ultramarine, cadmium yellow light, and just a touch of burnt sienna. Apply this to the second to left tree trunk.

**20** For the background foliage, switch back to your muted green mix. Keep subtly altering your mixes, by introducing a little more of one color or another. This will keep the picture fresh, with lots of delicate changes of color.

**18** To soften unsightly marks, wet the area with clean water and then dab it with a piece of kitchen towel. Try not to remove all the accidental marks. Little spots and runs of paint can bring the painting alive and help capture the texture of foliage, grass, and the ground.

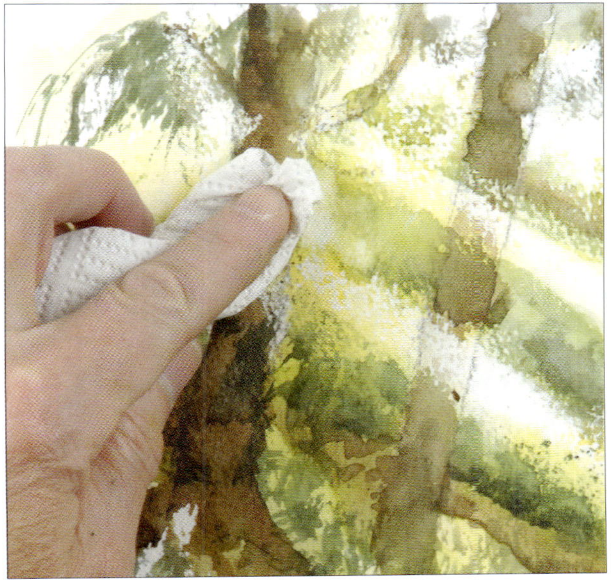

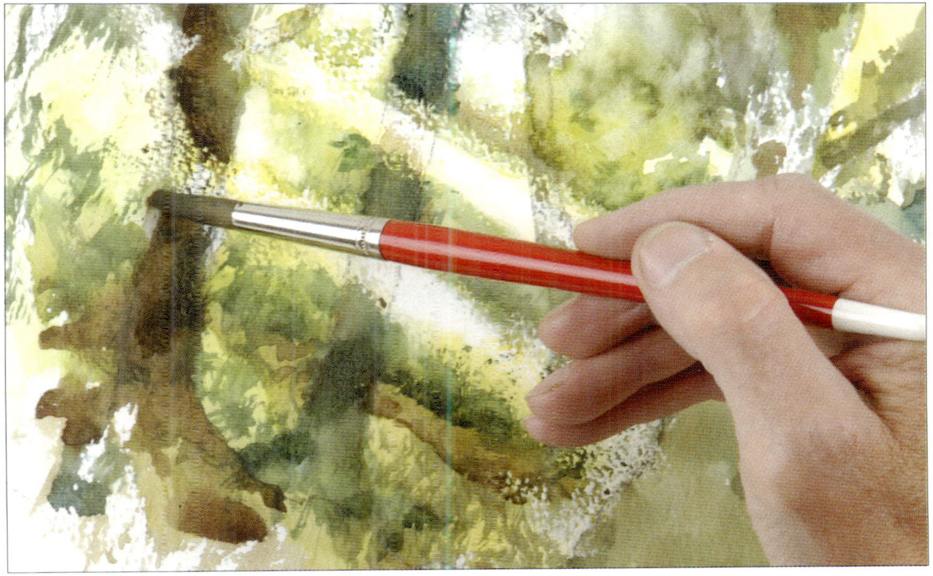

# basic techniques / **stippling**

1 Stippling involves building up color and tone with lots of small dots of paint. It is a great way to convey the form, texture, and fall of light on an object—and it works perfectly for an orange, with its pitted peel. Start by applying a flat wash of orange with a medium-sized round brush. Do not worry if your orange is not perfectly circular—oranges very rarely are!

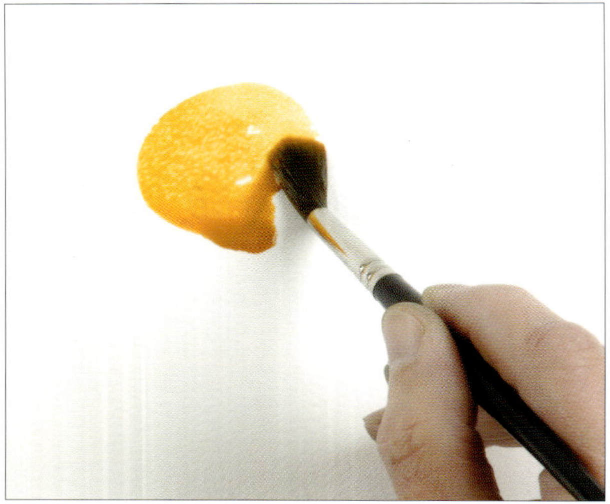

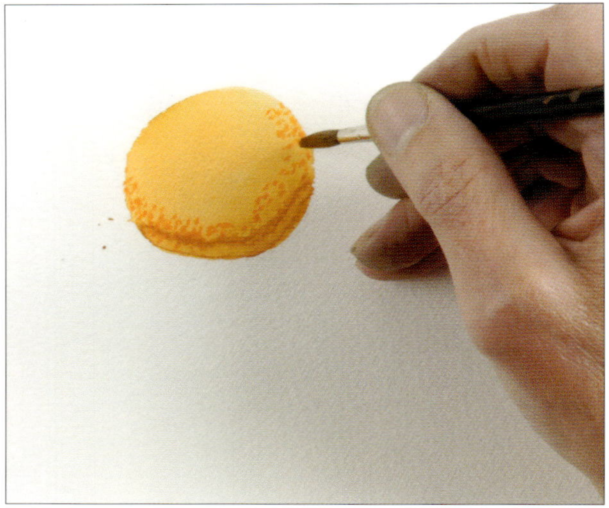

3 Continue building up the stippled dots. As the light is coming from the left, darken the right side of the orange as well as its underside. To do this, paint the stippled dots close together.

2 Darken your orange mix with, for instance, burnt sienna or burnt umber. Apply this with the point of a small round brush to the shadowed underside of the orange. Simply dab color on to the paper with the pointed end of the brush to create the stippled effect.

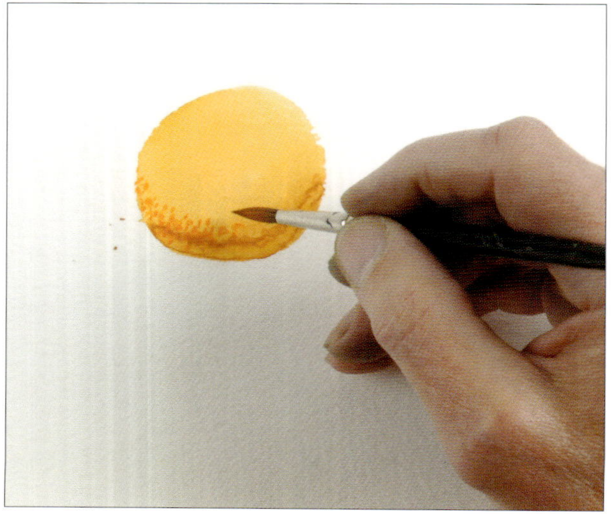

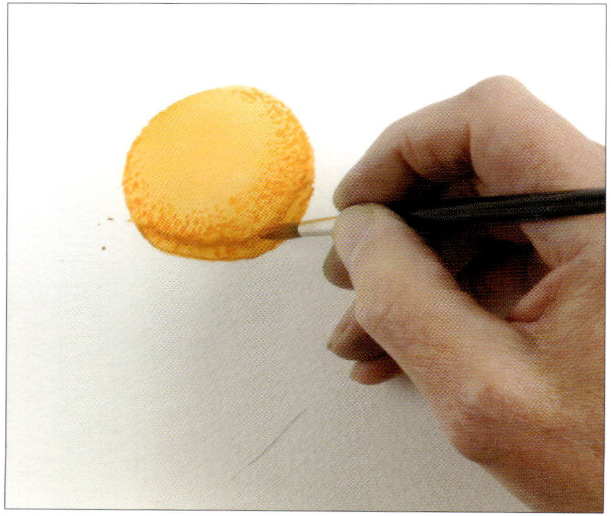

4 Establish a curving line that runs just inside the bottom and right edges of the orange. Below this line, some light will be reflected back from the white tabletop—so this area will be slightly paler than the rest of the shadowed side.

21 Now emphasize the shadow areas on the left by applying your deep green mix (ultramarine, cadmium yellow light, and a touch of burnt sienna). Use a well-loaded brush and don't be afraid to run color over the base of the far left tree.

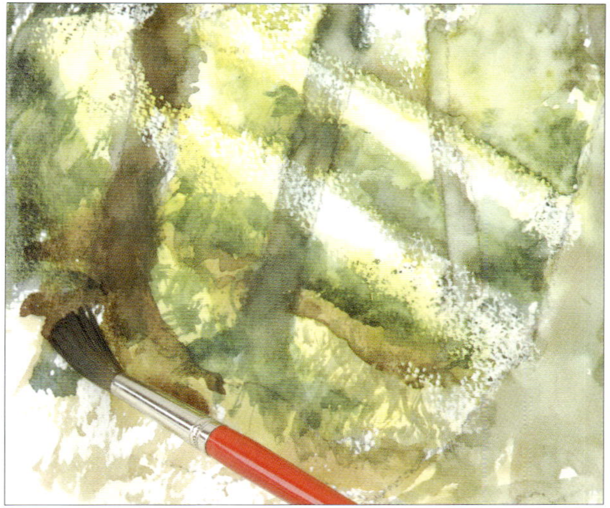

22 Bring your green mix down to the bottom left corner of the image. This large wash will help lead into the viewer's eye into the sunlit center of the picture. If you see an unsightly edge, wet your brush in water and soften it.

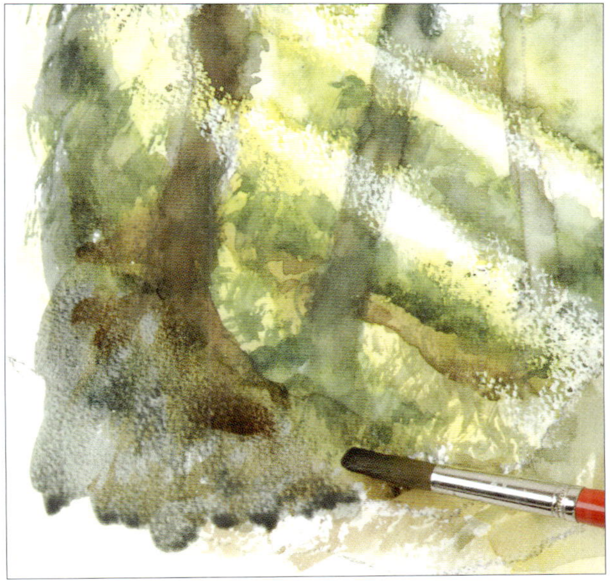

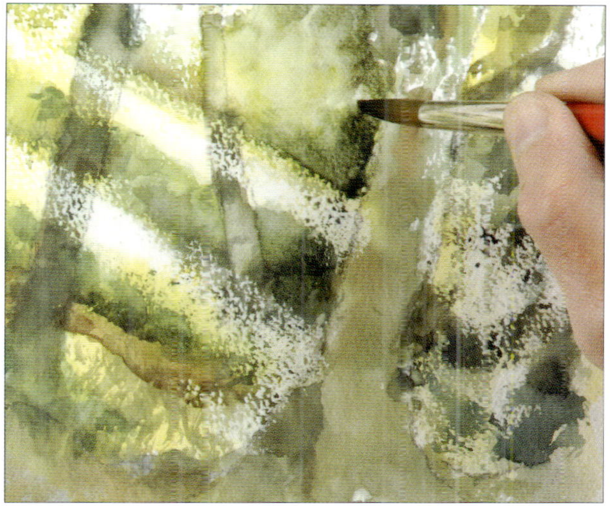

23 Continue using your deep green mix to pick out the dark tones in the background. This will help the tree trunks and the shafts of sunlight stand out. Note also how the paint creates a speckled effect over some of the areas of the wax—perfect for the shimmering quality of sunlight in this leafy glade.

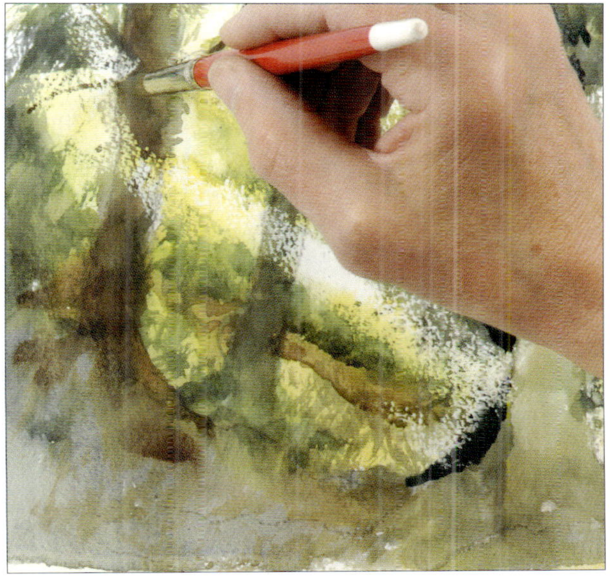

24 Returning to your brown mix, describe a few branches emerging from the trunks. Do not be too definite, but use a relatively dry brush and just graze the tip of the brush across the surface of the paper. Let the rough watercolor paper create textures for you.

5 Make a new wash, combining a green pigment with touches of your gray mix. Use this for the cardigan of the man on the right.

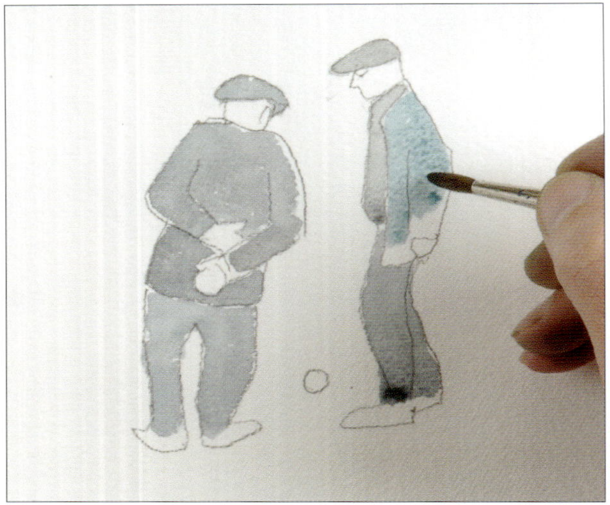

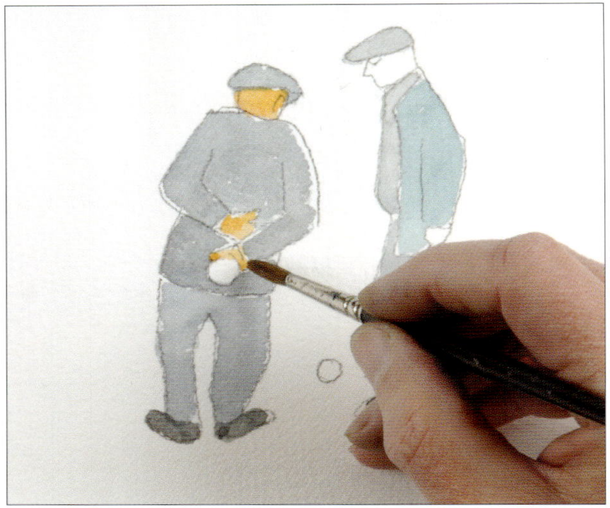

7 Now add the flesh tones on the hands and faces. Some manufacturers make a flesh-tone pigment—generally Naples yellow with a touch of vermilion. But this is hopelessly inadequate to deal with endless range of human skin tones. It's often best to experiment with mixing your own flesh tones. For these fair-skinned gentlemen, try creating a warm orange hue to convey their sun-tanned skin.

6 Strengthen your blue-gray mix to put in the shoes of both men. Painting the shoes in a dark tone helps anchor the men to the ground, stopping them from appearing to float in space.

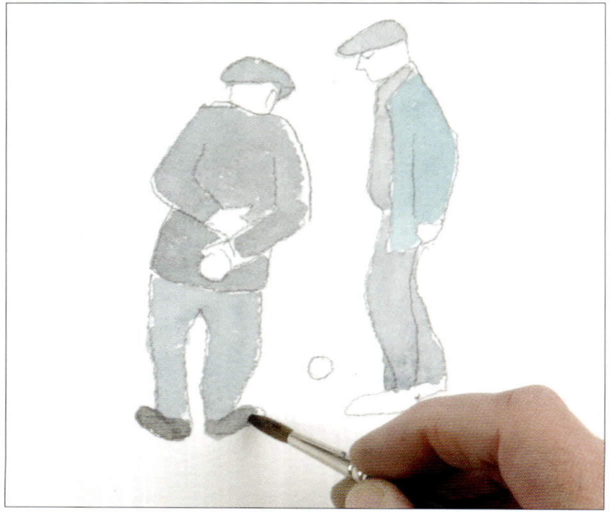

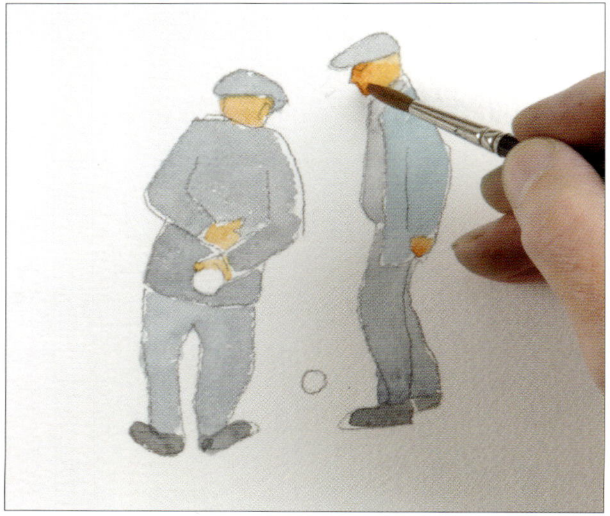

8 Note how the warm skin tones bring the image to life—they jump out at the viewer, especially as they are set against the cool blue and green-grays of the clothing.

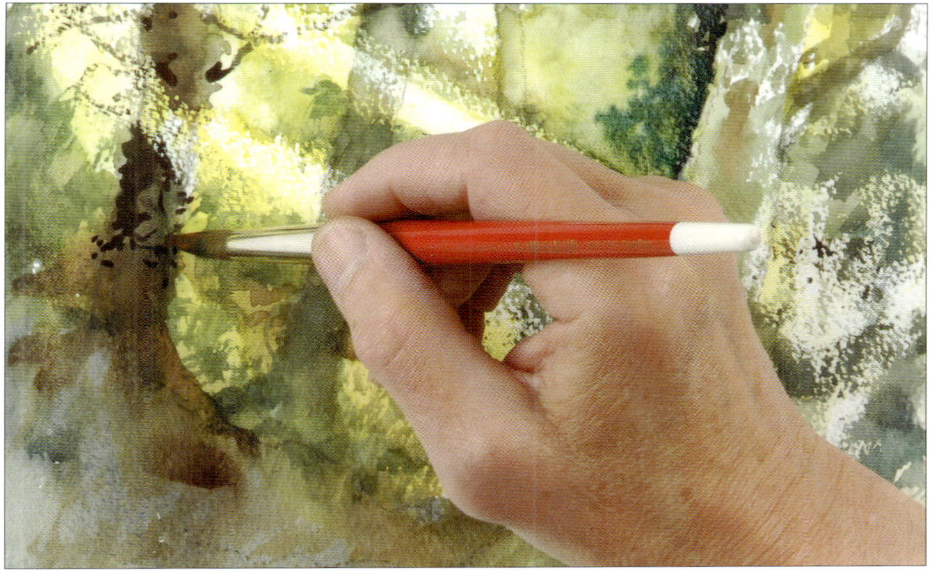

**25** Now mix in more burnt sienna and a touch of ultramarine into your brown mix. Use this to build up the ivy on the tree on the left. Dab the tip of the brush onto the paper to attain crisp leaf-like shapes.

**26** Now dip the brush in clean water and use the water to soften areas in the background that appear too bold. Use the water to lift out highlights to the trunk of the farthest trees.

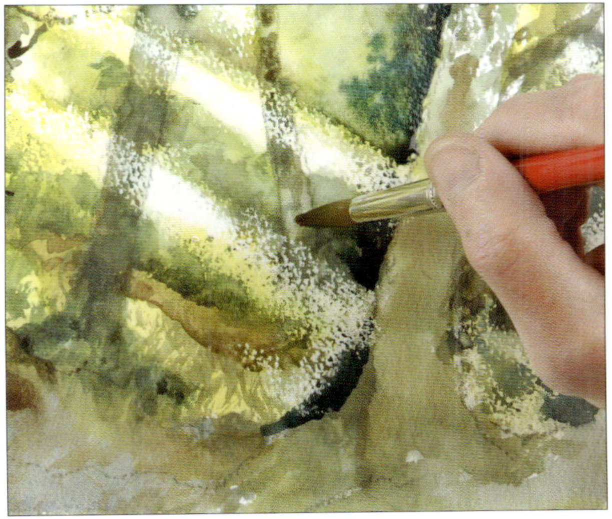

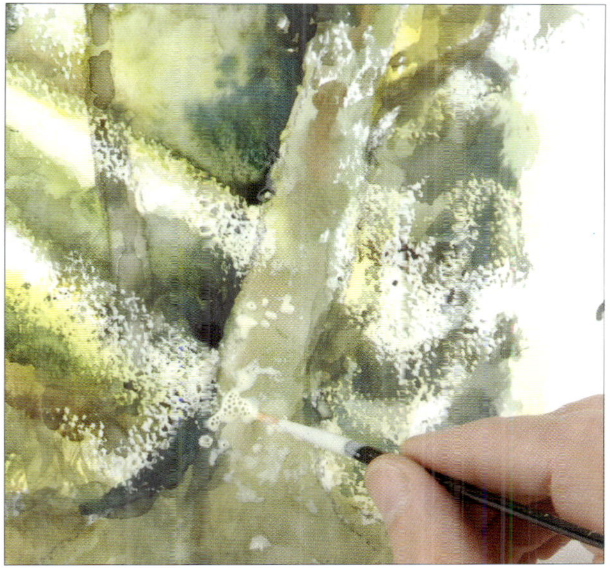

**27** Now apply some masking fluid to the tree trunk on the right of the painting. Use an old brush that you keep specially for this purpose and paint in little dabs to the tree trunk on the right. This will preserve some light areas that will give an impression of both the bold, mottled texture of the bark and the sunlight coming through the leaves.

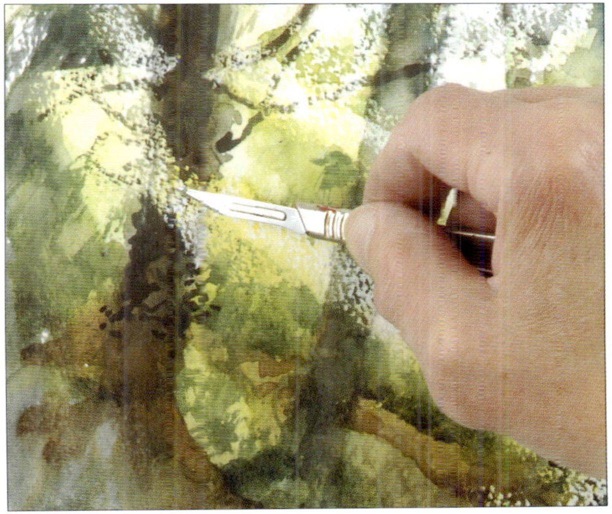

**28** When working with wax resist, you are likely to make a few mistakes. Luckily, correcting them is easily done. Here, the artist has decided it would look much more dramatic and realistic, if the shaft of light traveled behind the foreground tree on the far left. So he is gently scraping off the wax on this tree with a craft knife.

# basic techniques / **simple figures**

1 You can create wonderful figure studies in watercolor—either by sketching people quickly or by building up a series of wet-on-dry washes to create a detailed study. Watercolor washes often look best when combined with pen and ink or, as here, pencil. Start this exercise by drawing the outline of a man in profile.

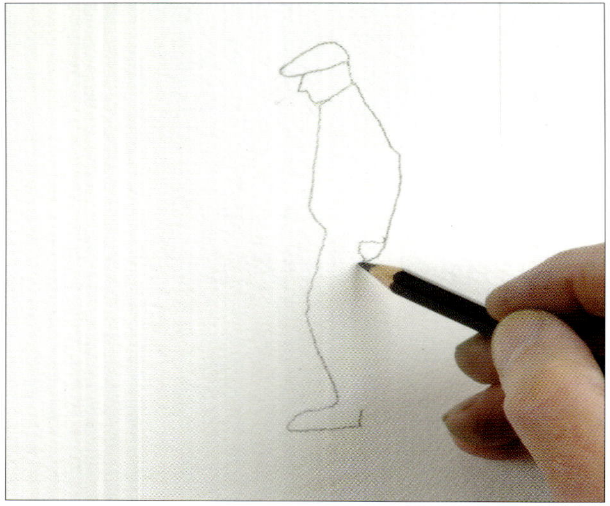

2 Now draw a man with his back to us. People tend not to stand bolt upright—especially old people. So draw the man leaning slightly. Note that he leans to the right—so that the eye is led into the picture not off to the edge of the paper. As a result, it looks as if the two figures are talking. In between the men, draw a petanque ball.

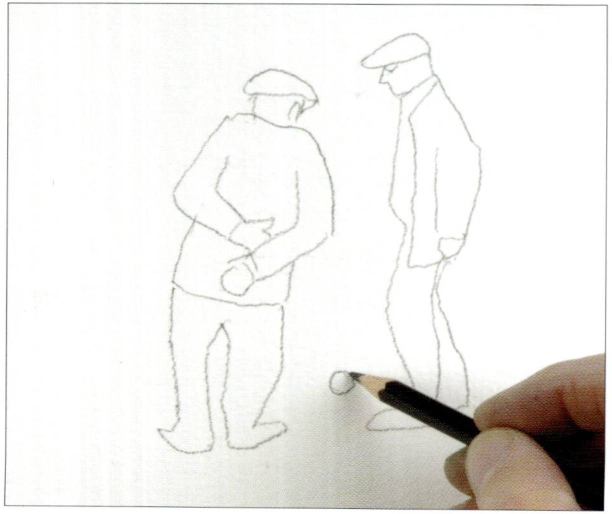

3 Use a wash of blue-gray for the leaning man's top and cap. You can build up wash after wash so you attain deep shadows and a sense of three-dimensional form. For this study, however, we are keeping it simple and using single washes.

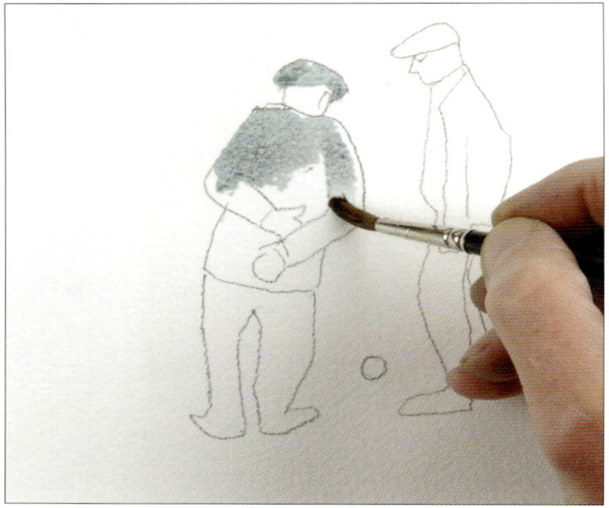

4 Add a touch more blue to your mix to paint the man's pants. Then use the same mix for the shirt of the man on the right.

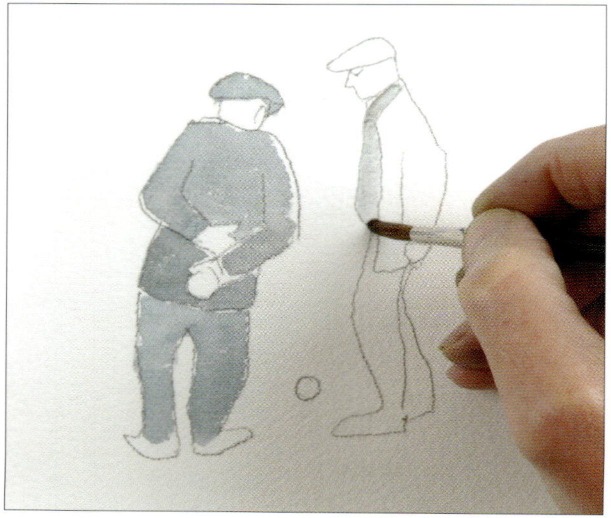

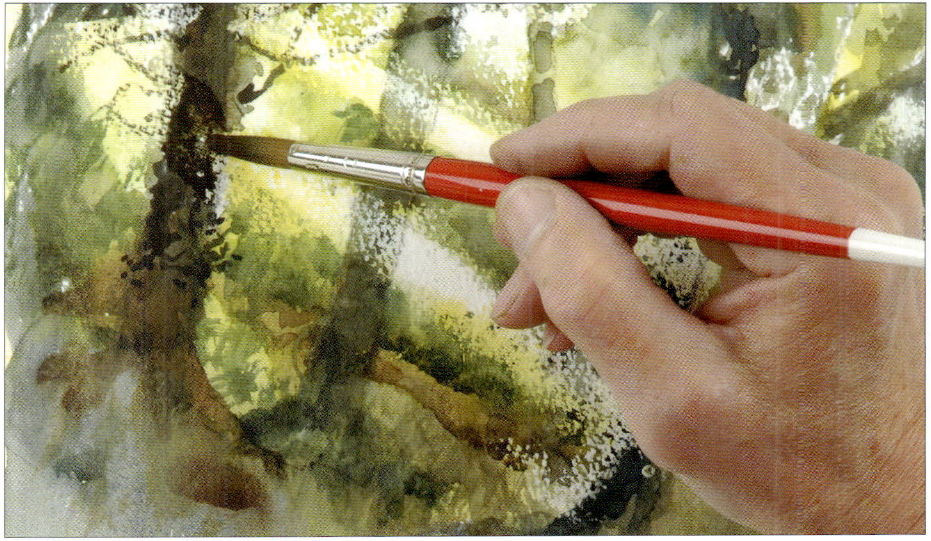

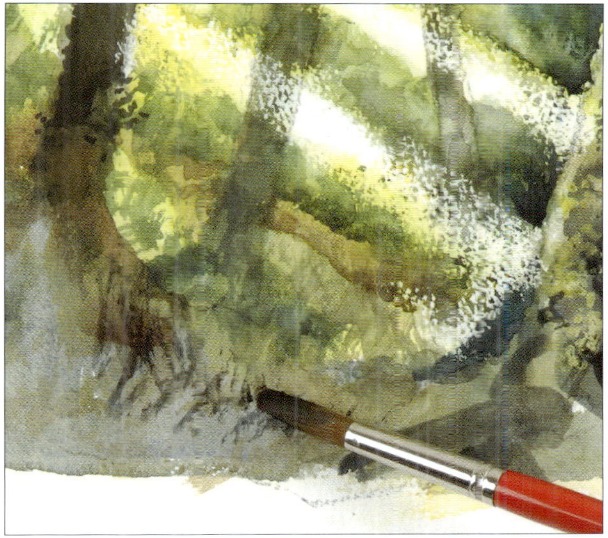

**31** Now put in some foreground grasses. Wipe off any excess paint on a scrap piece of paper. Then apply the remaining dryish color to the paper using small flicking movements of the wrist. Vary the direction of the strokes.

**29** Then, with the No.12 brush, the artist applies the brown mix to the area he has scraped off. Note how the tree now leaps forward in front of the shaft of light, giving the picture an impression of depth.

**30** Add some ultramarine to your brown mix and apply it in bold brushstrokes to describe the roots of the near tree. Remember, as the sun is coming from the left, put the darkest tones on the right side of the tree.

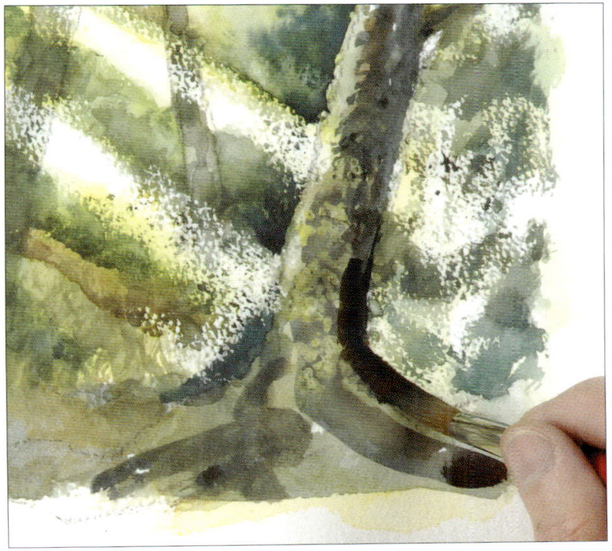

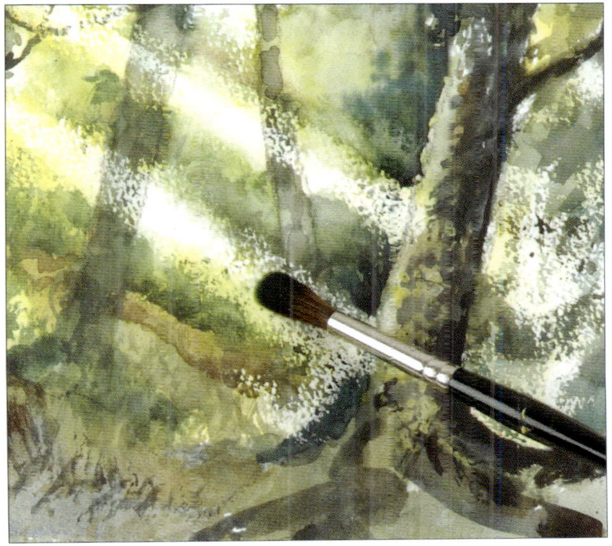

**32** To really give the impression of the shimmering light, use the No. 8 brush to graze color over the areas of wax. Note how the wax has not completely covered the paper, and so paint adheres in specks in the "tooth" of the paper.

# basic techniques / **lifting out**

Painting clouds in watercolor can be done in two ways. You can apply a wash of color for the sky, let it dry, and then paint clouds over the top. To do this, you mix white paint with touches of other color, maybe pink and yellow for the sunlit tops of the clouds, and blue and purple for the shadowed undersides. The addition of white paint makes the watercolors opaque, so hiding the blue wash below. Alternatively, instead of adding paint, you can take it away. With a kitchen towel or a damp brush, you can lift out paint from a sky wash while it is still wet. The white paper you expose then stands for the clouds. This is the technique used in this exercise.

1 Tilt your drawing board slightly toward you and mix a large wash of blue with lots of pigment. With a decorator's brush, apply the wash across the top of the paper. Do not worry if it does not cover all the paper.

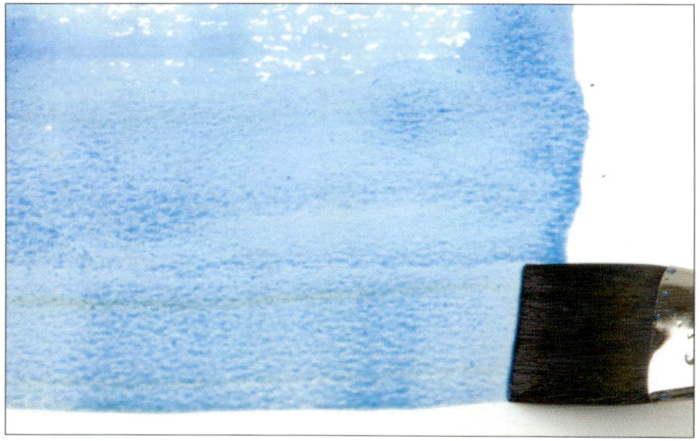

2 Continue applying your blue wash with horizontal strokes, overlapping them slightly to attain a fairly flat wash. Now you have to work quickly before the wash dries!

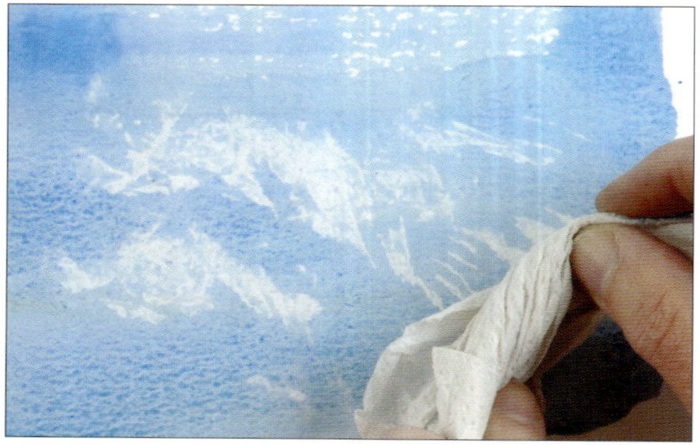

3 Use kitchen towel to dab out the color and create clouds. When dry, kitchen towel will lift out nearly all of the paint, but picks up progressively less paint as it gets damp. Use it dry for the sunlit tops of the clouds and damp for the undersides.

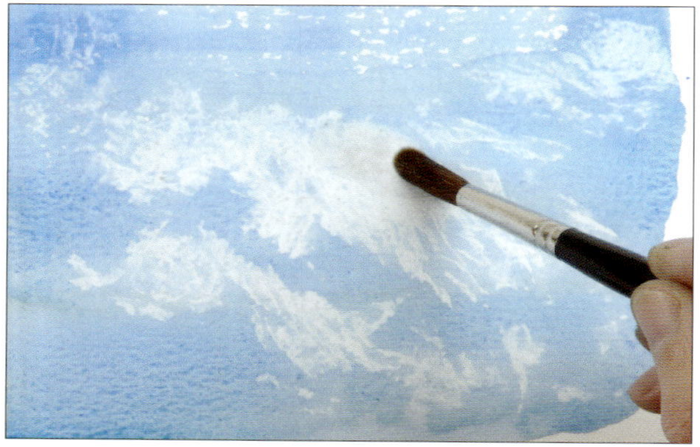

4 Now roll the side of a clean, damp brush across the sky to take back more color. Manipulate the paint so that you attain pleasing cloud shapes. Wipe the brush on kitchen towel before using it to create clouds in a different part of the sky.

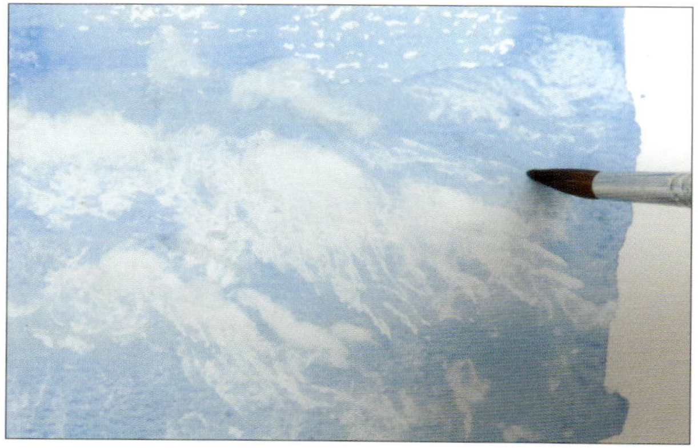

5 You now have a sky full of differently shaped clouds. What's more, there is a sense of energy and movement—as if the clouds are racing across the sky.

**33** Now strengthen the shafts of light by grazing the brown mix diagonally down to the bottom left corner. Again use a relatively dry brush and drag the color gently over the paper.

**34** Keep building up the shadow areas. Aim for a large variety of tones, from the white of the paper to the dark foreground trunks. Emphasize some shafts of light by dragging a damp clean brush diagonally down to the bottom right corner.

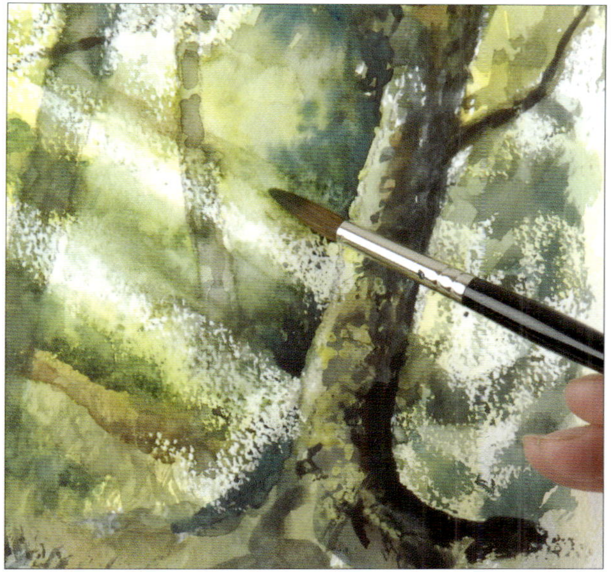

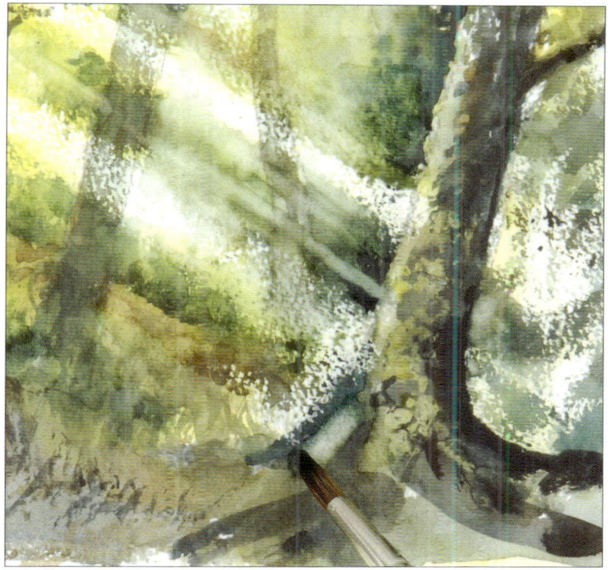

**35** Continue using your brush dipped in clean water to remove some paint at the bottom of the foreground tree. Make sure your brushstrokes follow the root forms.

**36** Now, with a finger, gently rub the area of the tree trunk where you applied the masking fluid, and remove the dried coating to reveal the preserved lighter areas underneath.

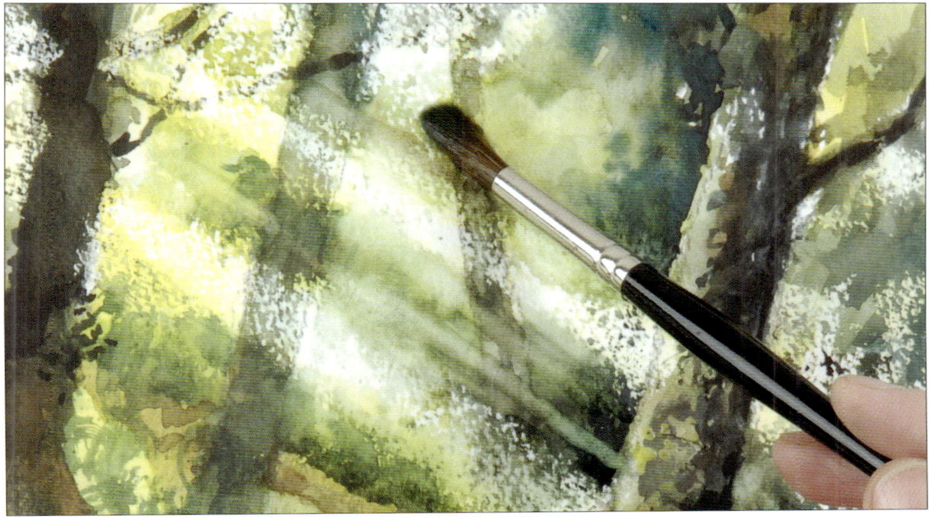

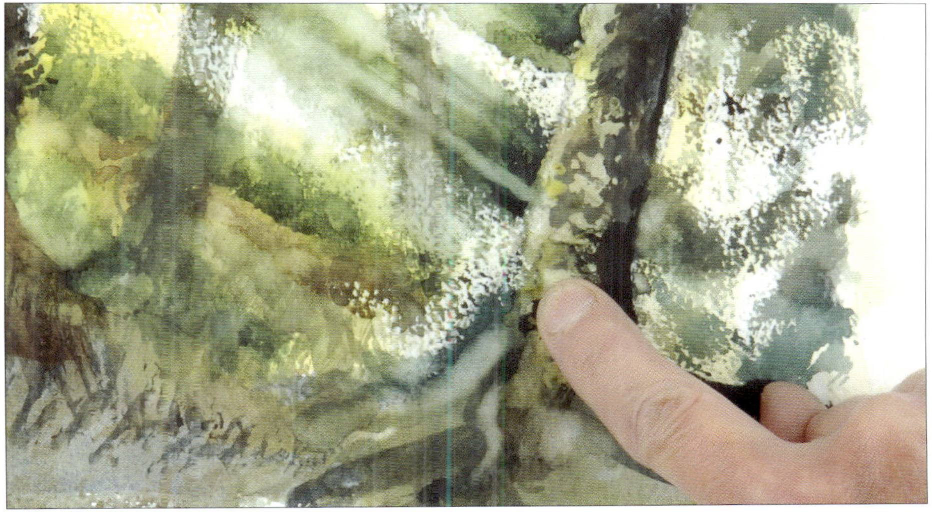

5 Use a medium round brush to apply your dark mix to the rock on the right. Do not obliterate the original sponge texture—instead paint around it, adding solidity to the textural marks.

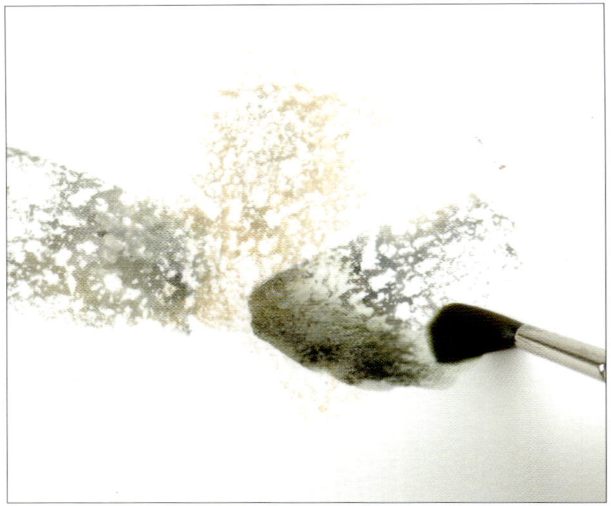

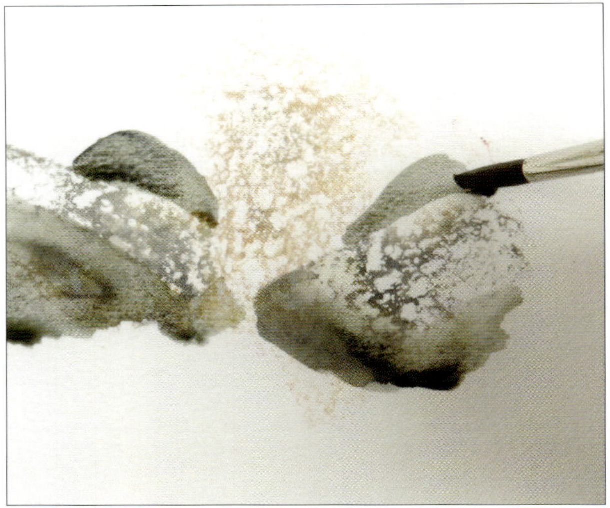

7 Continue building up the dark mix. Let the paint pool at the bottom of your brushstrokes—this will give an impression of the shadowed undersides of the rocks. Vary the color of the mix if you want—by introducing a cool green or blue pigment that plays off against the warm red rock.

6 Also brush the dark mix to the rock on the left. Use sweeping curved strokes so the rocks look as if they have been smoothed by the sea.

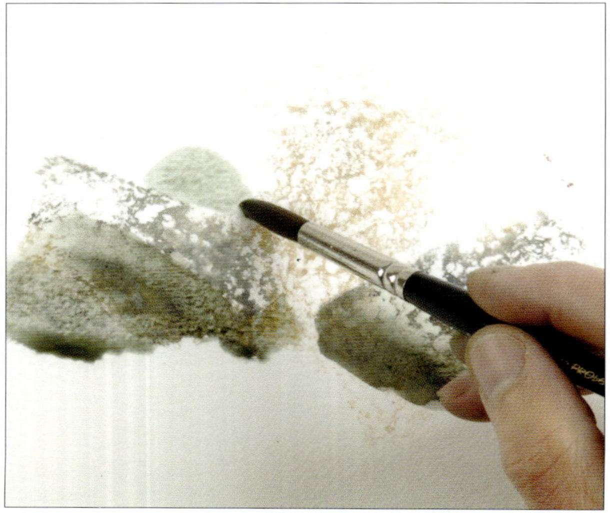

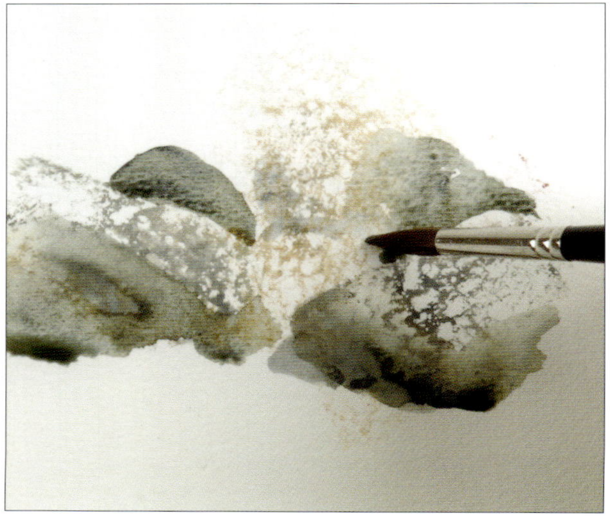

8 Finally, tie the whole picture together by dipping your brush in water and smoothing out some of the brushmarks over the textural areas. The final picture has an exciting mix of smooth brushstrokes and textured spongework.

**37** Using your brown mix and the tip of the No.1 brush, draw two or three thin branches. Try to add each branch with an unbroken brushstroke. Also, to create a sense of depth, make sure the distant branches are thinner and paler than those in the foreground. For the distant branches, you can even lift the brush off the paper in places.

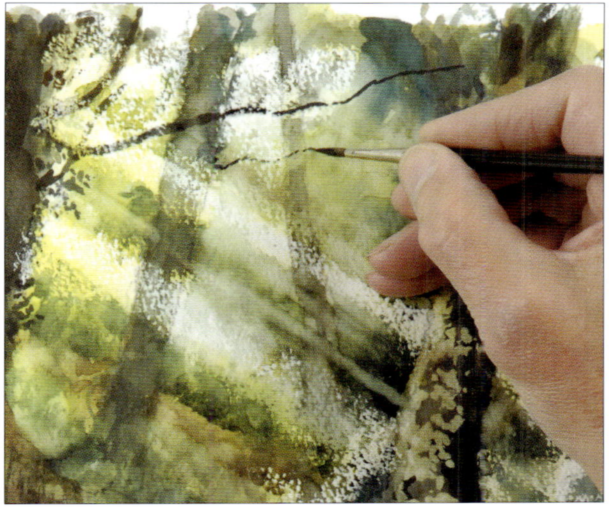

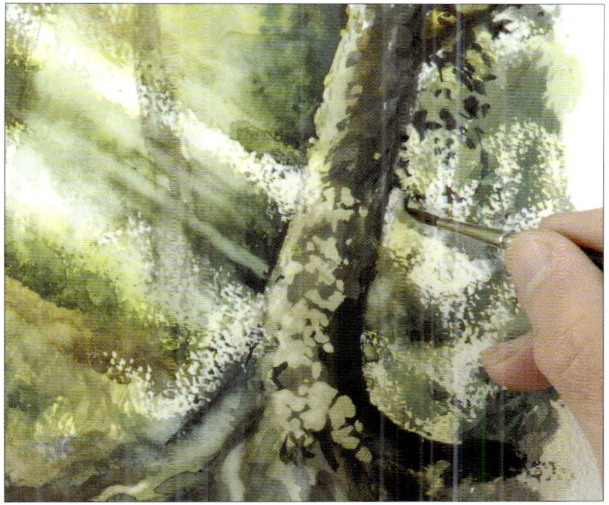

**39** Describe the ivy foliage on the right tree. Remember, you will see some leaves head-on and others at oblique angles so vary the size and shape of your marks.

**40** To finish, build up the tone of the foreground. Use the muted green mix to deepen the shadows in the roots of the foreground tree. You want lots of contrast so the foreground details leap forward.

**38** Add more ivy leaves to the bottom of the far left tree with your deep green mix. Work quickly, dabbing the paint on with the tip of the brush. Remember adding lots of texture in the foreground will contrast with the hazy shapes in the distance, resulting in a picture with a true sense of three-dimensional depth.

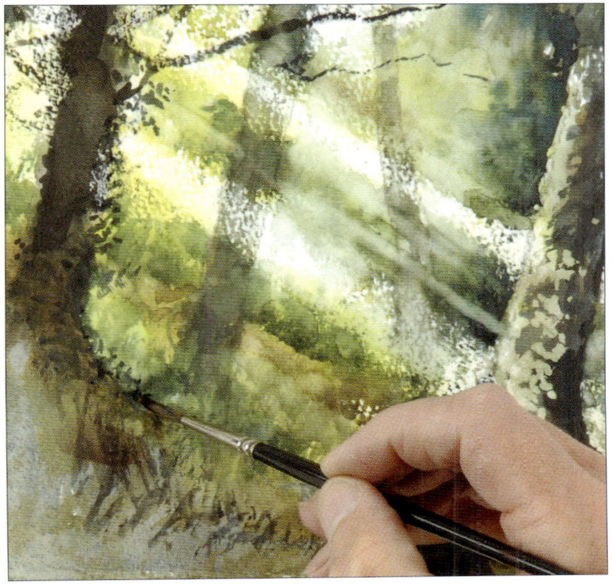

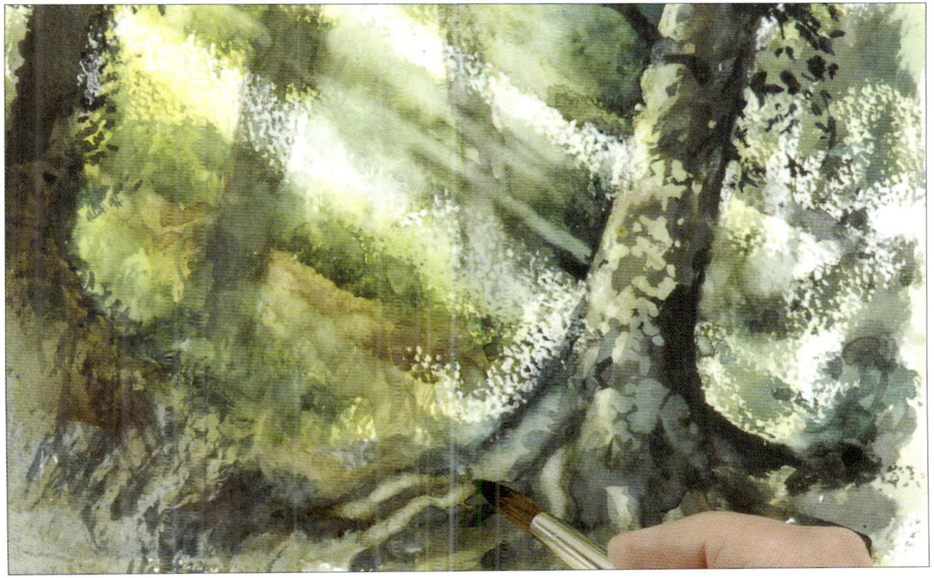

# using sponges: synthetic

1 Synthetic sponges create more predictable textures than natural ones. However, if you apply several layers of paint with a synthetic sponge and then enhance this with brushwork, you can create some stunning and varied effects. In this study of rocks, start by mixing a warm reddish brown color—raw sienna or burnt sienna are ideal.

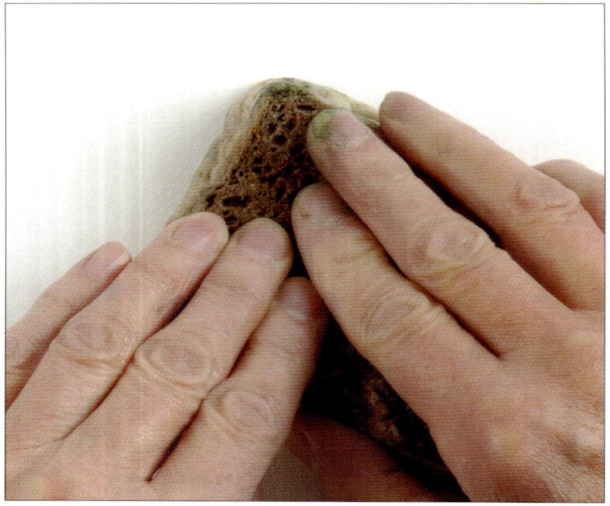

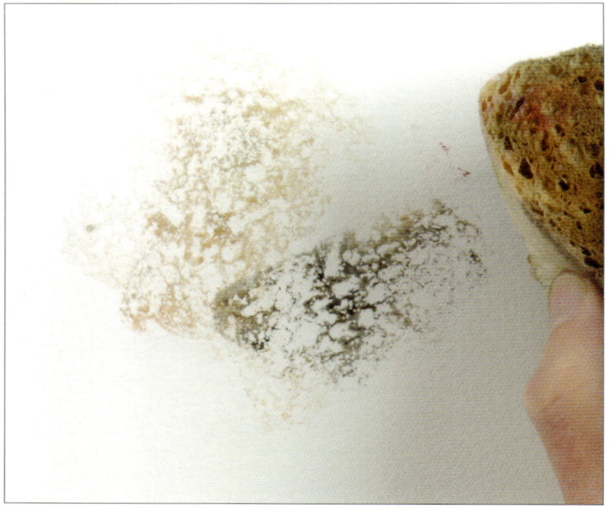

3 Now mix a darker color, for example raw umber. Dip a different part of the sponge into this mix and apply it to the right of your first mark.

2 Dip your sponge into the warm red mix and then press it onto your paper. You can create different effects by varying the amount of pressure you exert.

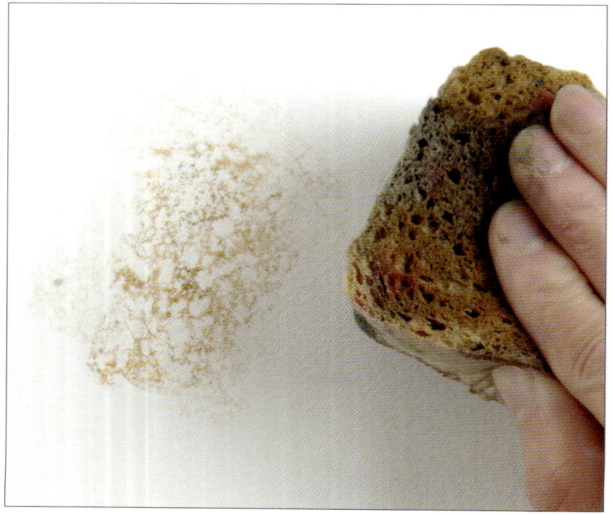

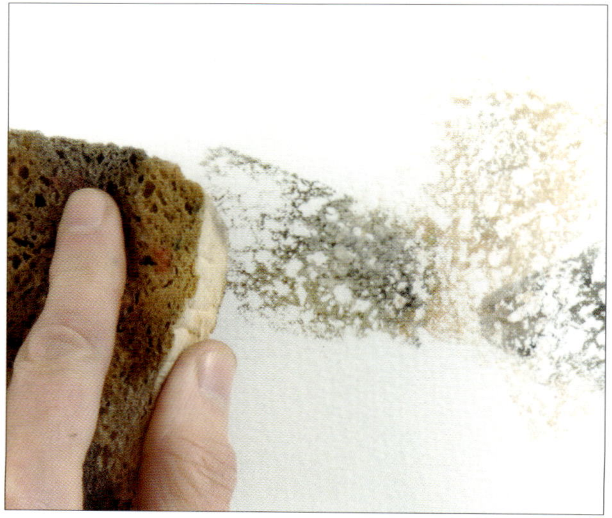

4 Add another dark mark to the left of your red mark. You now have the beginnings of three rocks. Next, you need to use brushwork to complement the textures created by the sponge.

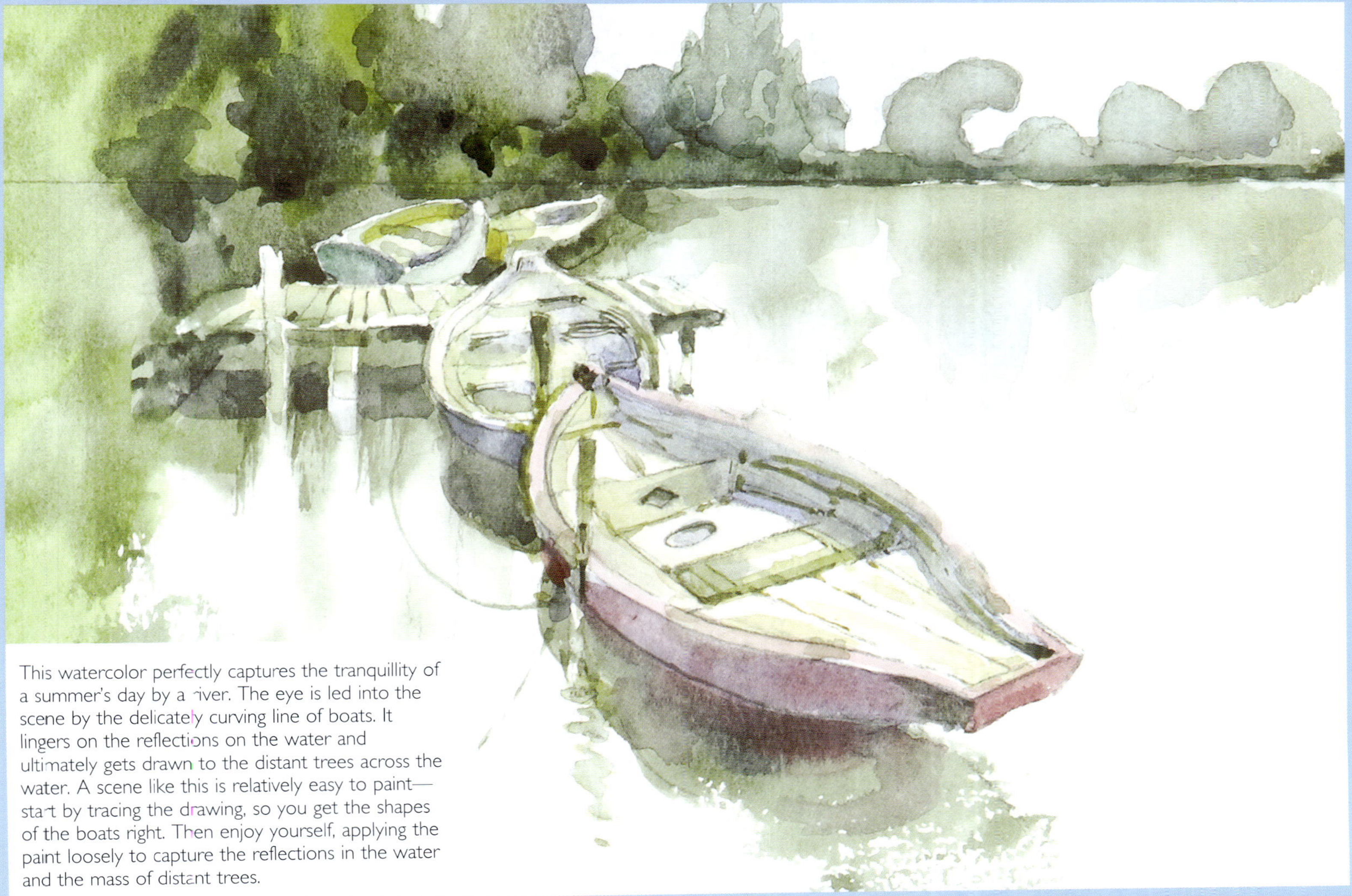

This watercolor perfectly captures the tranquillity of a summer's day by a river. The eye is led into the scene by the delicately curving line of boats. It lingers on the reflections on the water and ultimately gets drawn to the distant trees across the water. A scene like this is relatively easy to paint—start by tracing the drawing, so you get the shapes of the boats right. Then enjoy yourself, applying the paint loosely to capture the reflections in the water and the mass of distant trees.

**MATERIALS**

**Drawing board**

**Watercolor paper**

**Watercolor palette**

**Watercolors: ultramarine blue, viridian, burnt sienna, Payne's gray, permanent rose, cadmium yellow**

**Brushes: No.10 round, rigger brush**

**Jar of water**

**Tracing paper**

**HB pencil**

**Ruler**

**Eraser**

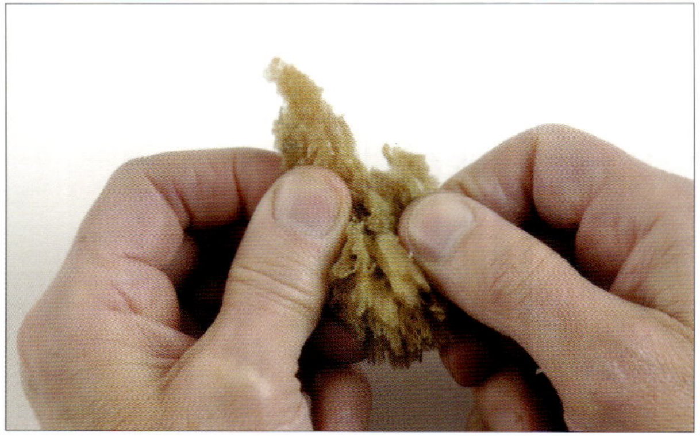

1 Painting with sponge creates textures that cannot be made using a brush. Natural sponges are preferable to synthetic ones—they are softer, more absorbent, and have an endless variety of surface textures.

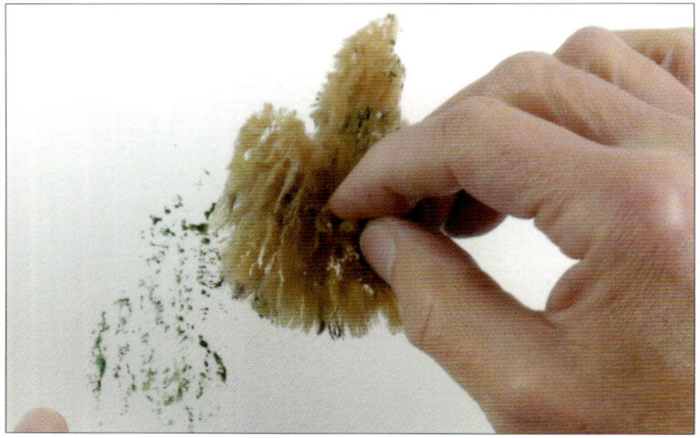

2 For this exercise, try painting a couple of trees with the help of a natural sponge. In your palette, mix a dryish green wash and dip your sponge in it. Practice making a couple of marks on scrap paper. Then apply the sponge gently on your drawing paper.

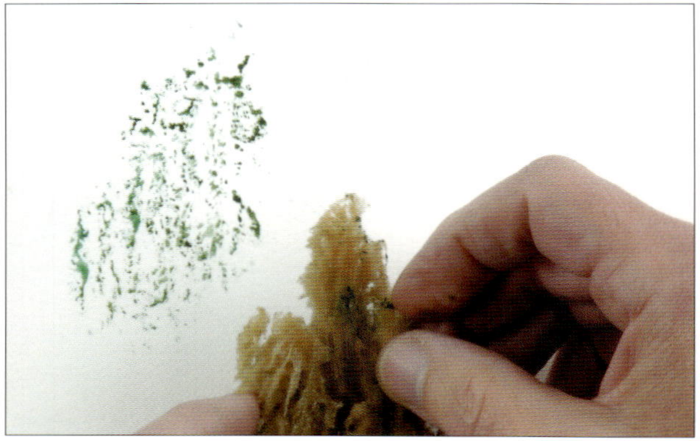

3 Continue dabbing the sponge on the paper. Note that the marks you make become finer as more paint is deposited on the paper. It is possible to achieve some very delicate effects in this way.

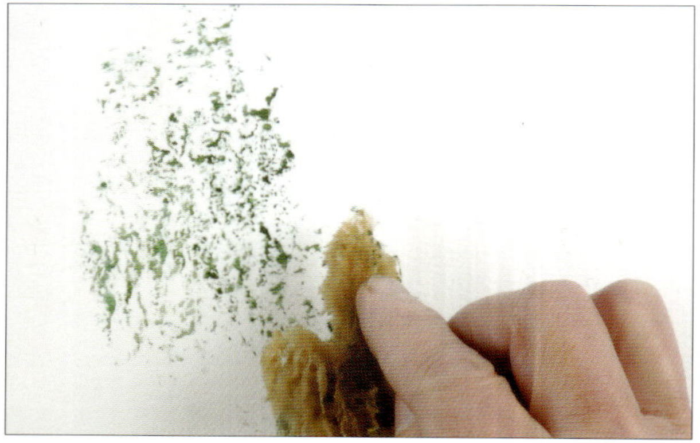

4 Continue building up the texture with the sponge. Reload the sponge with paint when the marks become too faint. Vary the way you hold the sponge, squeezing it into a ball for bolder marks and letting it spread out for more subtle effects.

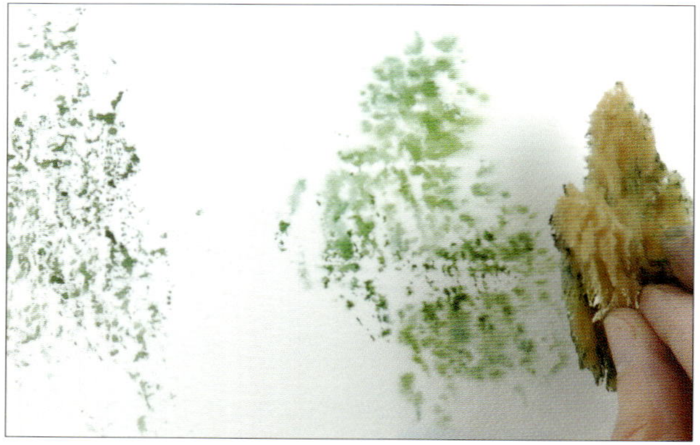

5 Create another tree. Add some yellow and more water to the wash. When you apply this color, press harder and try to move the sponge slightly across the paper. This will create broader marks that distinguish the new tree from the first one.

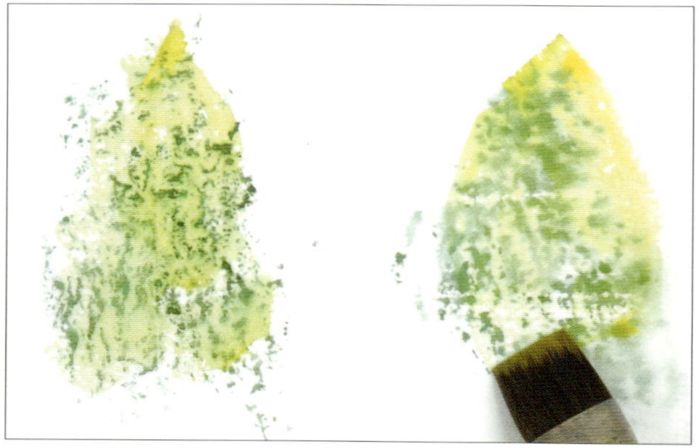

6 Let the all sponge marks dry. Then with a large flat brush and a very watery mix of yellow, paint over the textures you have created. The wash will appear to soften the sponge marks and create the perfect impression of two trees.

1 With the HB pencil, trace the outline of the boats from the opening page of this project. Place the tracing paper on your watercolor paper and go over it with a sharp-pointed tool—for example, a stylus or a hard pencil. You will then be able to follow the indentation in the paper to do your drawing.

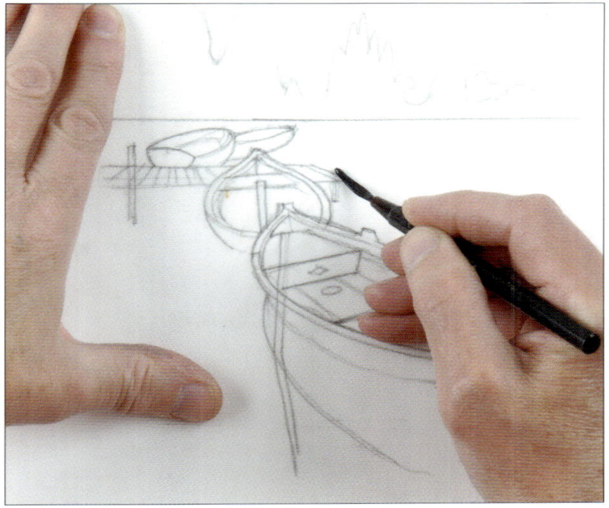

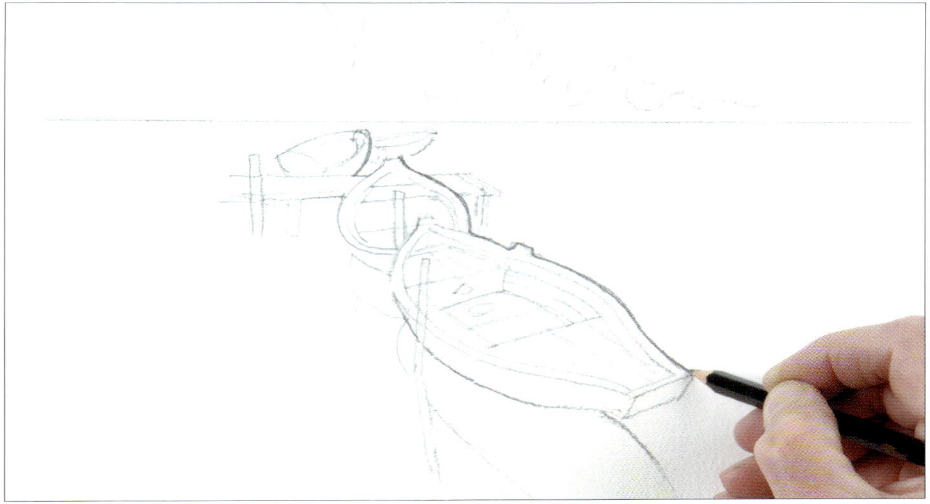

2 Work over the indentations in your paper with the HB pencil. First, draw in the horizon with a ruler. Then draw the boats and the jetty. Define the internal features of the boats —the planks and the benches—not just their outlines.

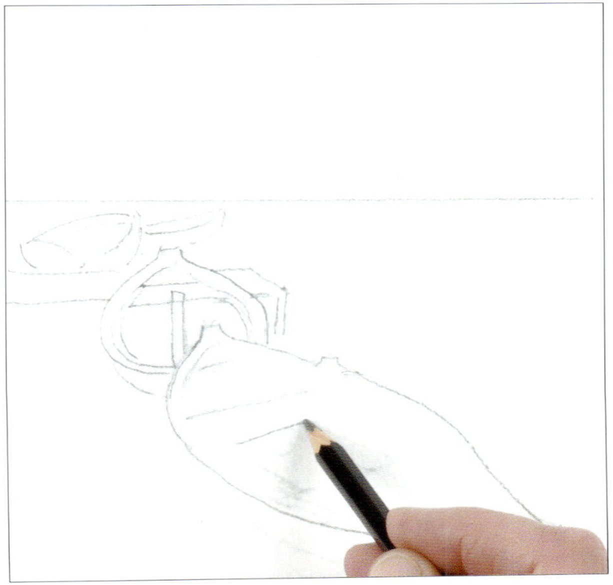

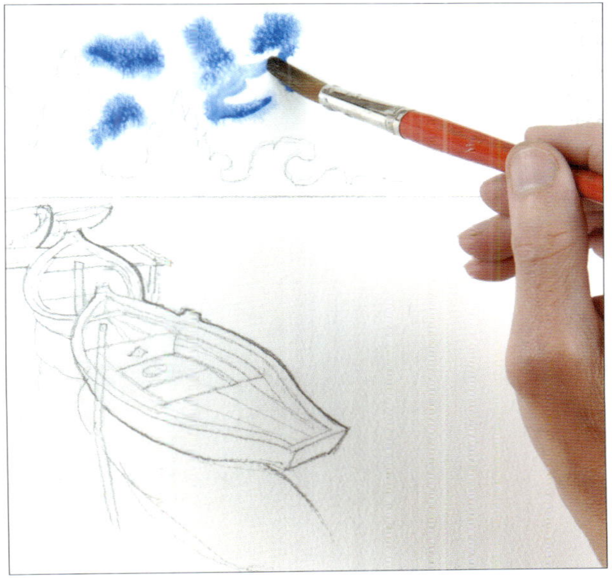

3 Add the outlines of the trees above the horizon. They do not have to be as detailed as the boats. Next strengthen the line defining the right edges of the boats. Varying the weight of some lines can make the drawing look less mechanical.

4 Now, using the No.10 brush and clean water, wet the sky, taking care to avoid going into the tree area. Then mix up a wash of ultramarine blue and begin to dab this over the sky.

5 Mix a gray wash and, with a small round brush, add this color to the tops of the birds' bodies. Do not add color all over the birds' bodies—the exposed white paper can stand for the pale feathers.

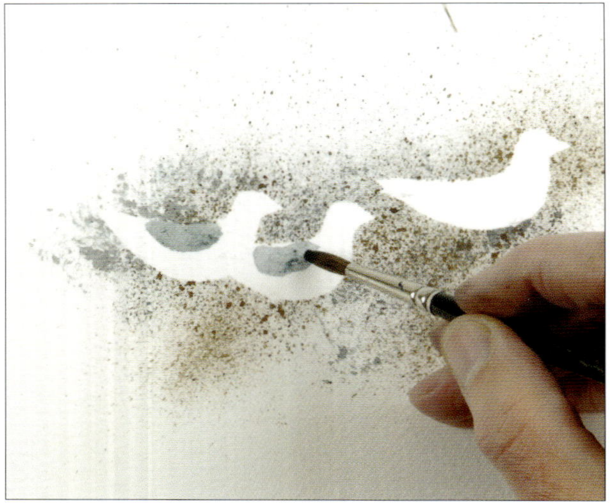

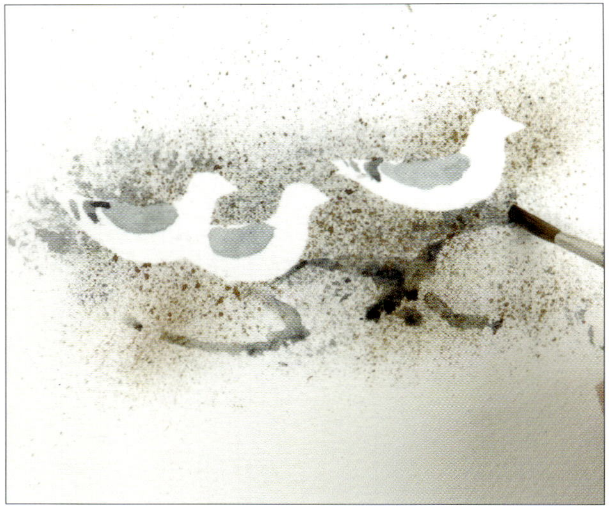

7 Add darker paint to your gray mix—for instance, Payne's gray or burnt umber—to vary the color of the outlines. Do not complete the outlines—otherwise, they will begin to compete with main subject of the painting, the birds.

6 Continue with the gray mix to indicate tail feathers and the rocks the birds are standing on. Do not fill the rocks with color; you only need to suggest the outlines—the viewer's imagination can do the rest!

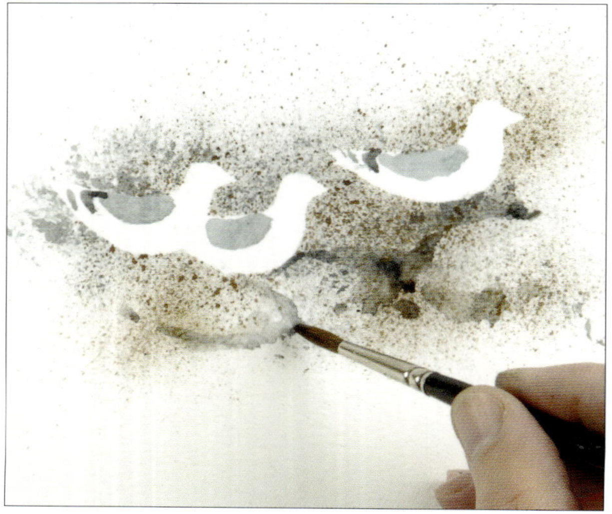

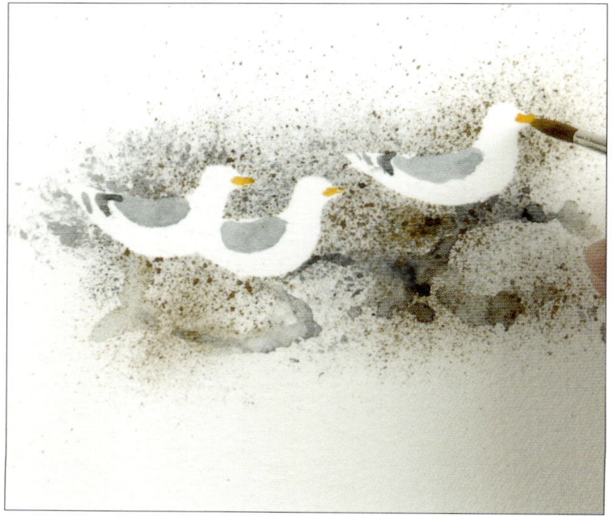

8 As a final touch, mix some yellow paint and use this to indicate the birds' beaks. The spattering really brings the final image to life—although the birds are static, the image is full of movement. The contrast of tones—from the exposed white paper of the birds' bodies to the dark outlines of the rocks—further enlivens the picture.

5 Continue building up the sky by adding the ultramarine on to the damp paper. Leave some white paper showing in between your brushstrokes—this gives a good impression of wispy clouds.

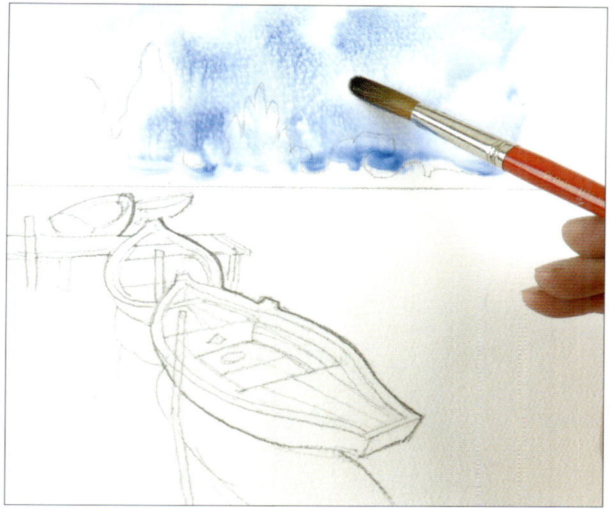

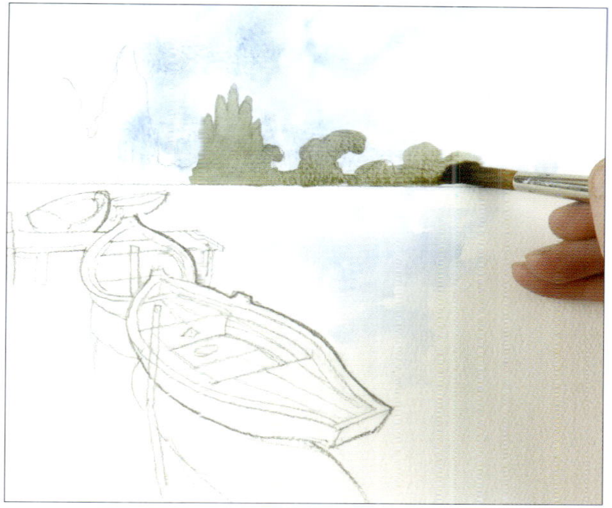

7 Now make a muted green mix using viridian, touches of burnt sienna, and Payne's gray, and lots of water. Add this into the tree area. Give some trees curved outlines and others straighter ones.

6 Now dampen the water area and apply the ultramarine here. Again try to dab the paint in different areas. Do not cover the water area with a flat, uniform wash of paint, and avoid putting too much color next to the horizon.

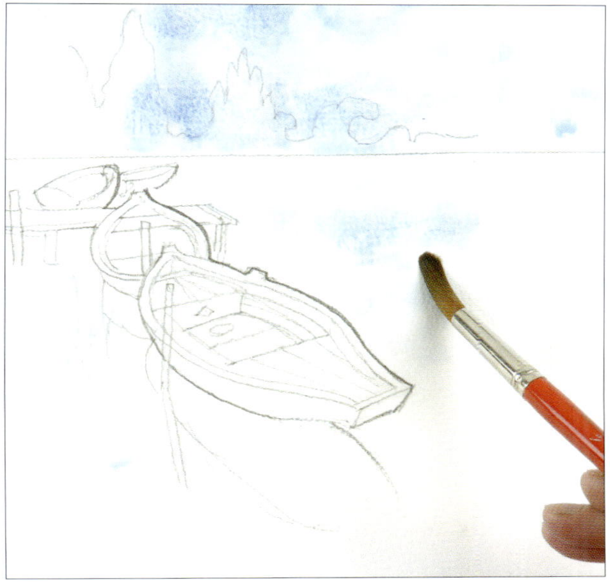

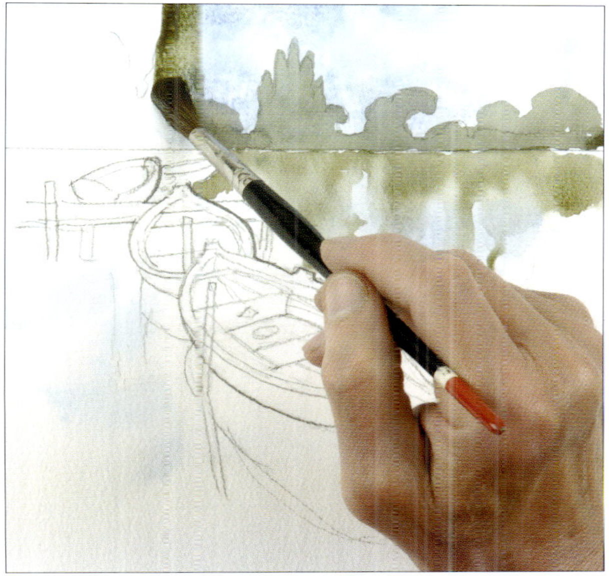

8 Apply the muted green mix under the horizon to show the trees' shadows in the water. Let the color bleed into the ultramarine on the damp paper. This wet-in-wet technique gives a great impression of gently moving water. Then add the tall pine tree above the boats with a bold brushstroke.

1 Spattering is a fun way of creating lively areas of texture and color. In this exercise, it is used with stenciling and sponging to capture a beach scene. First, draw three seagulls in silhouette on scrap paper and cut them out. Stick these stencils to your drawing paper, using a little paper glue to hold them temporarily in place. Then begin applying a dry mix of blue-gray with a natural sponge over the top of the birds.

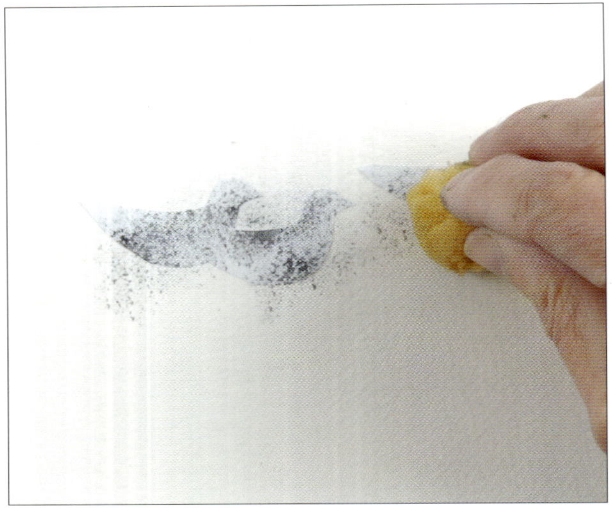

2 Continue applying color with the sponge. Squeeze the sponge into a tight ball and press firmly to intensify the texture in places.

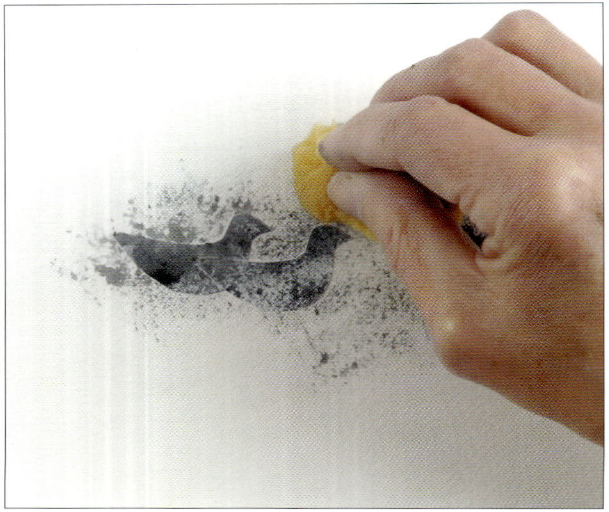

3 Now mix some brown paint and load a large round brush with this color. Hold the brush above the picture and use the handle of another brush to dislodge droplets of the paint. Vary your spattering technique by dragging the handle slowly through the hairs, hitting the hairs quite sharply and tapping the two brush handles together. This will alter the size and density of the droplets. Practice first on scrap paper.

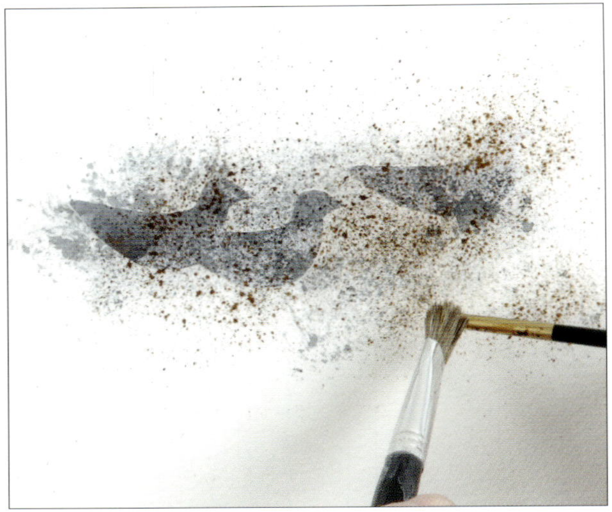

4 Let the spattered paint dry and then use a craft knife to pull up the paper stencils. The seagulls now stand out as white silhouettes against a beach of pebbles.

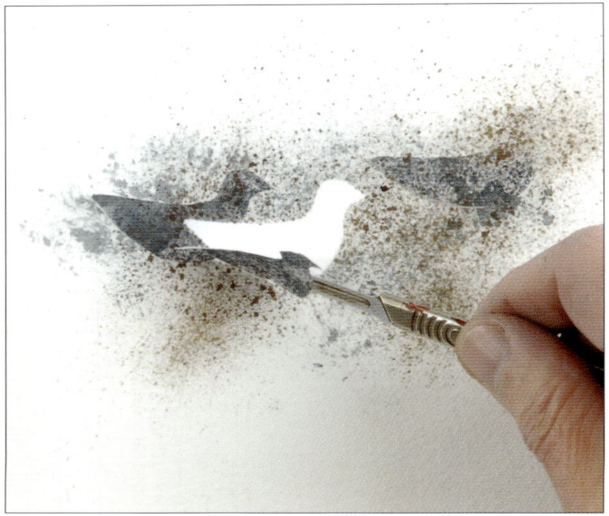

9 Add more viridian to your mix to build up the tone of the trees on the left. These trees are nearer to us than those on the right and giving them a stronger tone will make the come forward in the picture. Use the tip of the brush to begin rendering the shadow of the trees in the water.

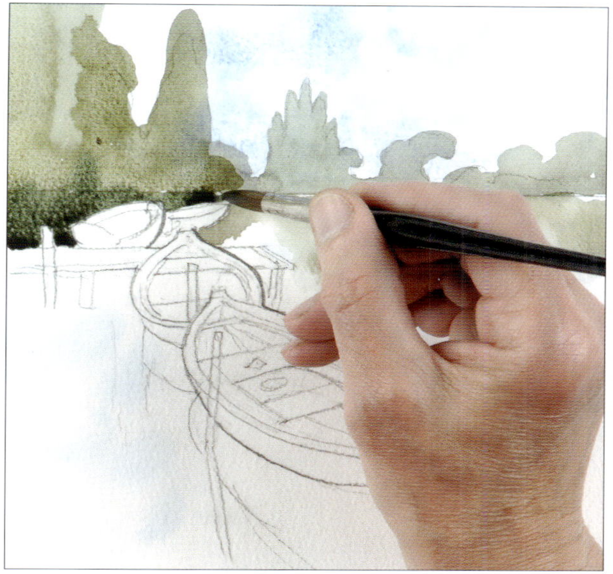

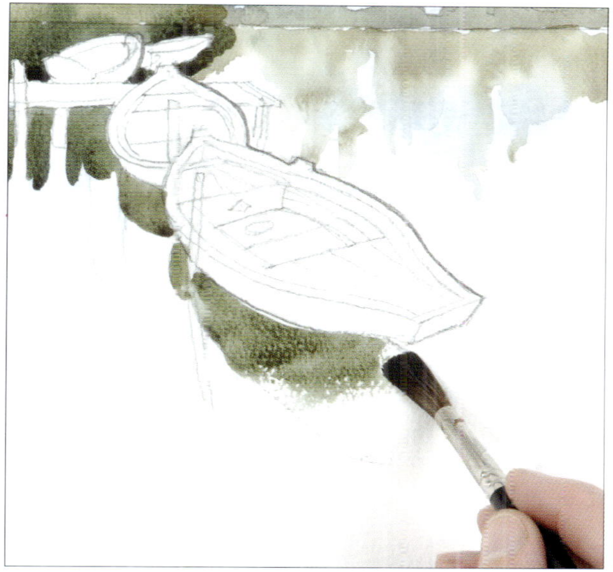

11 Add a little more water to your mix as you work down to the foreground, putting in the shadows of the boats. Make sure these shadows are curved like the boats themselves.

12 Now dip your brush in clean water and use it to "tease" some of the shadow tone under the jetty into the foreground. You should attain a pale blue-green color.

10 Add more viridian and a touch of ultramarine to your mix as you apply paint to the water. The shadows of the trees in the water should be as dark as the trees themselves. Carefully work around the boats and the jetty.

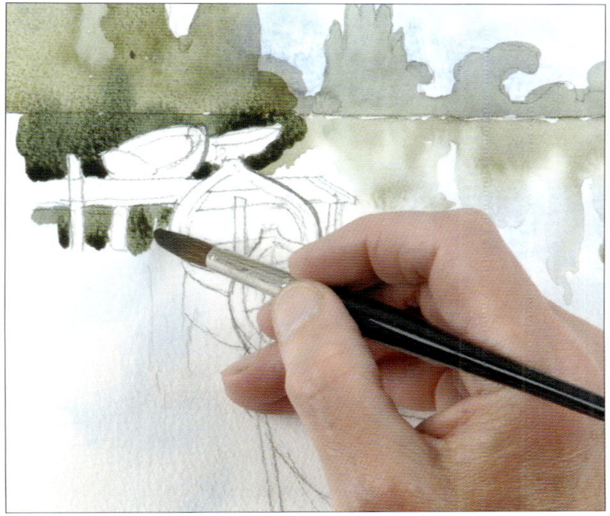

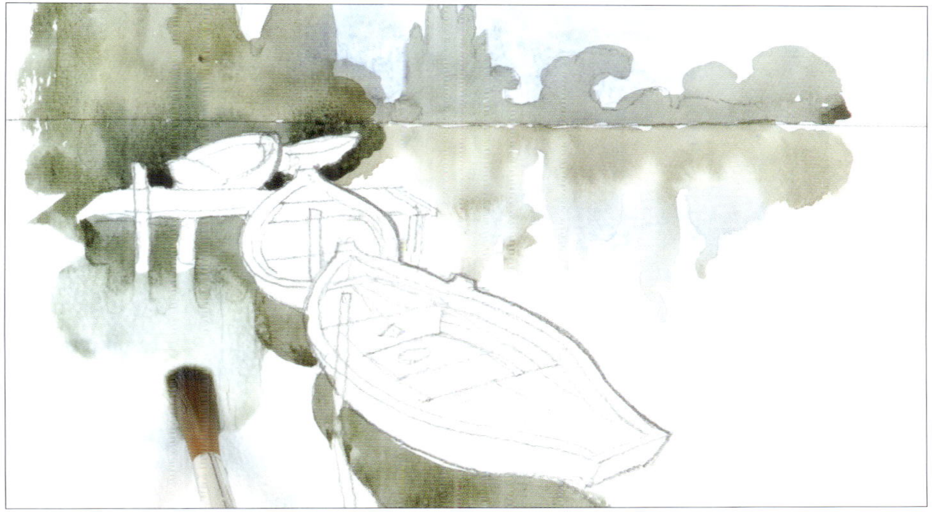

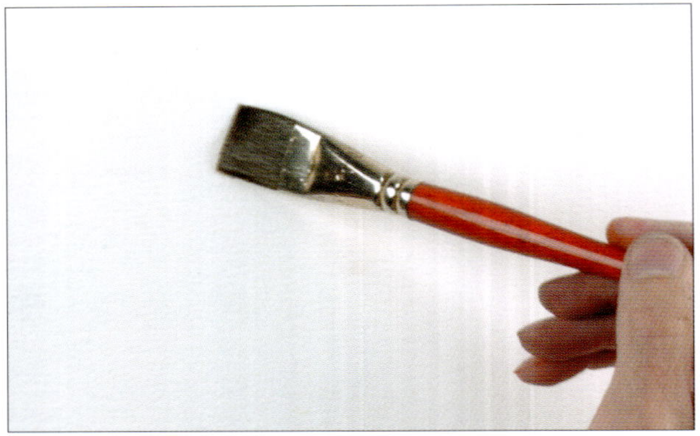

1 First, lay down a wash of clear water across the page with a wide, flat brush. Apply the water by pulling the brush across the paper in horizontal strokes to form bands. This is the technique for applying any flat wash to paper.

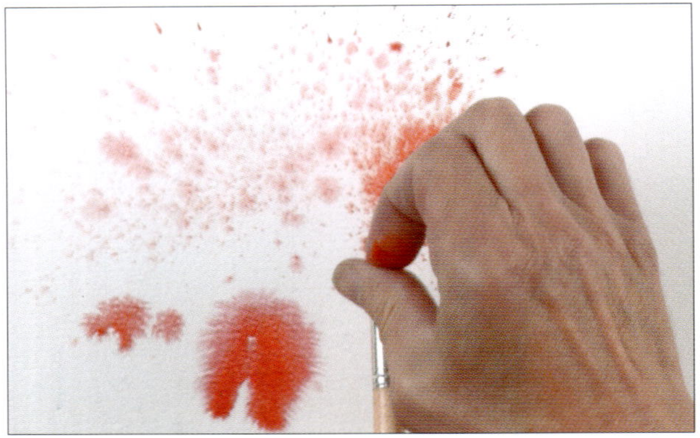

2 Dip a stiff hog-hair brush into your paint. Don't mix the paint too thickly, or it will tend to stick to the brush. Then pull your index finger across the hairs. Remember to pull your finger toward you—otherwise, you will cover yourself in paint.

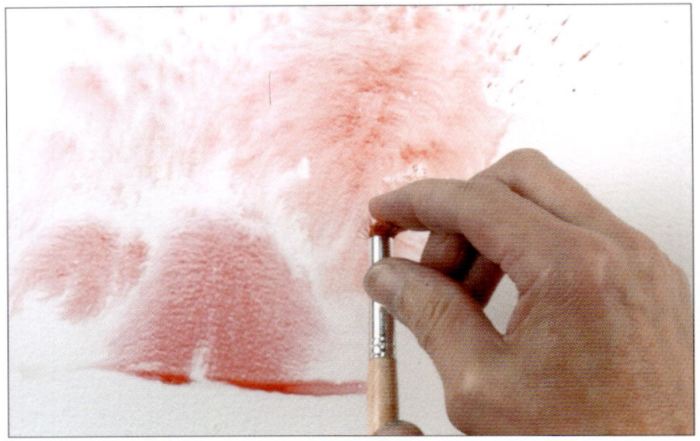

3 This creates an explosion of color across the page, which expands and merges as it spreads in the water. Repeat the spattering process to increase the effect. The overall result is to liven up an otherwise flat color with a textured effect.

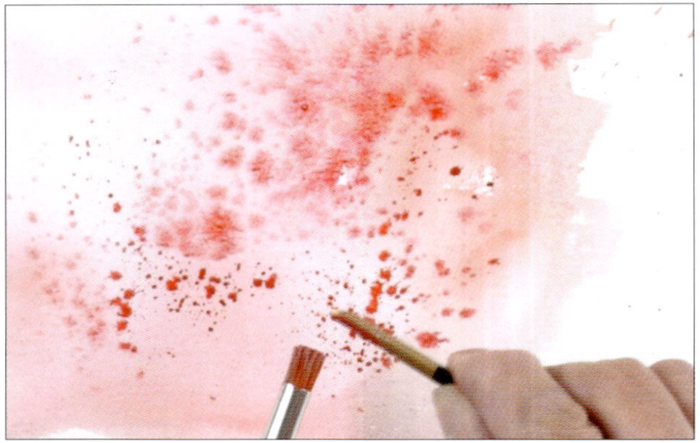

4 As well as using your finger, you can also use the handle of another brush. As before, simply pull the handle toward you to spatter the paint over the paper. Successive applications of spattered paint create more and more texture on the paper.

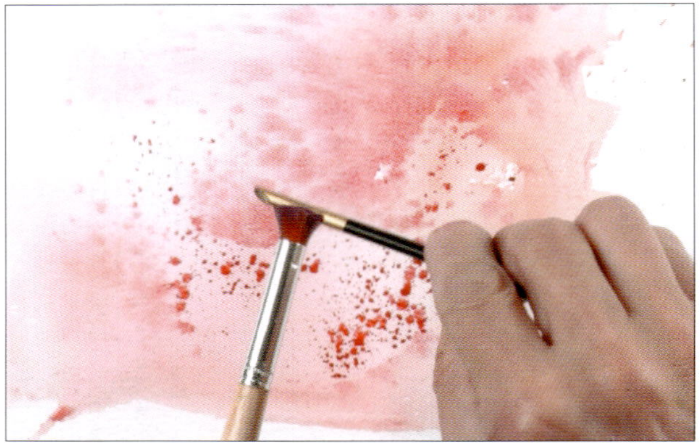

5 You can add almost any colors you like, building them up one after the other. As a guide, though, you should only use colors with the same tonal range—this will give your image a more unified look.

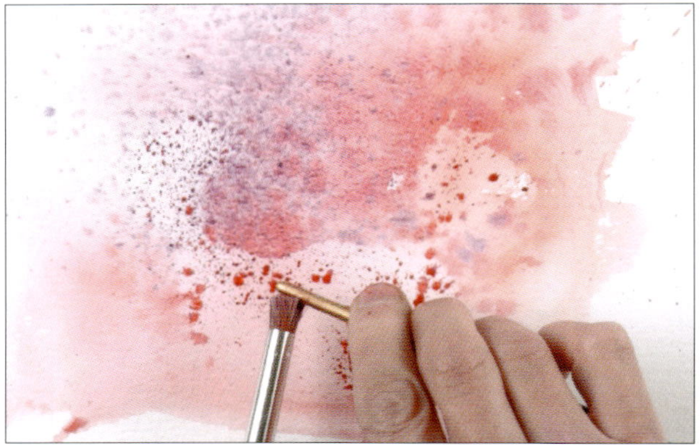

6 Add the last color, in this case violet, by dipping just a few bristles on the edge of the brush into the paint and carefully spattering it with the handle of the brush. This creates a lighter spray of paint, in contrast to the larger drops underneath.

**13** Build up the shadows under the jetty by adding more viridian into your dampened paper. Then wipe your brush. With the dry brush, drag some viridian, mixed with a touch of Payne's gray, across the bottom left corner of the picture with the side of your brush. This gives an indication of the grasses on the bank.

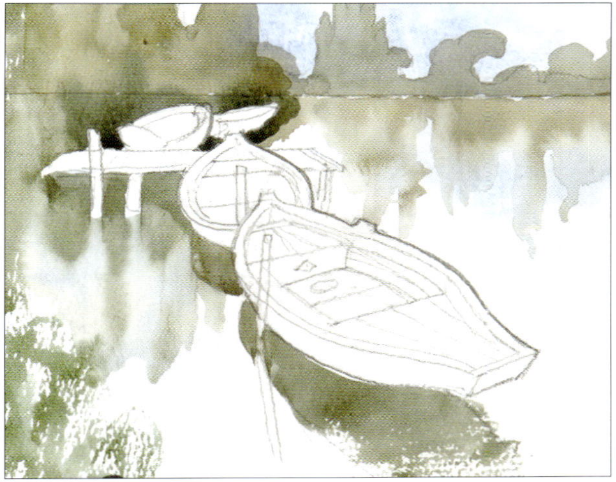

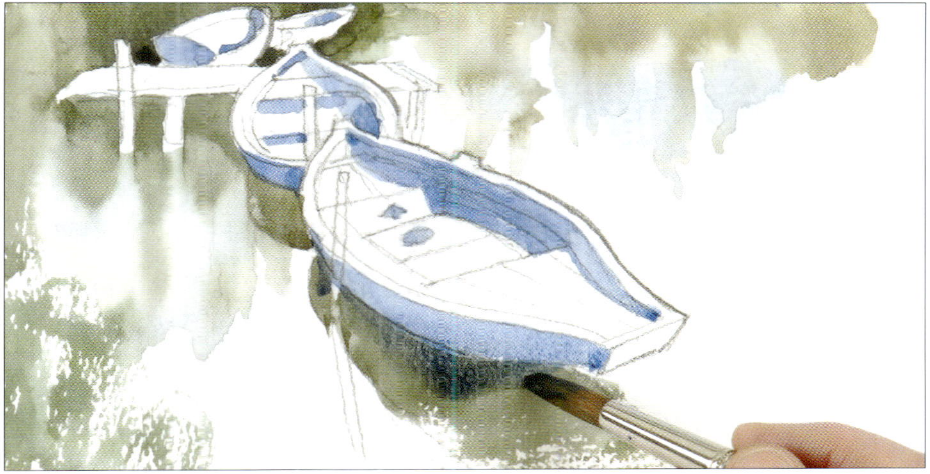

**14** Now use ultramarine to begin defining the shadow tones on the boats. As the light is coming from the right, surfaces that face left will be in shadow. Also remember to put shadow tones under the benches in the boats.

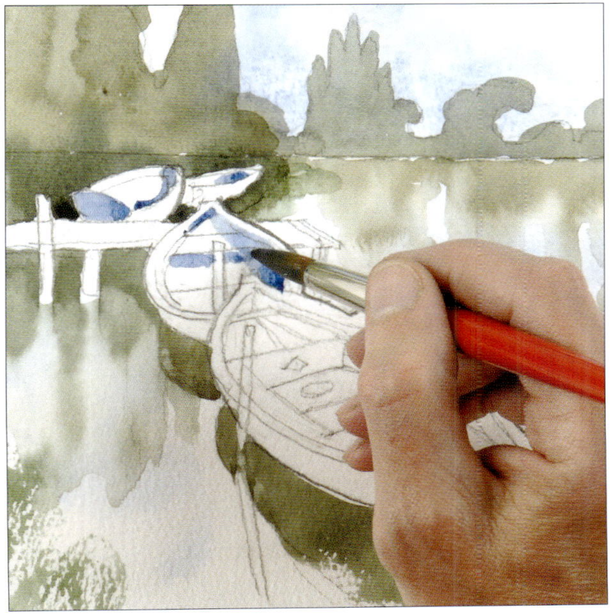

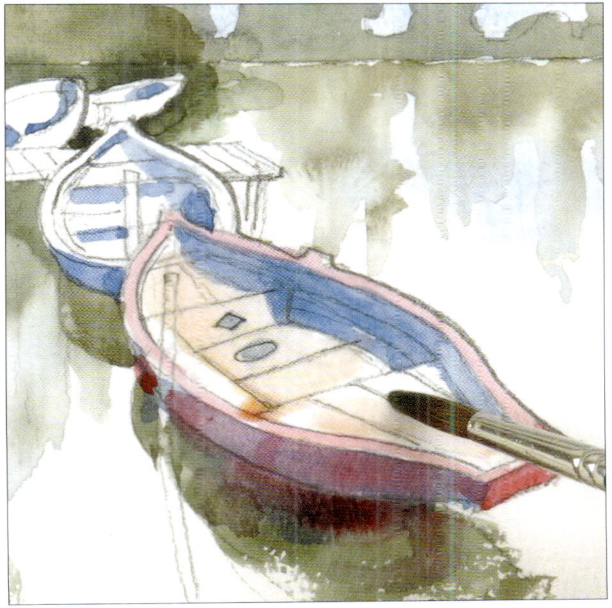

**15** Complete the shadow tones inside the boats. Then use ultramarine to strengthen the shadow cast by the foreground boat. Note this shadow will be darkest directly under the boat.

**16** Now start describing the color of the boats. Use a wash of permanent rose for the outside of the foreground boat. This color will also be reflected in the boat's shadow in the water, so add it there too. Switch to a weak wash of burnt sienna to render the woodwork inside the boat.

1 Spattering is, quite literally, flicking paint onto an area of your painting. It can be used to dramatic effect. For this example of the technique, the wet paint is spattered onto a dry surface In order to practice the technique, first apply a flat wash of a single color on your paper. Leave this to dry.

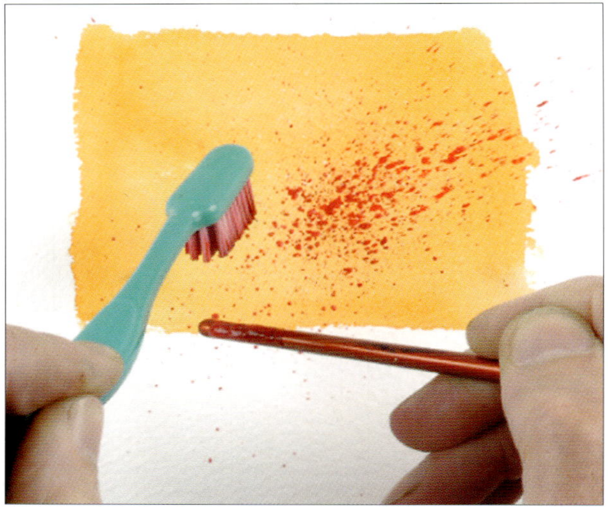

3 Allow the bristles to flick forward by bringing the paintbrush handle toward you. Repeat the process until the toothbrush has no paint left or you are happy with the result.

2 Load an old toothbrush and use the handle of a paintbrush to draw back the toothbrush bristles.

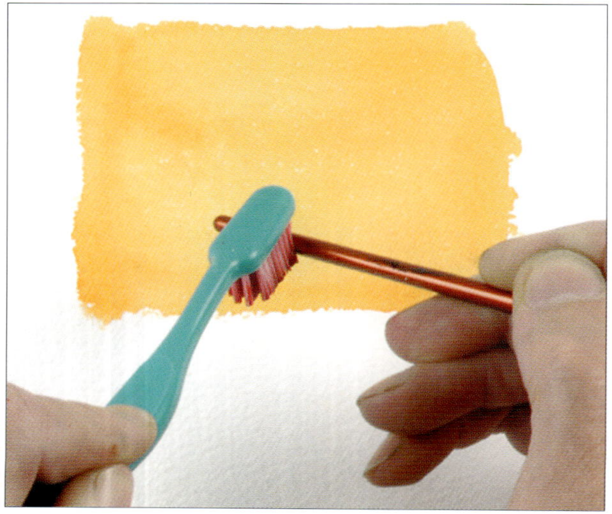

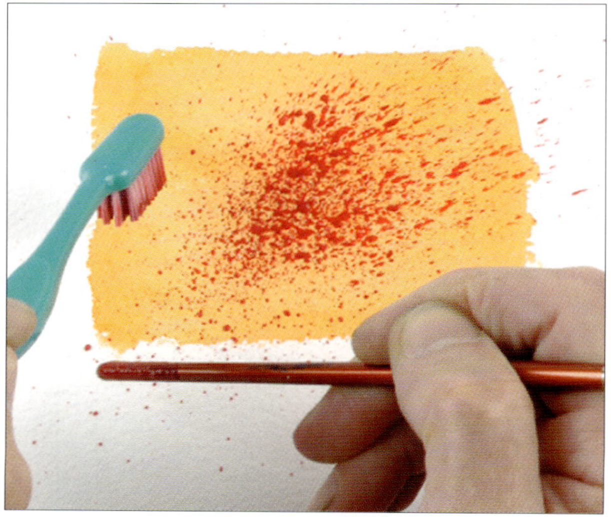

4 You don't have to stay with one color, you can change to different colors, but it is always wise to stick with colors from the same range.

**17** Continue adding dilute burnt sienna to the insides of the boats. Then add a touch of viridian to the outside of the boat directly above the jetty. This bright emerald-green color will help pull the viewer's eye into the picture.

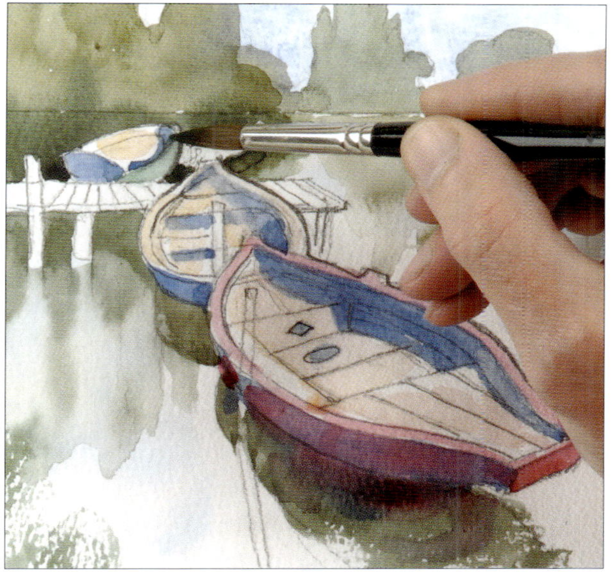

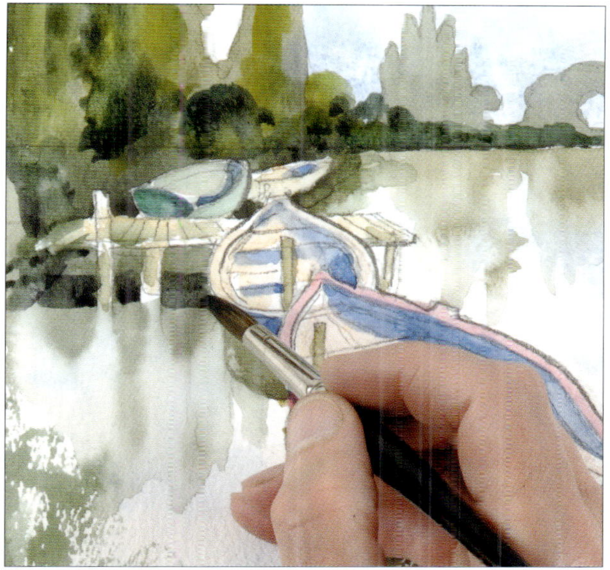

**19** On the far left of the composition, use a cool green viridian/ultramarine mix to strengthen the shadows of the trees in the water. Also use this mix to help to define the top of the jetty and to put in the shadow tone under the jetty.

**20** Build up the insides of the boats with a dilute mix of cadmium yellow. Note how this yellow creates a wonderful green when it is applied over the blue shadow tones.

**18** Develop the trees in background. Vary the color by adding a yellowish-green made from cadmium yellow and a touch of ultramarine. Then create a cooler green from viridian and ultramarine. Apply this mix with progressively larger brushstrokes as you work from right to left along the shoreline.

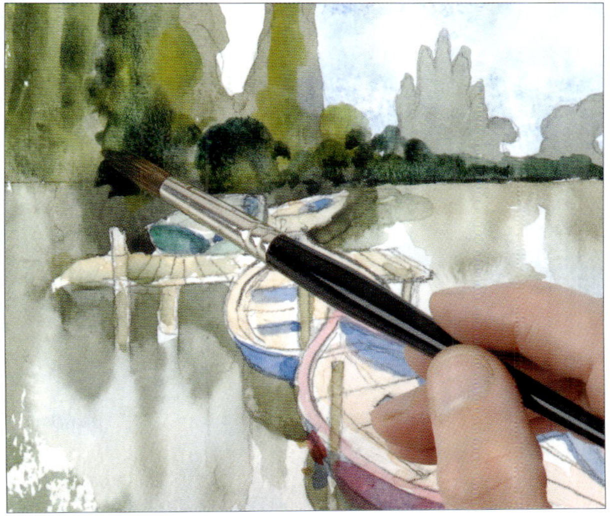

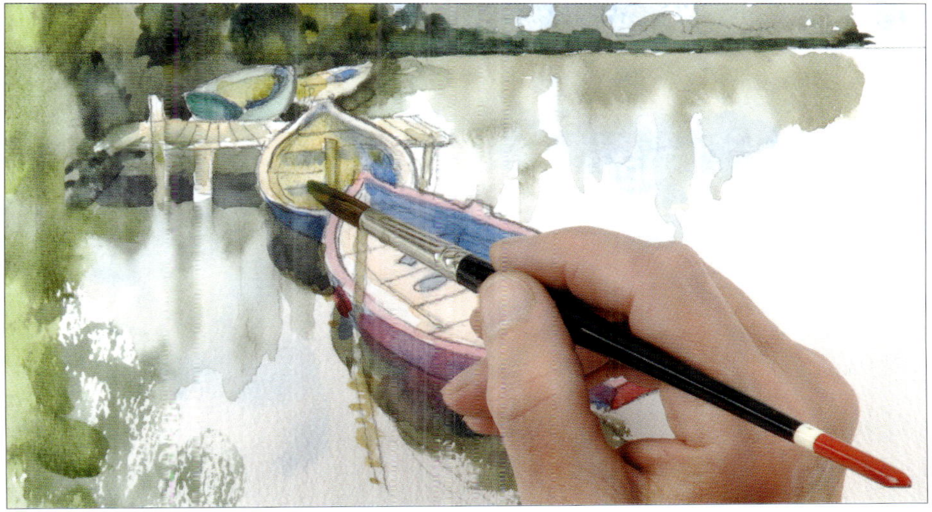

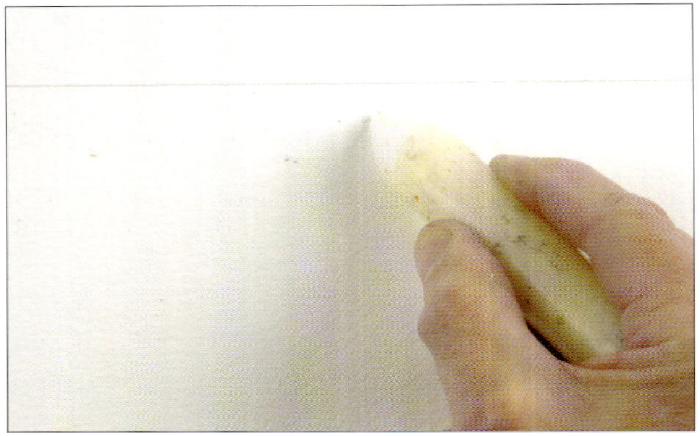

1 Like masking fluid, a household candle can be used to preserve the white of the paper. You simply draw with it like a crayon—using the edges at the base, laying it flat, or, as in this sea scene, sharpening the candle to a point with a craft knife.

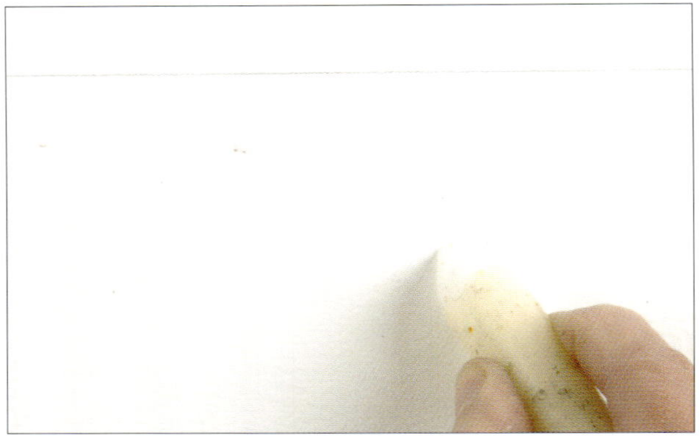

2 To attain a lively impression of frothy surf, draw the point of candle across the paper in a series of gently curving, broken lines. Vary the angle of the point so you attain a range of marks. Tilt the paper to see where the wax is on the paper.

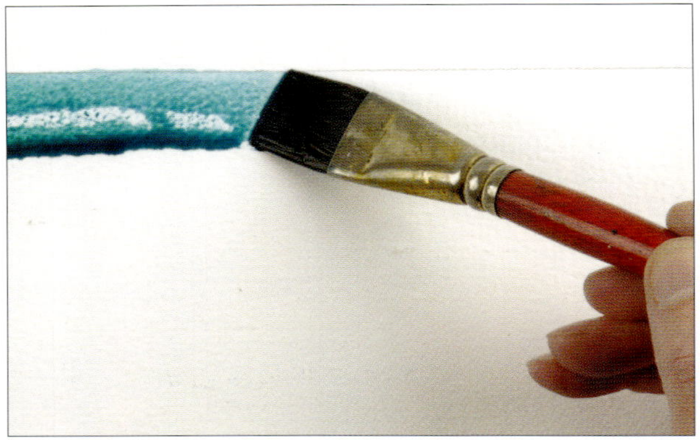

3 Draw a horizon line at the top of your paper with a ruler and pencil. Then mix a blue-green wash and, using a large flat brush, paint it over the wax.

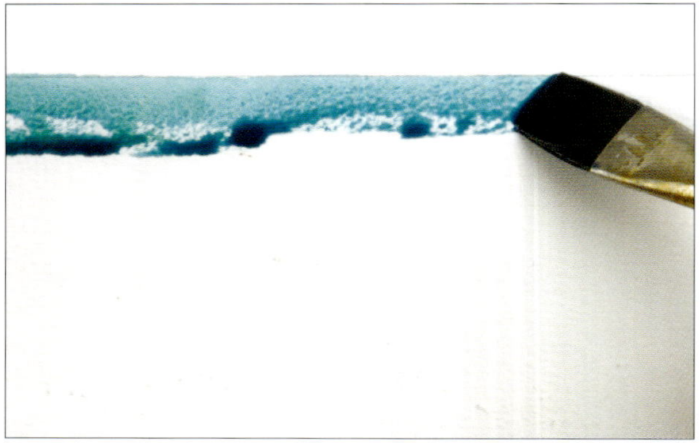

4 As you apply the wash, you will see where the wax has coated the paper as it will repel the wash. However, the paint will be able to penetrate tiny gaps between the wax creating a beautiful mottled texture— to accentuate this effect, use rough paper.

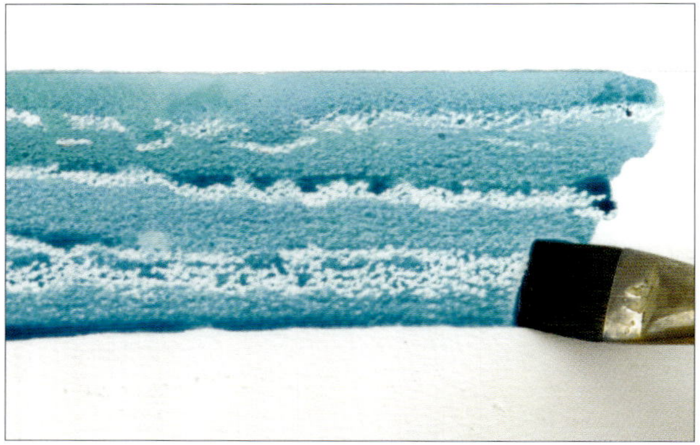

5 Continue applying the wash. Note the variety of marks. The thin broken lines in the background were created with the sharpened point of the candle. The broader marks in the foreground were created with the side of the point.

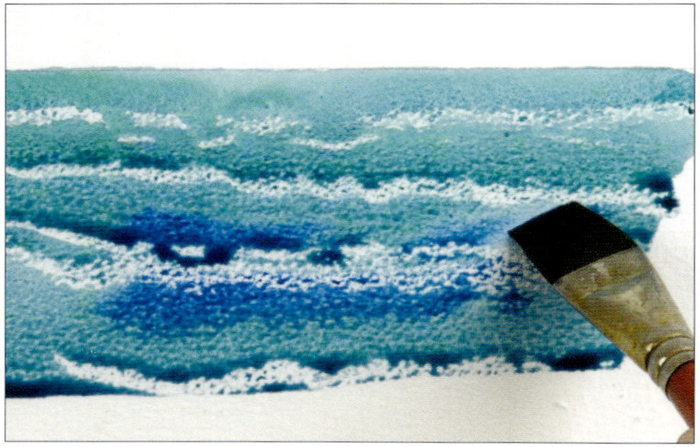

6 You can apply as much color over the wax as you wish, it will continue to repel the color. Note, the wax cannot be removed easily—it becomes part of the picture, adding textural interest as well as bright white areas.

**21** Strengthen the permanent rose mix on the foreground boat. As this boat is nearest to us, it should have the brightest color and the deepest tone. The viewer's eye should immediately be attracted to this boat, before it travels into the rest of the scene.

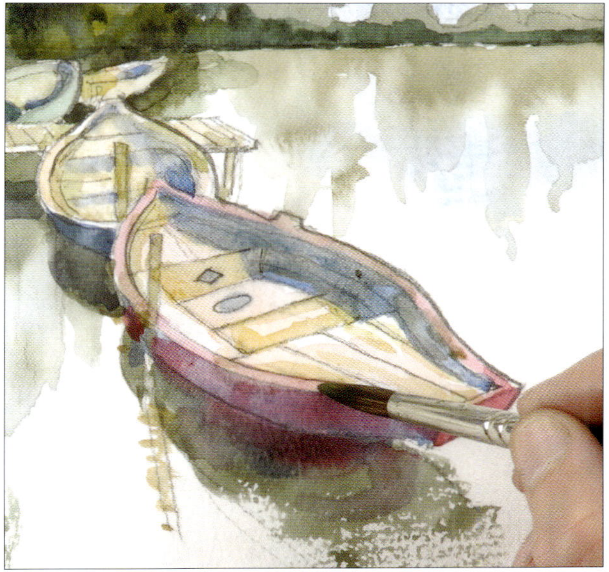

**22** Add some viridian to the trees in the background. It's important to keep varying the greens here so the trees do not appear dead and lifeless.

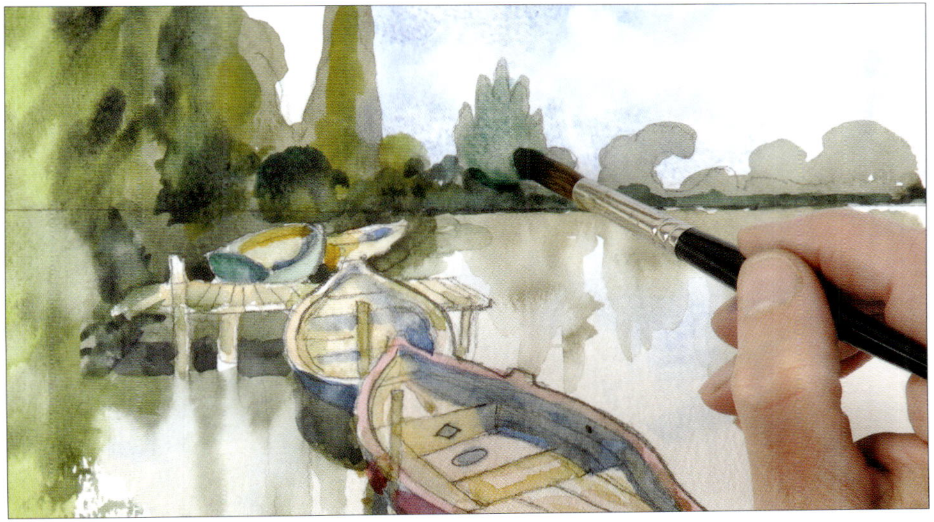

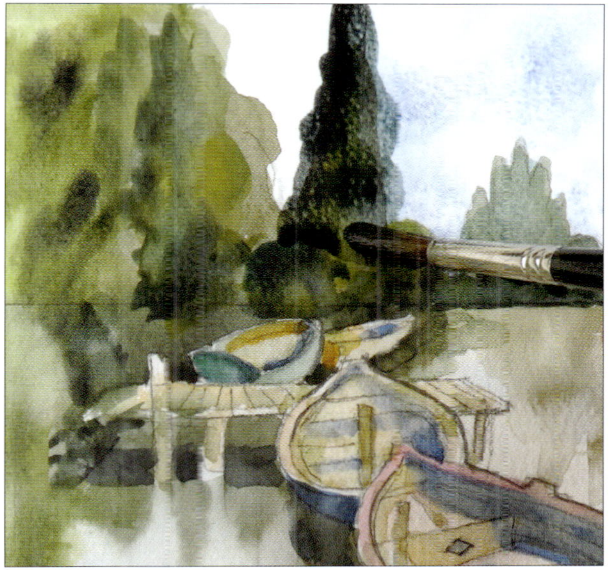

**23** Now strengthen the tall tree with your viridian/ultramarine mix. This is a pine tree so it needs to have a dark tone and a cool green color.

**24** Mix more water into the viridian/ultramarine mix. Use this to redefine the shadows of the trees in the water. The colors should merge into one another seamlessly to give the illusion of gently moving water.

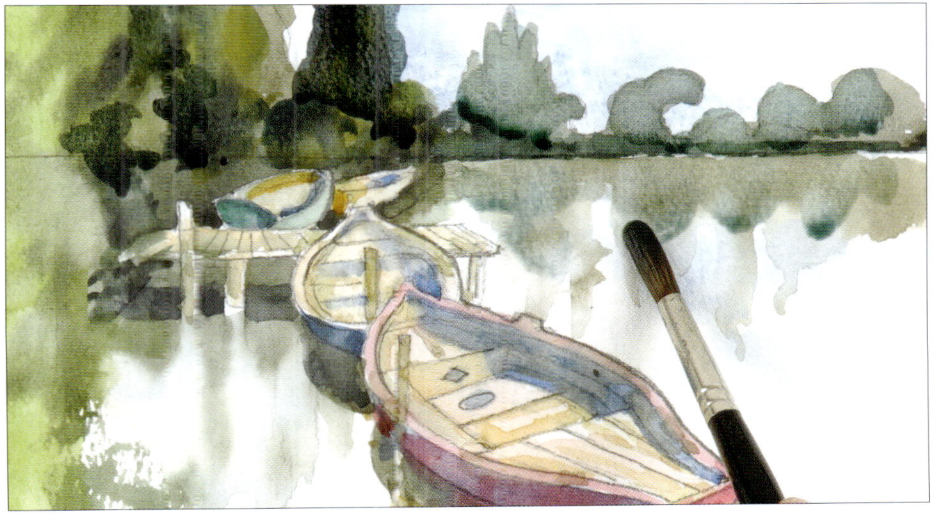

**5** Use horizontal strokes to create a flat wash of green over all the masked-out area. Leave to dry—if necessary, use a hair dryer to speed up the process.

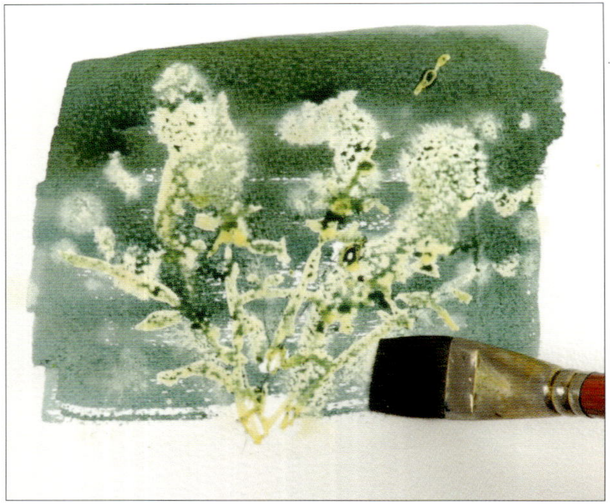

**6** Check that the paint is thoroughly dry, including any drips that have collected on the fluid. Then remove the fluid by rubbing it with your fingers. You may have to rub firmly—eventually the fluid will roll up into a ball and reveal the untouched white paper beneath.

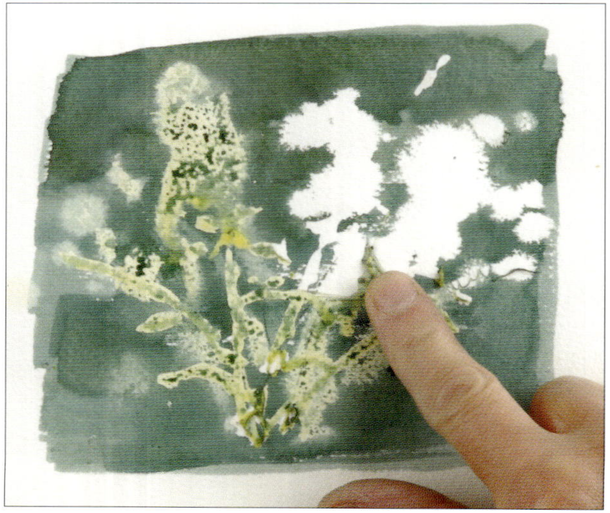

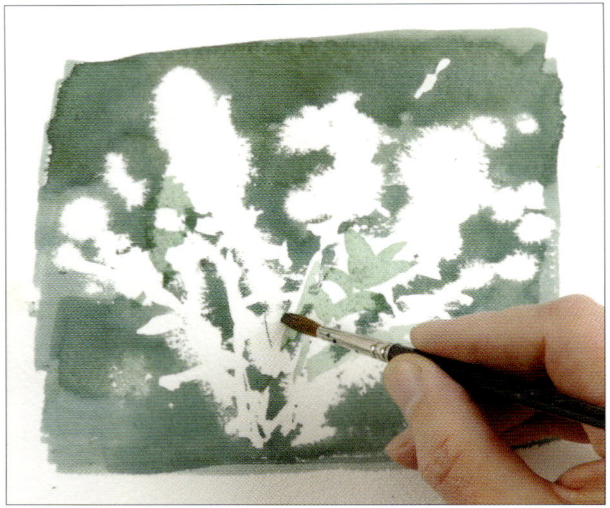

**7** Mix a light green wash and use it to render a few small leaves with a small sable brush. The sharp edges of these strokes contrast well with soft edges elsewhere. You now have a lively study of plants, full of exciting shapes and bold contrast.

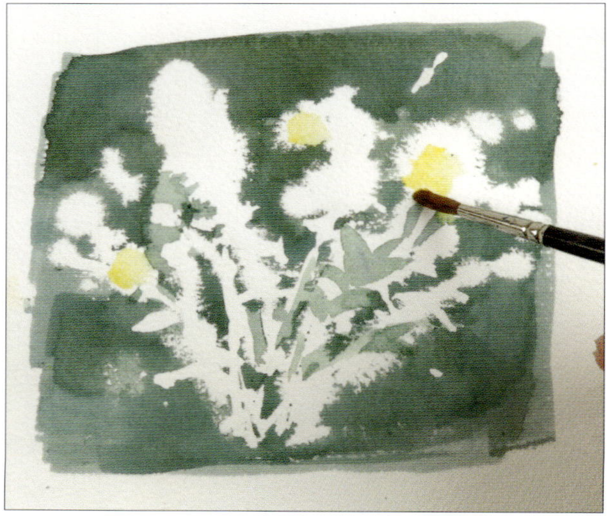

**8** For a final touch add some flowers. Mix some yellow paint, then dampen some of the white areas at the top of the plant with a clean wet brush. With the same brush, drop the yellow mix onto the damp areas—the color will spread and create the effect of flowers in bloom.

25 Now clean up the pencil lines with an eraser. Only rub out lines that are obtrusive or detract from the painting. Leave most of the pencil work inside the boats—it conveys important detail and information.

26 Now with a small brush, add details on the boats and jetty. Use the viridian/ultramarine mix to indicate the individual planks on the shadowed side of the foreground boat.

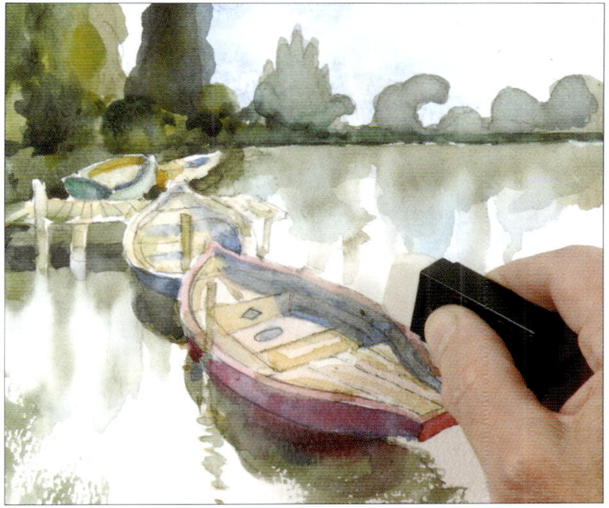

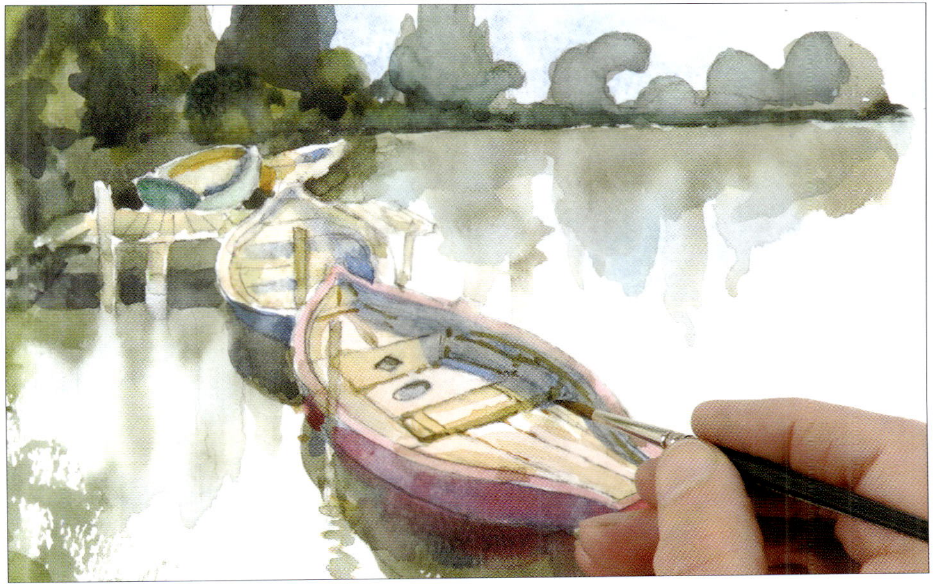

27 Continue with the cool green mix to add details to the boat in front of the jetty. Add two small horizontal strokes inside the boat to indicate the seats. Also add touches of green to the mooring post near the foreground boat.

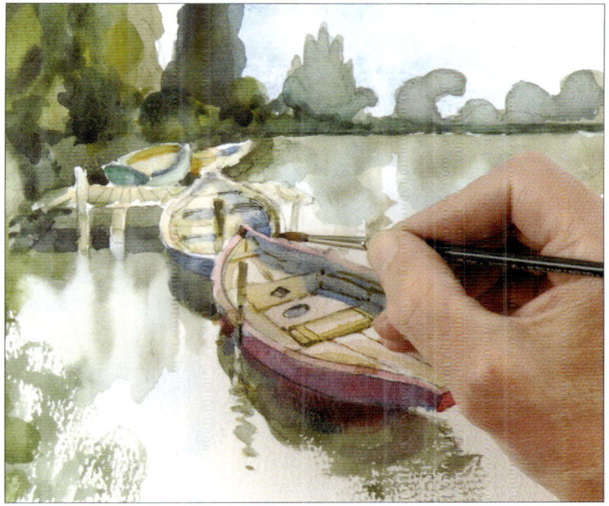

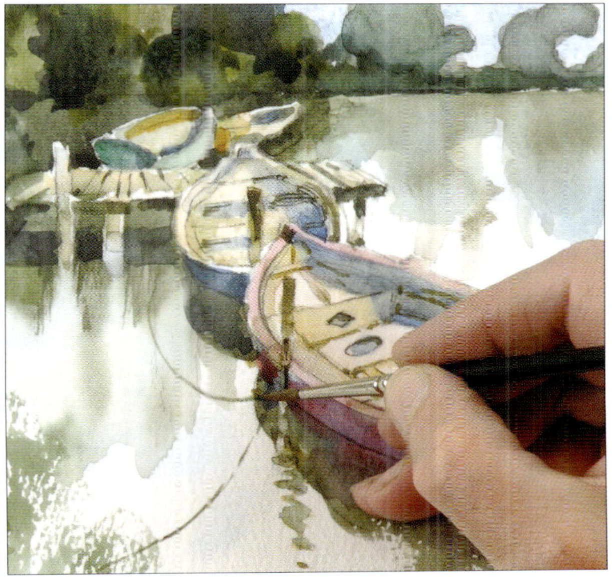

28 Now with the tip of the rigger brush, paint the mooring ropes. Just graze the brush over the paper. If your strokes are too bold, the ropes will look unrealistic and command too much attention. Try to take the brush off the paper in places, so you "lose" and "find" the line.

# resist techniques: using masking fluid

1 Masking fluid allows you to protect areas of a painting that you wish to keep white. You paint it on the paper and, when dry, it prevents subsequent washes of color reaching the paper. After finishing the painting, you can remove it by rubbing gently with a finger. For this plant study, wet the paper before applying the fluid—this will create soft-edged effects, perfect for the foliage.

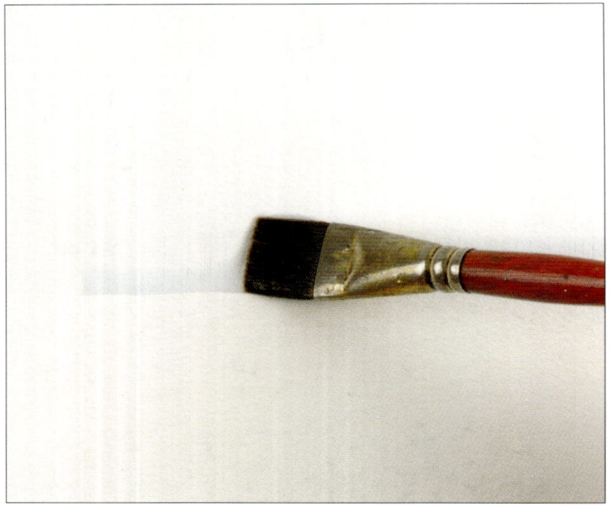

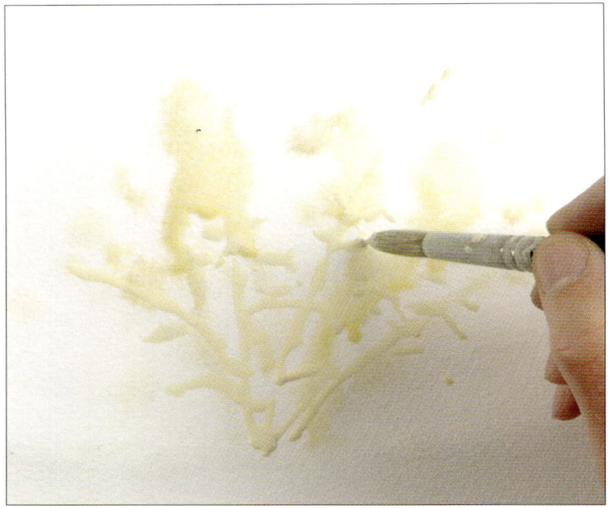

3 Now apply thinner strokes with the masking fluid, to indicate stems and smaller leaves. The fluid will dry to leave a yellow-colored residue. Do not worry if the residue is thicker in some areas than others—so long as it covers the required areas of paper.

2 Paint on the masking fluid using an old or inexpensive brush (the fluid tends to stick to the bristles and will eventually ruin a good brush). Brush on a variety of leaf shapes emerging from the center of the bottom of your picture.

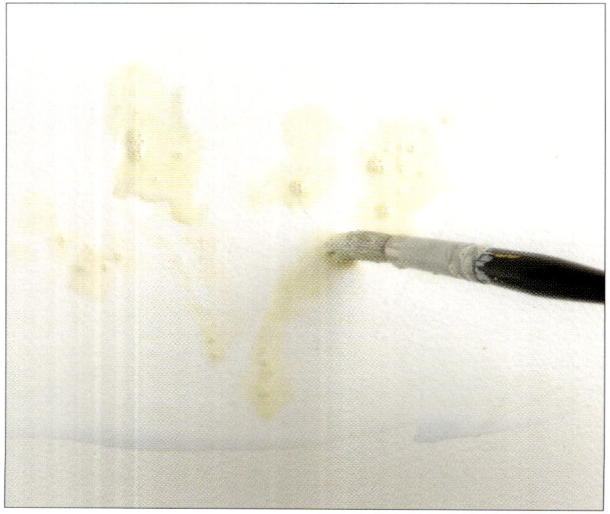

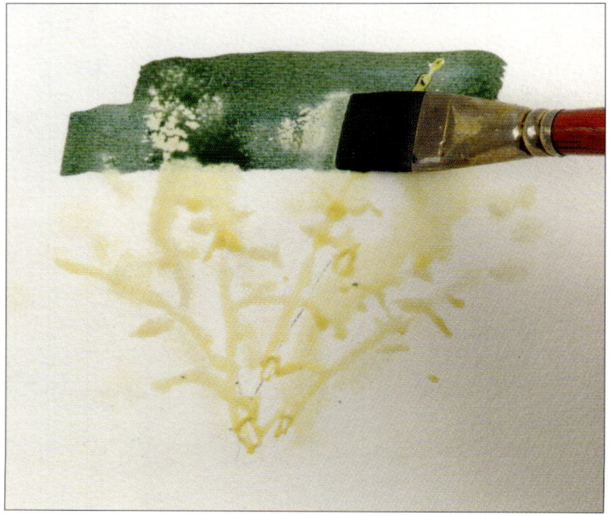

4 Mix a deep green and apply it with a flat brush over the masked-out area. While the paint stains the paper, it is repelled by the fluid—no matter how small the quantities of masking fluid are.

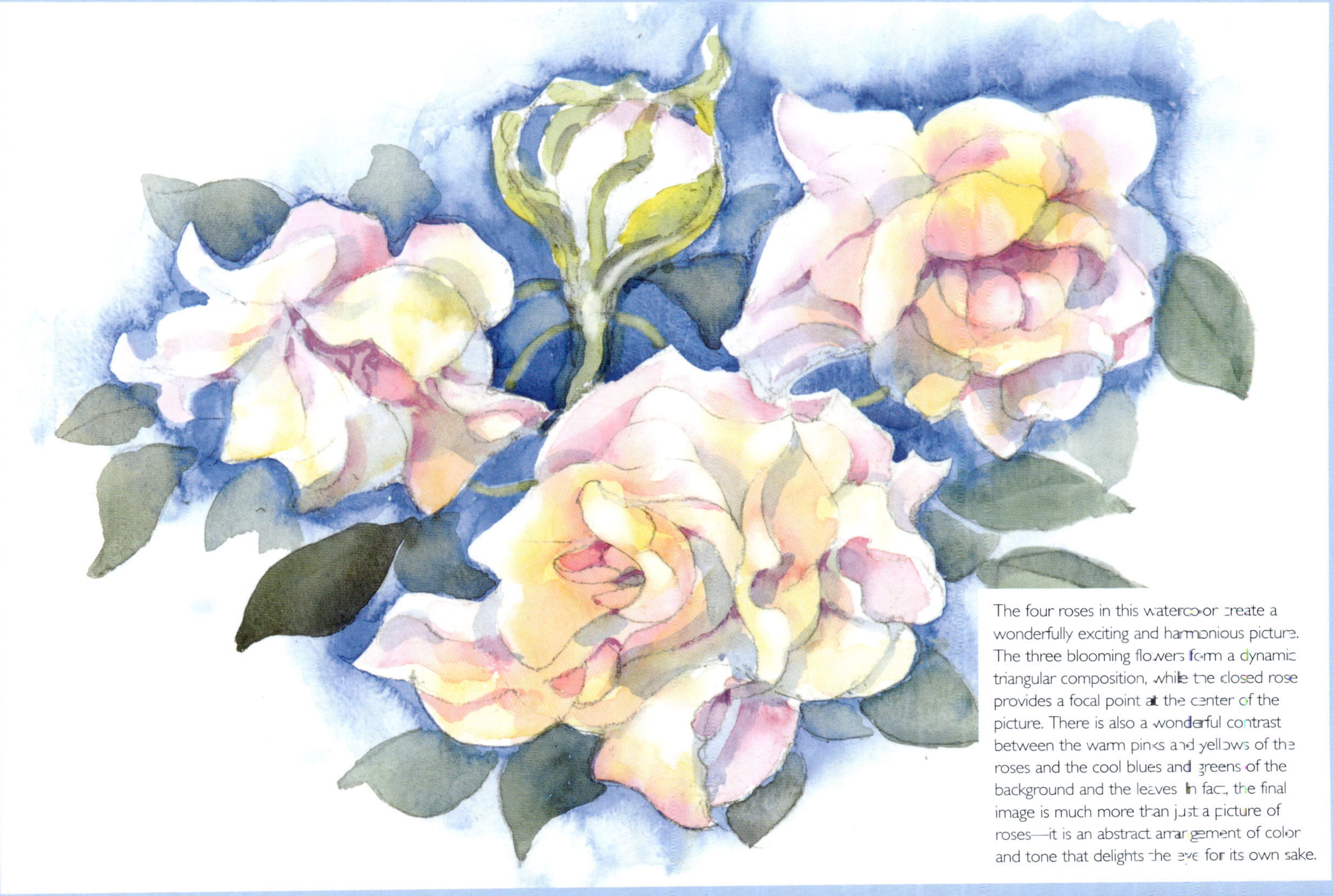

The four roses in this watercolor create a wonderfully exciting and harmonious picture. The three blooming flowers form a dynamic triangular composition, while the closed rose provides a focal point at the center of the picture. There is also a wonderful contrast between the warm pinks and yellows of the roses and the cool blues and greens of the background and the leaves. In fact, the final image is much more than just a picture of roses—it is an abstract arrangement of color and tone that delights the eye for its own sake.

## MATERIALS

**Drawing board**

**A sheet of thick watercolor paper**

**Watercolor palette**

**Watercolors: cadmium yellow, permanent rose, ultramarine blue, lemon yellow, viridian, burnt sienna**

**Brushes: No.12 and No.3 round and No.5 flat**

**Jar of water**

**B pencil**

**Eraser**

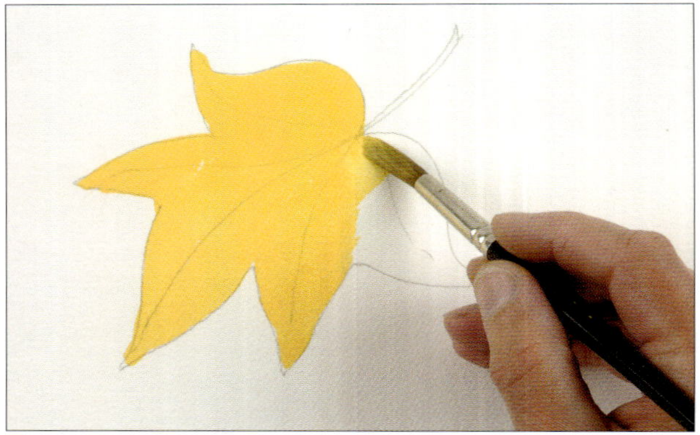

1 Scumbling involves using very dry paint to create textural effects. In this exercise, we are going to paint a leaf by laying down a flat wash of yellow, then scumbling red and orange over it. Draw the leaf with a pencil and then apply the initial wash.

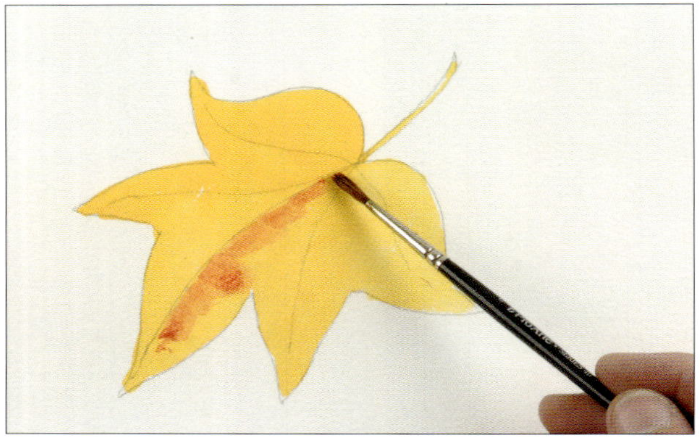

2 Mix a very dry wash of red. Alternatively, pick up undiluted paint, either squeezed from the tube or straight from the pan, on a damp brush. Gently scrub the red over the dry yellow wash, keeping the brush flat and letting the hairs fan out.

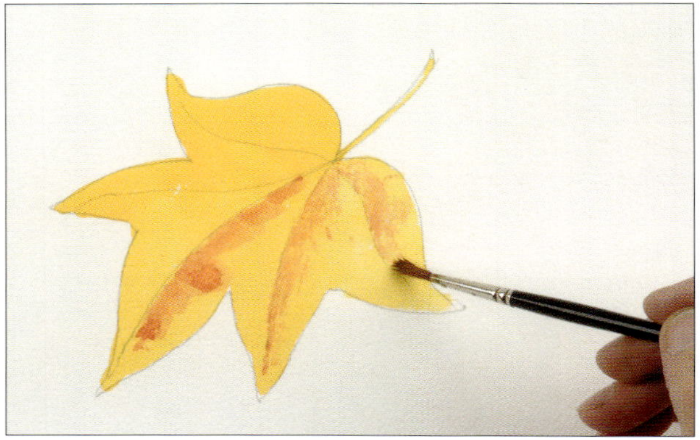

3 Continue adding dry color with the side of the brush. Follow the veins in the leaf.

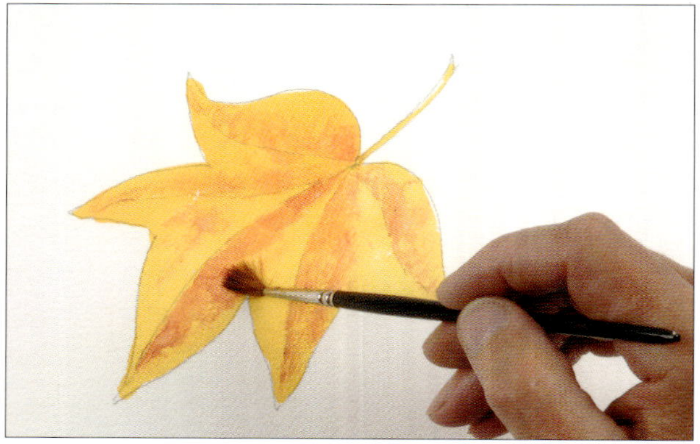

4 Scrub more color along the veins. Keep the paint as dry as possible. At times, it may appear that you are making little impression—but when you lift your brush, you will see a gradual build-up of color.

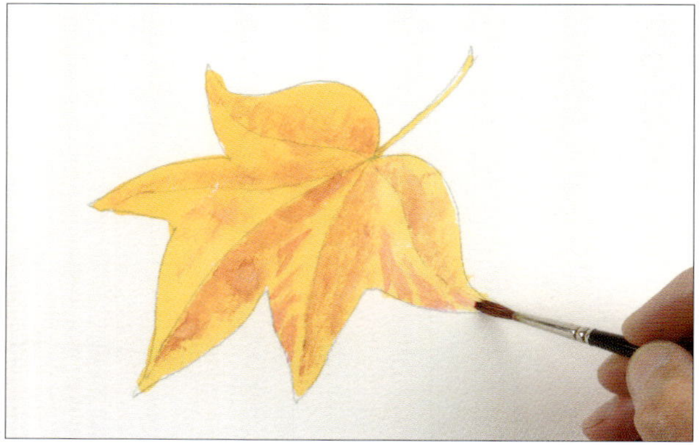

5 Vary the color by adding orange to your dry mix. Also add curved strokes emerging from the veins. They help give the impression that the leaf is not completely flat—it rises and falls in gently curving bulges.

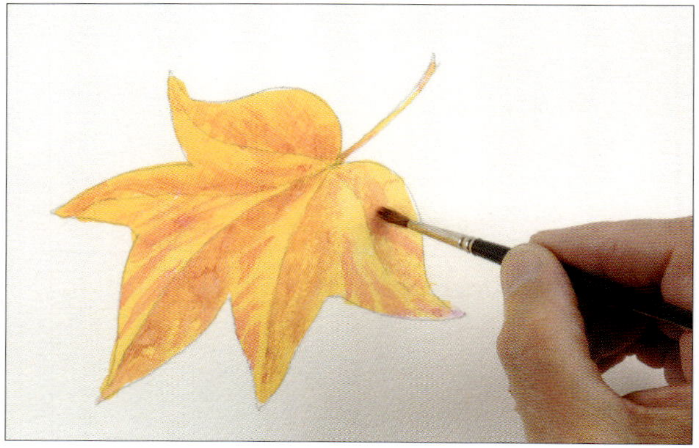

6 This technique perfectly captures the texture of a fall leaf. Try using a rough-textured paper—the paint will catch only on the raised "tooth" of the paper so tiny areas of the underlying wash show through and create a wonderful shimmering effect.

1 Begin by plotting the outlines of the three flowers with the B pencil. Note how they vary in size—the foreground flower at the bottom is the biggest and the background flower on the left the smallest. Together, the three flowers form a dynamic triangular composition.

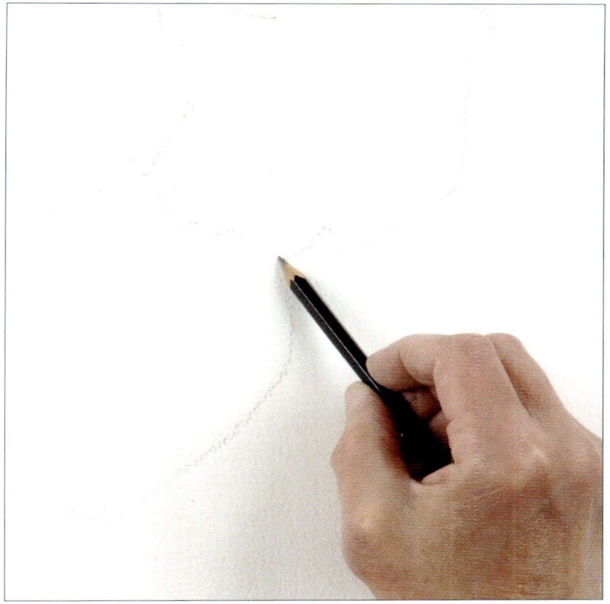

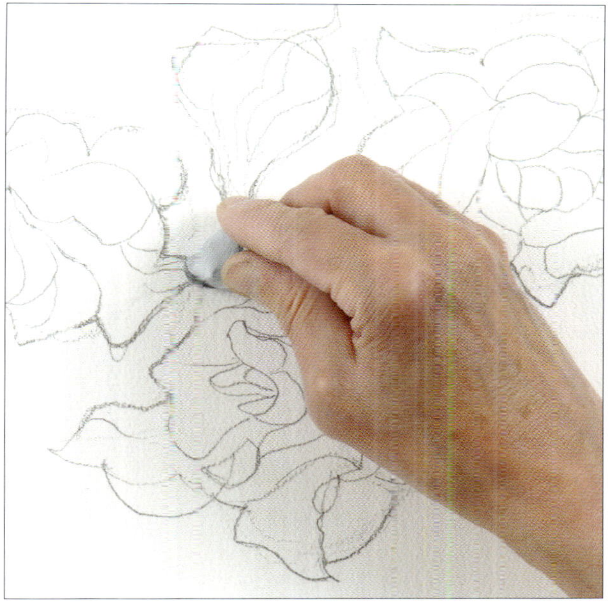

3 Continue building up the shapes of the petals in the three blooming flowers. Also draw the leaves that surround the closed flower. Then reappraise your drawing and make any corrections with an eraser.

4 Tape your paper to your drawing board and tilt it slightly toward you. Then with the No.12 round brush, dampen the flower area with clean water. Then apply a wash of cadmium yellow.

2 Now start drawing the petals, making sure they vary in size and shape. Note how we view many of the petals in the centers of the flowers at oblique angles while the petals around the edges are seen head-on.

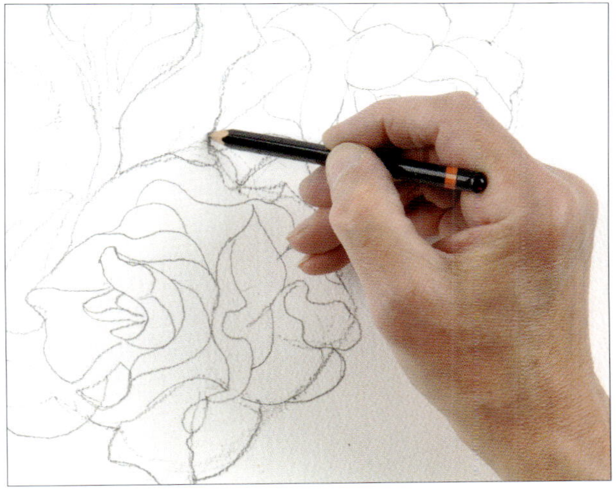

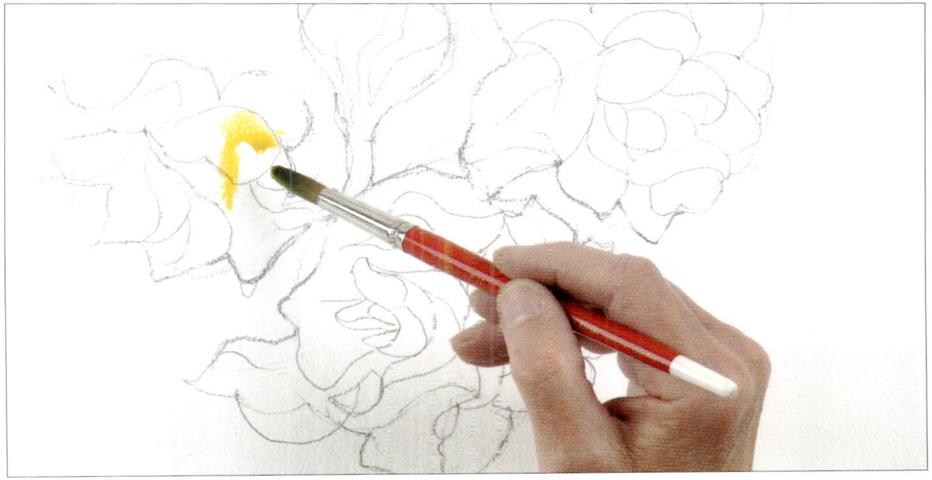

5 Working quickly and confidently, keep adding purple into the blue. The color will diffuse and go where it wants—so have a dry brush and some kitchen towel handy to lift out color that has run out of control! Do not over-manipulate the color, though. The beauty of working wet-in-wet is spontaneity—creating effects that simply cannot be made with a brush. Therefore, try tilting the board to control the paint rather than using a brush.

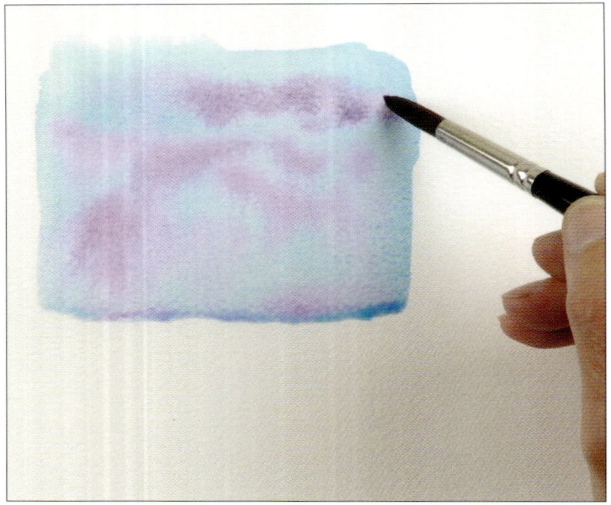

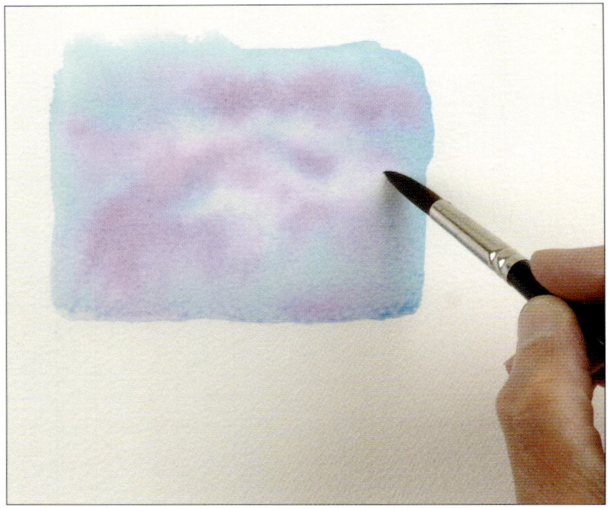

7 Continue adding water into the washes. The paler areas, created by the additional water, look as if they are the sunlit tops of the clouds, while the purple areas appear as if they are the shadowed undersides.

6 Clean your brush and apply clean water in places. This will remove color, letting the white paper show through—perfect to give the impression of paler clouds.

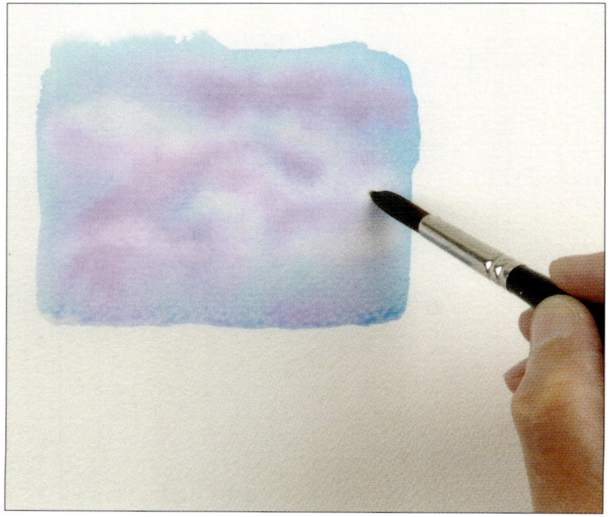

8 The final picture is a perfect rendition of clouds. Remember, clouds are not solid—they are made up of water particles and so are, in reality, sculptured mist. You can capture these qualities effectively by applying the paint wet-in-wet to create soft-edged washes and subtle changes in tone.

**5** Continue adding your cadmium yellow mix to the flowers. Apply the paint freely. Do not feel you have to follow the outlines of the petals or fill every inch of white paper.

**6** Now mix up a wash of permanent rose and introduce that into the flower area. As the paper is damp, the pigment will take on a life of its own and merge with the yellow.

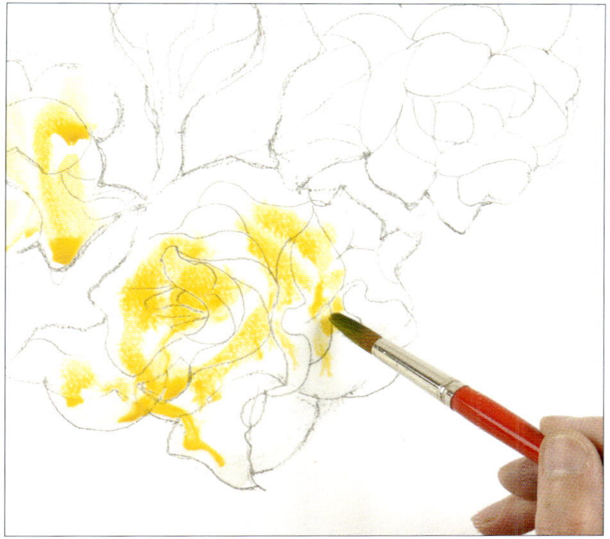

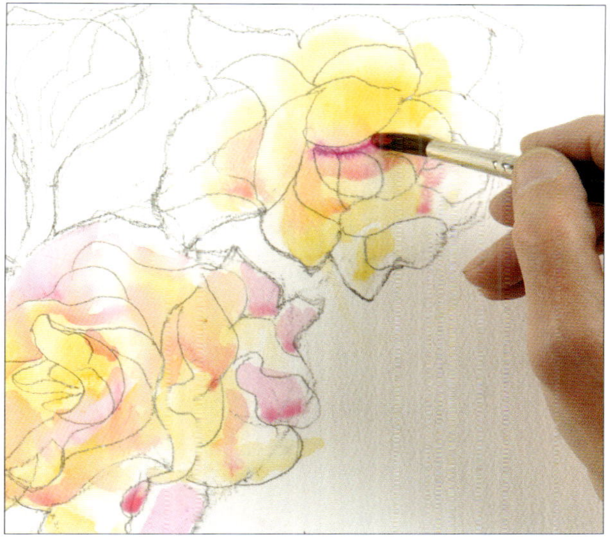

**7** Continuing adding the permanent rose. Look at the wonderful range of colors that start to appear, from sunny yellows and oranges through to salmon and rose pinks. Add some more permanent rose to your mix and paint the center of the top right flower.

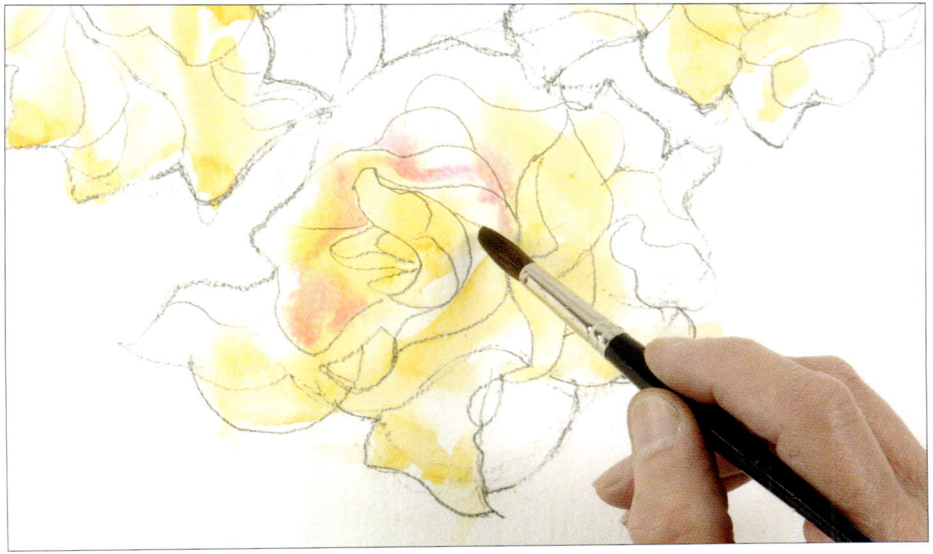

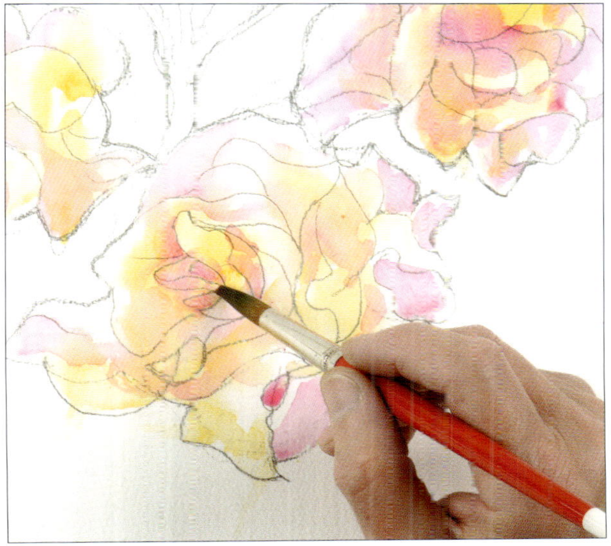

**8** Now apply permanent rose to the center of the bottom flower. The centers of the flowers are in shadow so they need the darkest tones. The outside petals receive lots of light so they are paler.

1 Wet-in-wet is a fabulously expressive technique. As you apply color to a wet wash, the paint takes on a life of its own, creating soft-edged shapes and wonderful new colors where the two colors mix. It is particularly suited to depicting water and skies. For this sky study, start by brushing clean water onto the paper. Before the paper dries, apply the first wash with the side of a round brush.

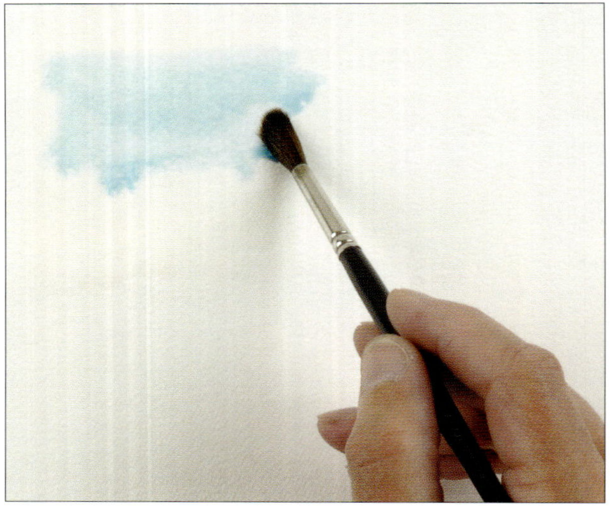

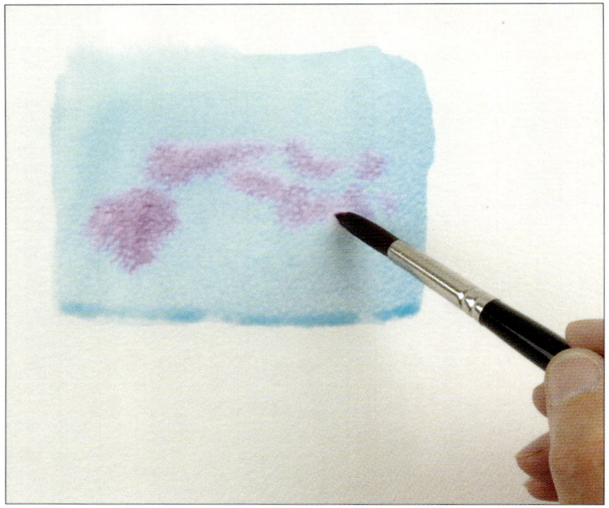

3 Now mix a purple wash and drop this into the blue. Do not over-dilute your mix—otherwise, the color will look pale and lifeless. Remember, the paper already contains a lot of water and watercolors become lighter when they dry. Start carefully, the paint will run out over the wet surface.

2 Paint a rectangular wash. Do not worry about the way you apply the paint—on the damp paper, the color will run in unexpected places and some areas will be darker than others. Tidy up the bottom of the wash by picking up excess paint on a clean brush.

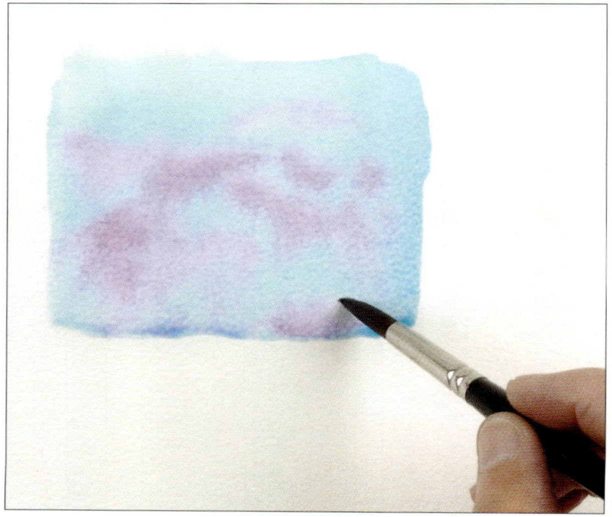

4 Note how pale pinks appear where the purple and blue washes mix. This is perfect for rendering realistic clouds. If you paint clouds with one flat color, they often look as if they have been stuck on the sky. By using the wet-in-wet technique, you can ensure they contain a range of colors and tones.

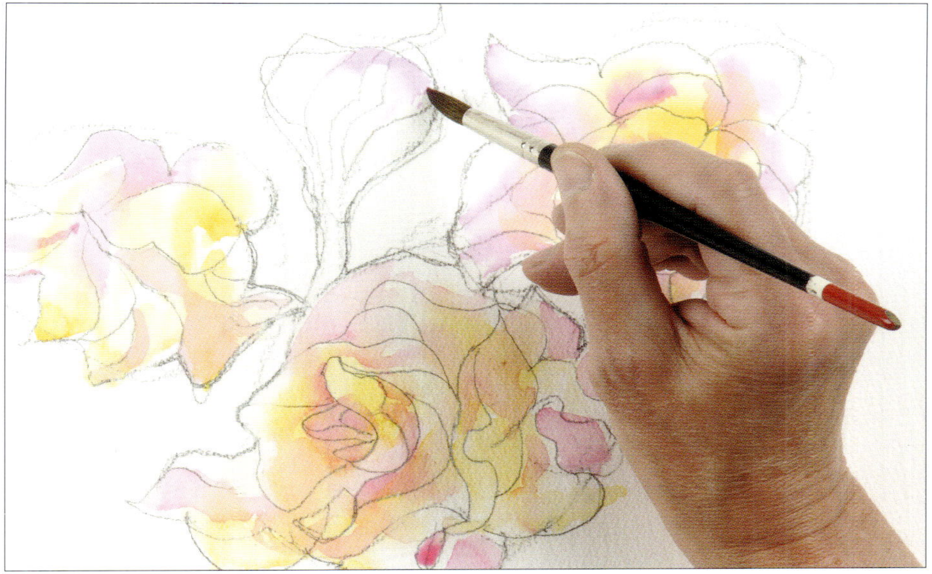

**9** Now begin to vary the color. In a separate well of your palette, mix up permanent rose with a little ultramarine blue to create a purple. Add this—here and there—across the flowers.

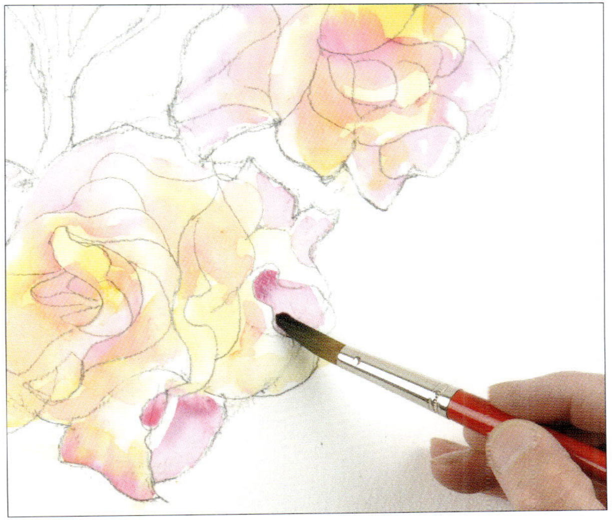

**10** Return to your permanent rose mix to build up the color on the bottom flower. To attain a lively interchange of color, intersperse every area of yellow with a dab or two of permanent rose.

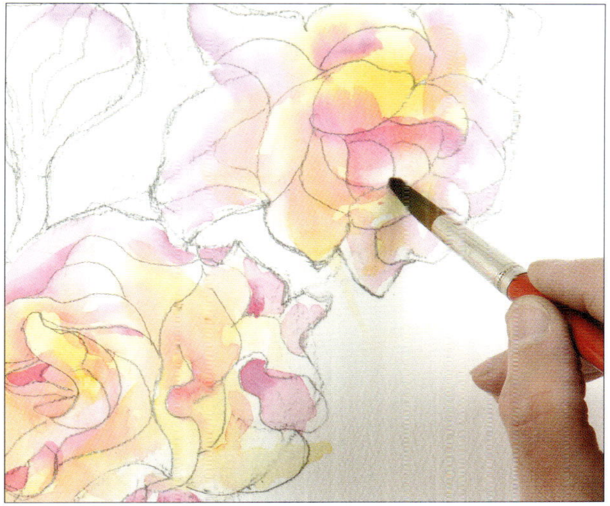

**11** Add more permanent rose to the center of the right flower. Look how strong the tone is at the center of the flower compared to the edges.

**12** Let all the washes dry. Then use your eraser to remove the outlines of the flowers. However, do not remove the outlines of the petals, as these add texture and detail to the painting.

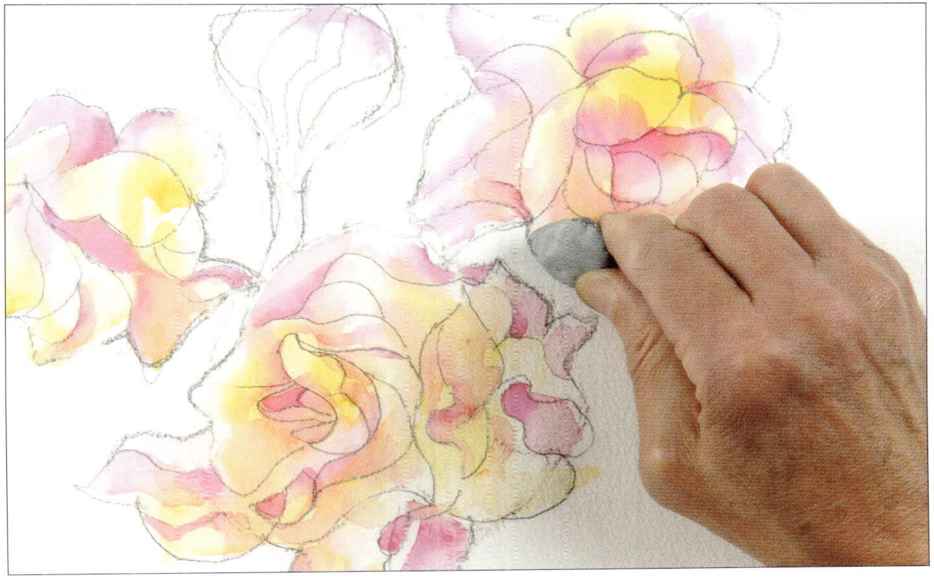

5 Add a third tree on the left and a fourth one on the right. Now let the green watercolor dry completely. Then apply a second wash of green across the bottom of the trees. This strengthens the tone and begins to give us an idea of the three-dimensional form of the trees.

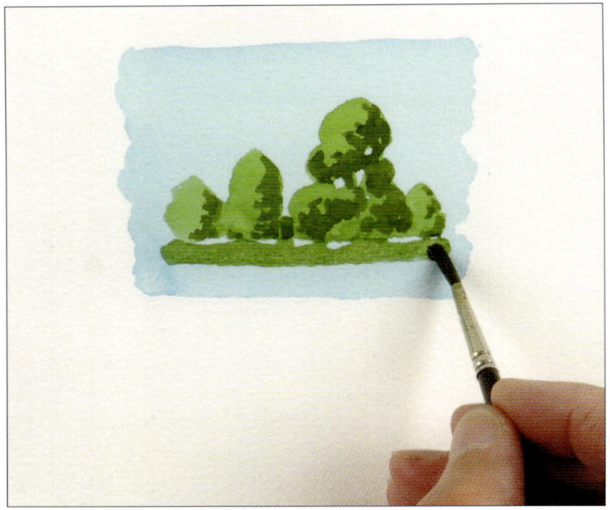

7 Add shadow tone to the right side of the three other trees. You can be really precise in applying these shadow tones as the dry underlayer "holds" the paint and prevents brushstrokes running out of control. This is the beauty of working wet-on-dry. Then add more green and more water to your mix and apply the color in one bold stroke in front of the trees, leaving touches of blue showing through under the trees.

6 Now intensify your green wash by adding Payne's gray (or a mix of ultramarine and burnt sienna). Use this mix to define the shadowed sides of the clumps of foliage on the main tree. As the light is coming from left, darken the right side and the underside of each clump of foliage. You can now perceive the form of the tree, with the sunlit areas of the tree advancing toward us and the shadowed sides receding.

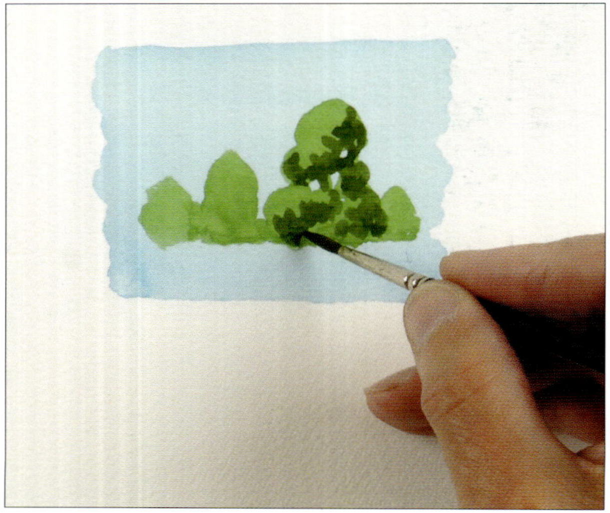

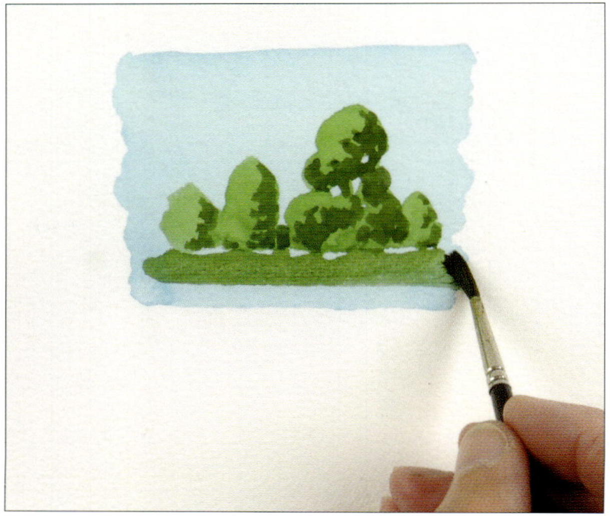

8 Extend the grass in front of the trees with one or two further brushstrokes and you have a pleasing study or summer trees. By working wet-on-dry in this way, you can create wonderfully detailed watercolors—but be warned, you can overdo it and end up with a fussy, lifeless painting.

**13** Now mix up a wash of ultramarine. Working carefully with the tip of the brush, paint the mix around the outside of the flowers.

**14** Continue painting the ultramarine mix around the flowers. The warm pinks and yellows of the flowers now really leap forward when set against the cool blue background.

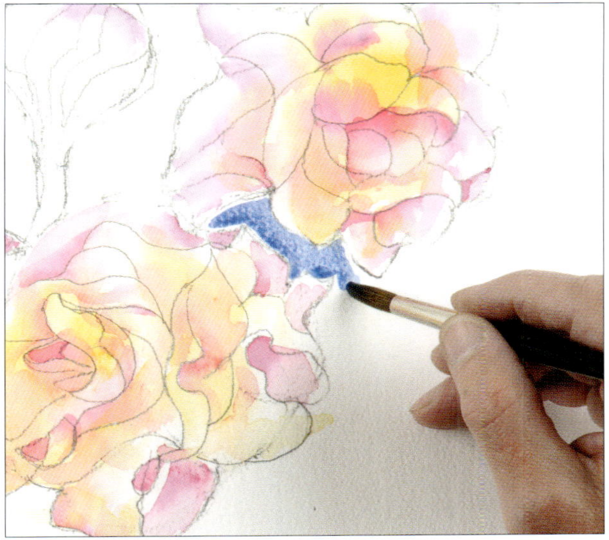

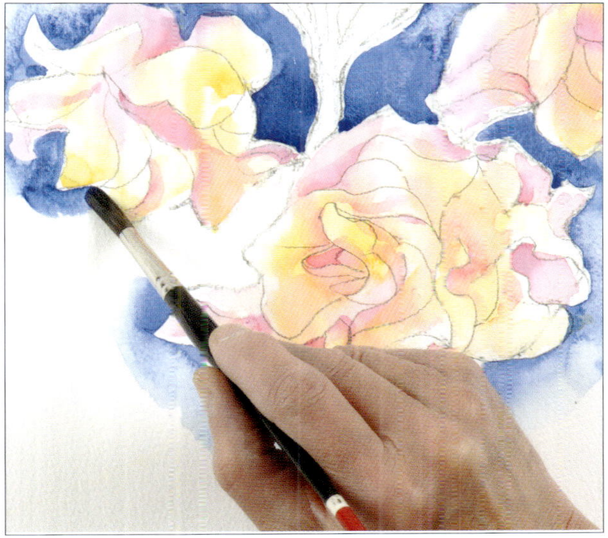

**15** Wet the exposed white paper with clean water so the ultramarine becomes progressively lighter toward the edge of picture. This creates a vignette effect that will focus attention on the subject of the painting—the flowers.

**16** In the closed flower, you can see the background through a hole in the foliage—so carefully add a small curved stroke of ultramarine.

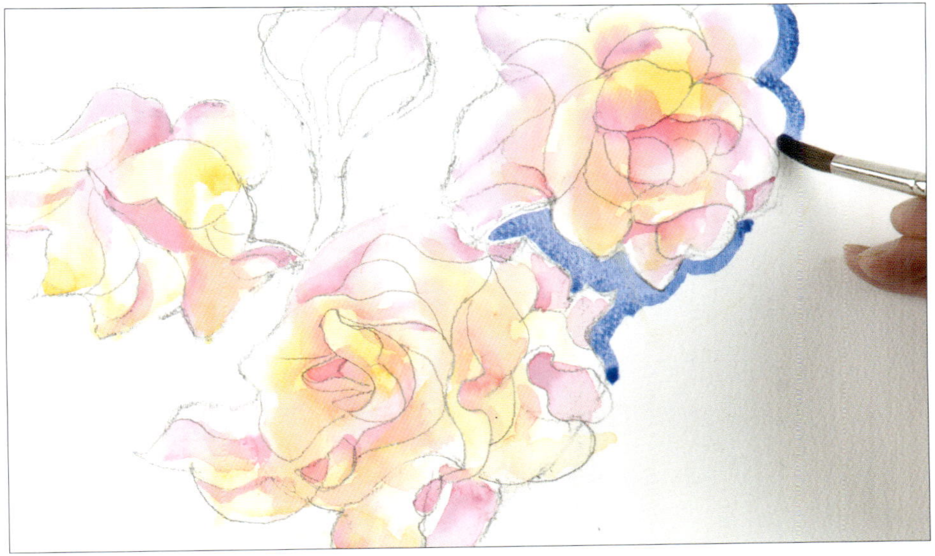

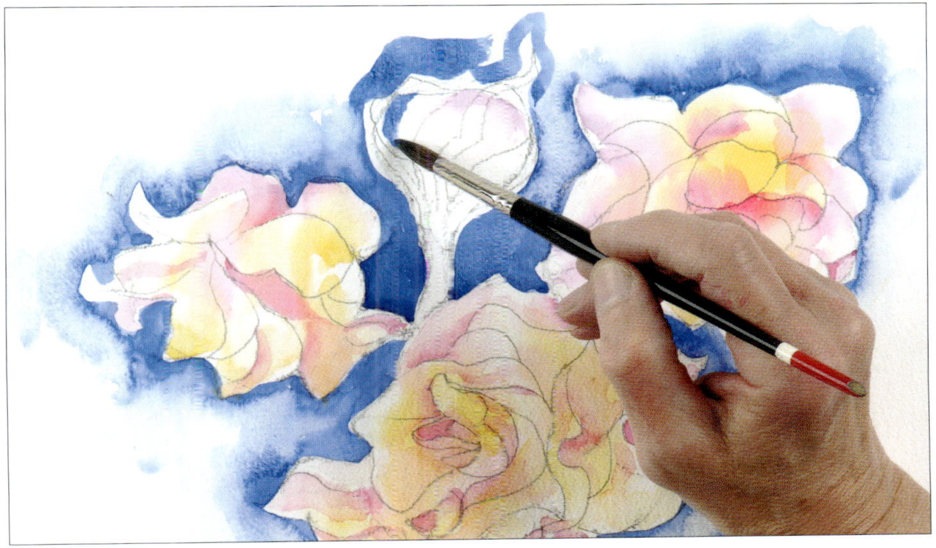

1 In this exercise, we are going to create a summer landscape, with trees in full leaf. Paint is only added when the underlying layer is dry—in this way, we will create crisp, sharp-edged washes of paint. First, lay in a flat wash of pale blue (cerulean is the ideal pigment, if you have it). Then let the wash dry completely.

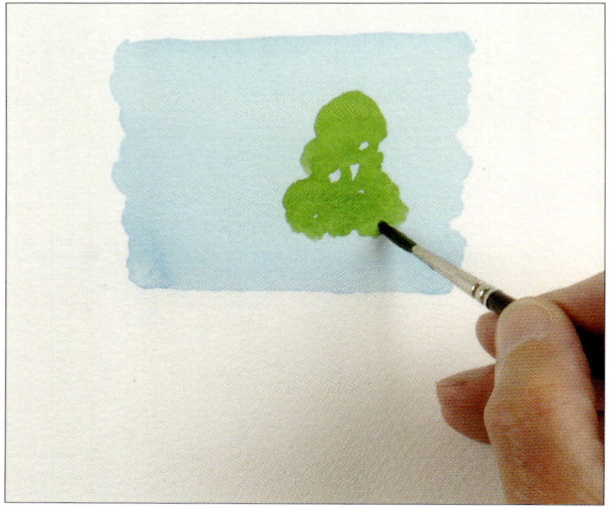

3 Work the green wash down the tree. Use small horizontal strokes and overlap them slightly so you attain a flat wash. As watercolor is transparent, the initial blue will influence the color of the green wash, creating a beautiful, luminous color.

2 When the first wash is dry, mix up a fresh green wash to depict the trees. Create curving shapes with one or two holes so the blue sky can show through in places.

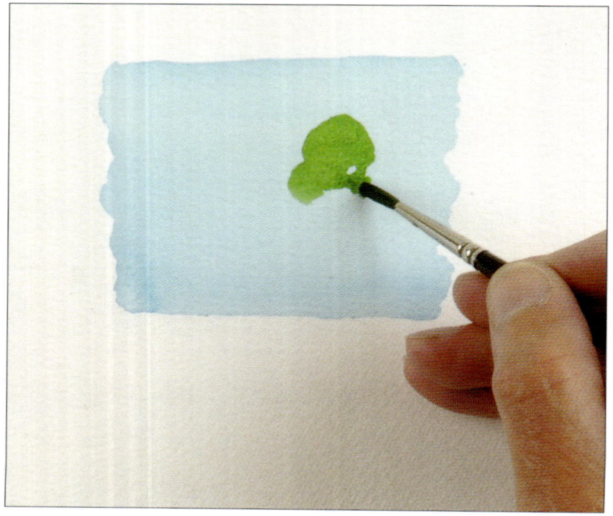

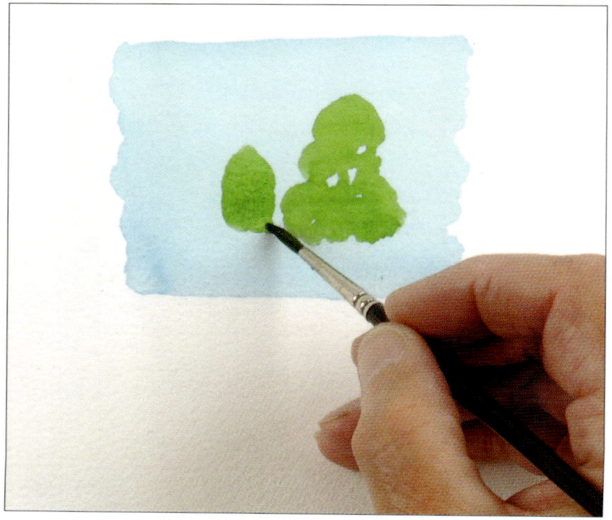

4 Add a smaller tree to the left. Make this tree a simpler shape—but again render it using a flat wash.

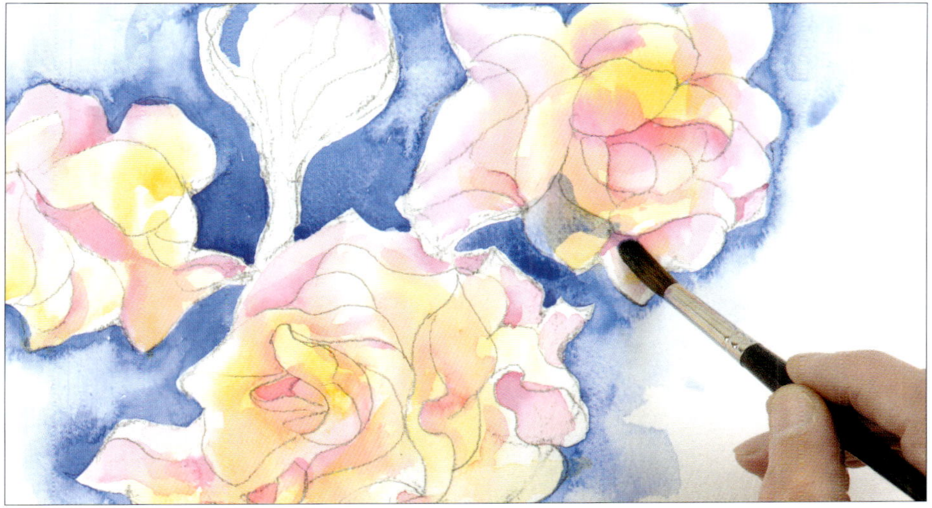

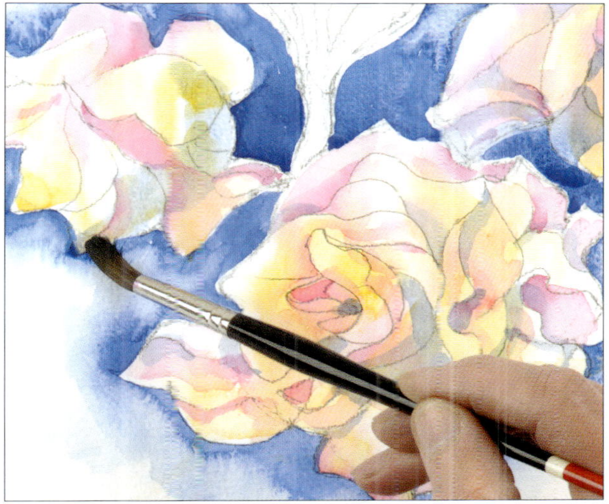

**19** Continue adding the ultramarine to the bottom of the left flower. Note how the ultramarine registers as blue on the white paper, but green when it is painted on top of the yellow and purple when it is painted over the pink. Building up transparent layers of paint in this way is known as glazing.

**17** Add more water to your ultramarine mix and use this to put in some shadow tones on your flowers. Do not try to follow the outlines of petals, but do make sure your brushstrokes have curved rather than straight edges.

**18** Break up the pinks and yellows on the top right flower with strokes of ultramarine. You can attain wonderfully subtle variations of color by laying the ultramarine on top of existing colors.

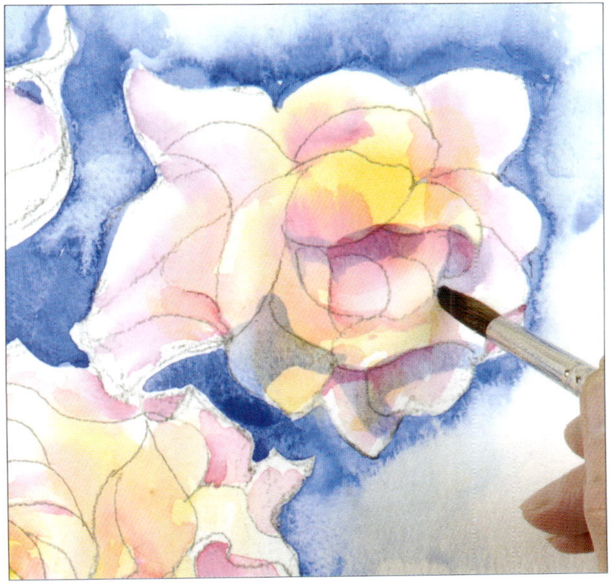

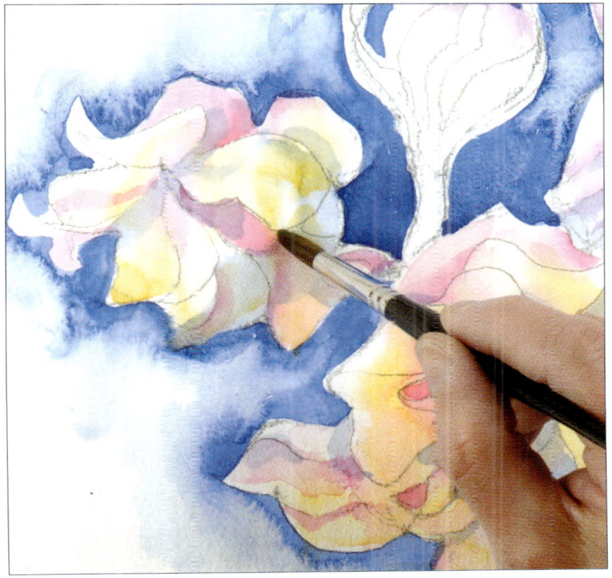

**20** Now add ultramarine to the top of the left flower. Think about creating a patchwork of different colors—subtle variations of pink and purple, yellow and orange, blue and green.

5 Clean your brush in water and dry it on a piece of kitchen towel. Then with the tip of the brush, carefully soak up the excess paint at the bottom of the pink wash. Let the paint dry. Now try creating a landscape in front of the sky.

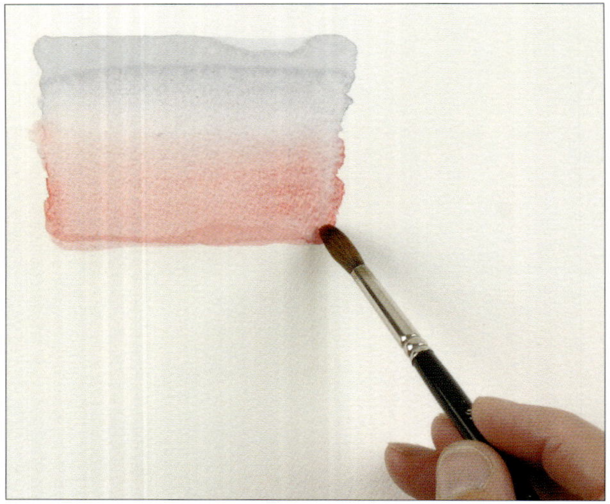

6 Add more pigment to your blue-gray wash to begin rendering a landscape—you want the tone quite strong here because the landscape features are silhouetted against the setting sun. Use the tip of a small brush to draw a long, vertical stroke for the land, and then add a cottage.

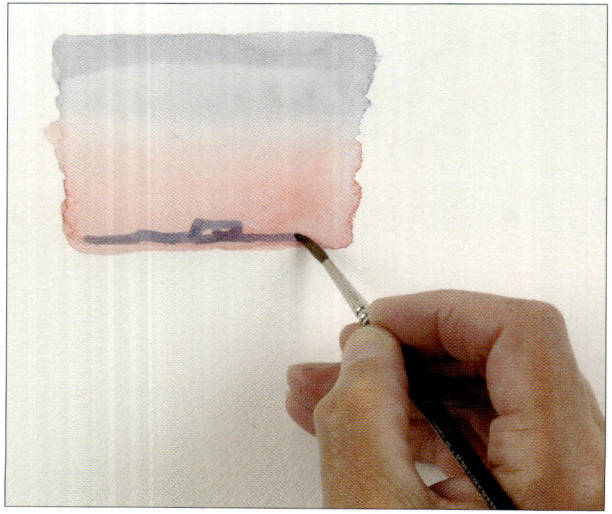

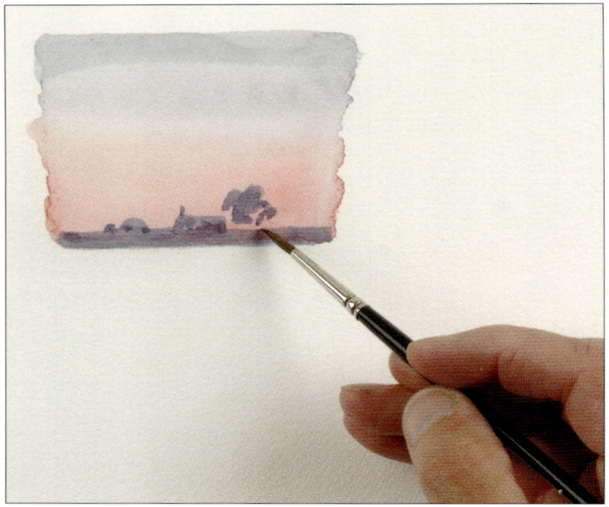

7 Landscape features set against a setting sun do not cast shadows, so keep your shapes simple and flat. A dark line right along the bottom of your flat wash will keep these features in the foreground.

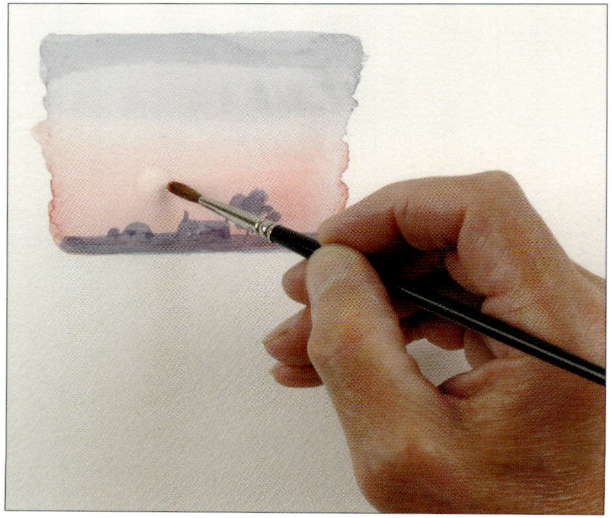

8 Continue to add detail—give the cottage a chimney and add some trees to break up the flat horizon line. Now you can give the impression of a watery sun emerging through the mist—simply apply clean water with the end of your brush to create a pale circle just above the landscape. Be patient if the color does not lift out straight away. If necessary, use a stiffer brush.

**21** Next use the B pencil to draw some leaf shapes emerging from behind the flowers. To make the leaves look realistic, vary the spacing between them and overlap them in places.

**22** Now mix up viridian toned down with a touch of burnt sienna. Use the tip of the brush to apply this mix inside all the leaf outlines.

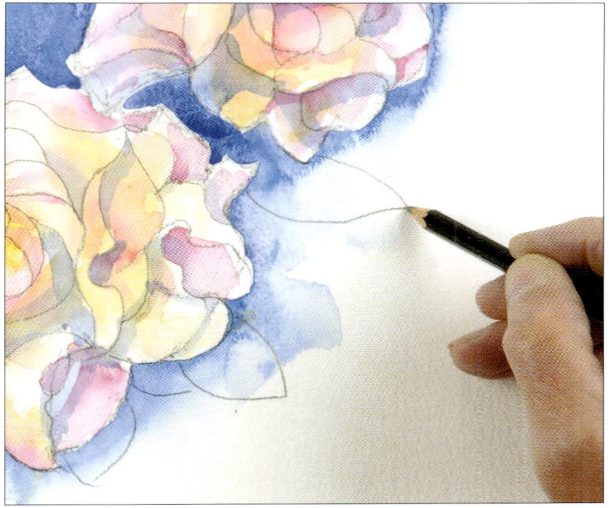

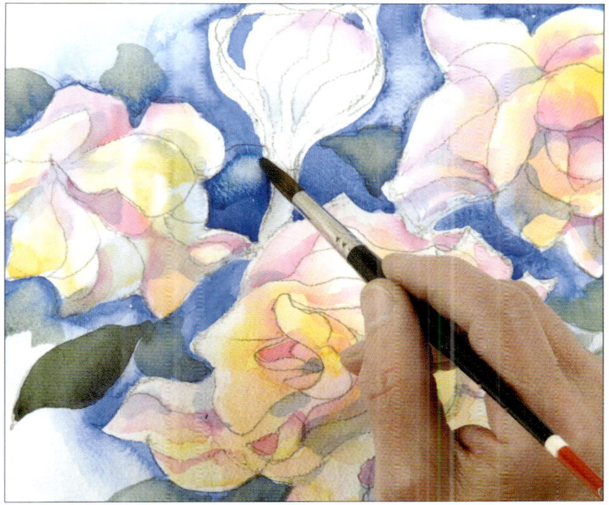

**23** Add some leaves in the space between the flowers. As the ultramarine is still wet here, the leaf shapes will have soft edges. This gives the impression that they are some way behind the flower.

**24** Keep painting the leaves around the edges. Try to describe each leaf with clean, bold brushstrokes. This will help capture the crisp feel of rose leaves.

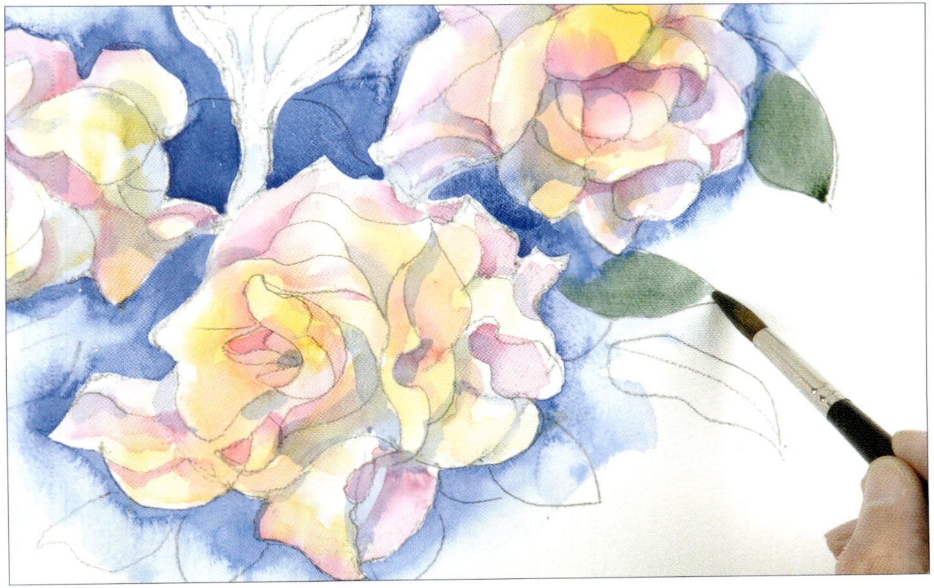

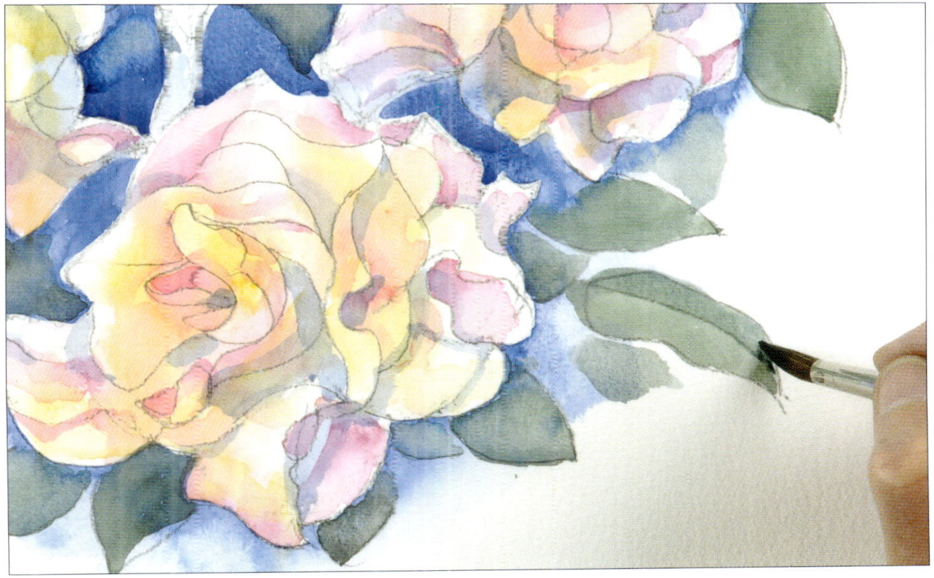

1 Now try blending two colors in one wash. This technique is particularly useful when creating atmospheric landscape effects—for instance, the sky and sea divided by a hazy horizon line. Here, we are going to use it to suggest the changing color of a sky at sunset. Mix up a blue-gray and a pink in separate wells of your palette, tilt your drawing board, and then brush the blue-gray across the top of the paper.

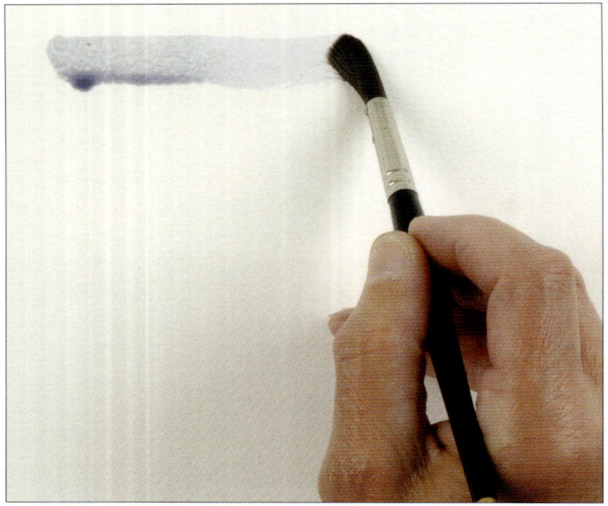

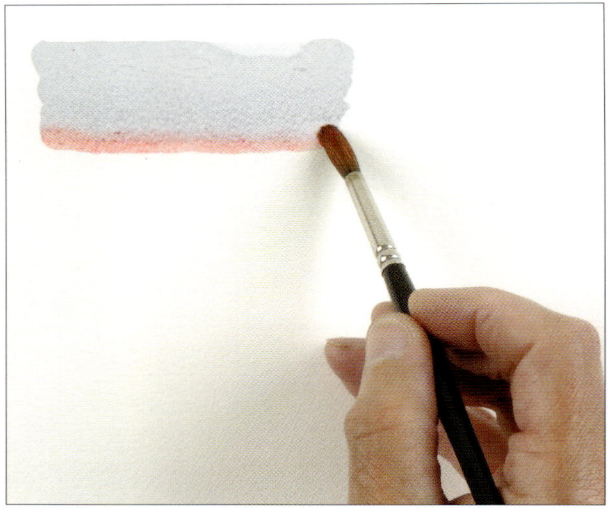

3 Before the paint dries, clean your brush in water and apply the pink so the top of the brushstroke just touches the bottom edge of the blue-gray wash. The blue-gray wash will begin to run down into the pink—creating a pleasing soft transition between the two colors. Let the color move of its own course—do not encourage it with your brush!

2 Load the brush with more of the same color and add another stroke just below the first one. Now clean your brush and use it to lift some of the excess paint that has run down to the bottom of the wash. More paint will run down to take its place so you will not attain a 'tidemark.'

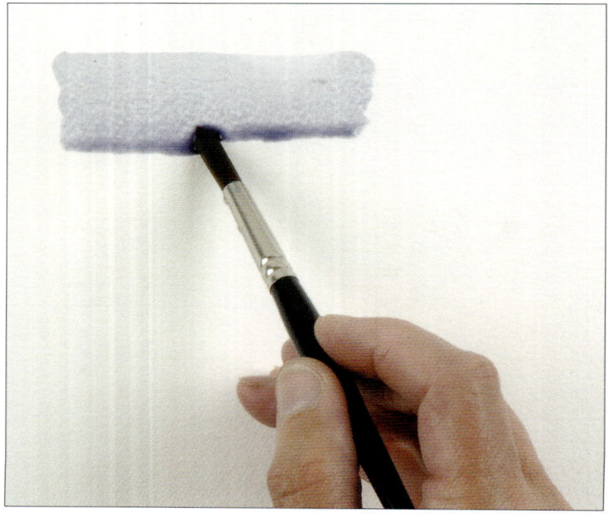

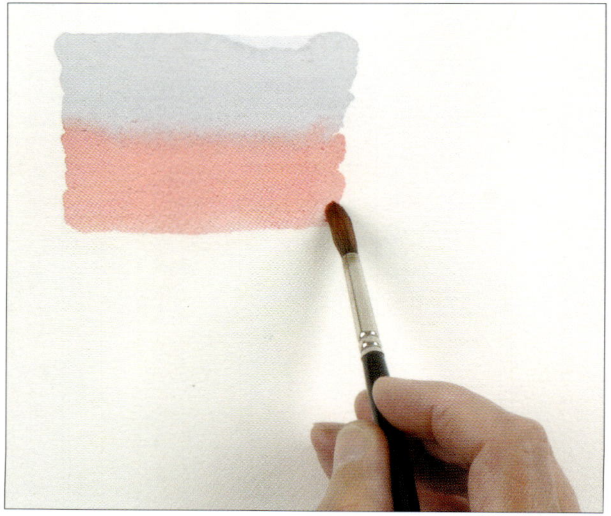

4 Complete the pink wash by continuing to work your brushstrokes, each one slightly overlapping, down to the bottom of the paper. Now you have a graduated wash—this can be seen as a sunset in a misty atmosphere.

**25** Now mix lemon yellow with some ultramarine to attain a fresh sap green color. Use this for the leaves clinging to the closed rose in the center. By roughly mixing the pigments, the color here varies from deep green through yellow.

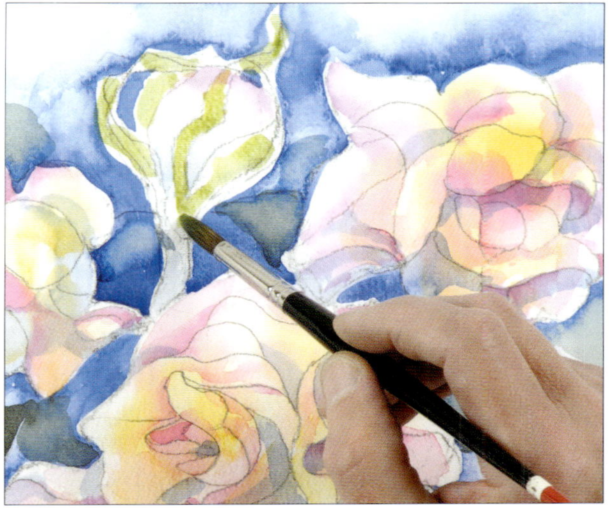

**26** Finish the foliage on the center flower. Note the leaves do not completely enclose the flower, so leave areas for the flower bud to show through.

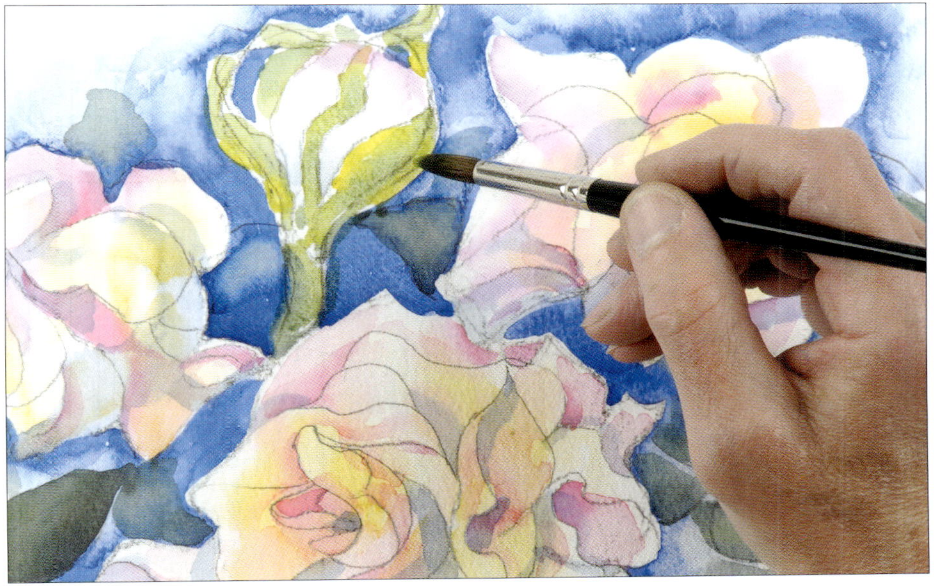

**27** Clean your brush and add more water to the edge of the picture to heighten the vignette effect.

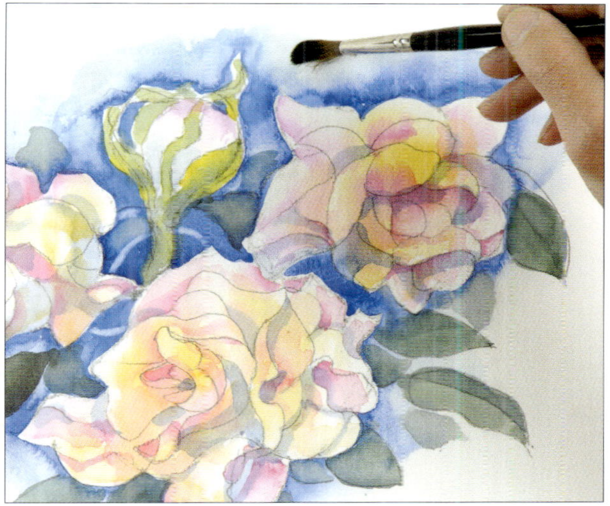

**28** Then wash your brush again and with its point "draw" fine lines into the ultramarine wash in between the flowers. These will lines will become stems.

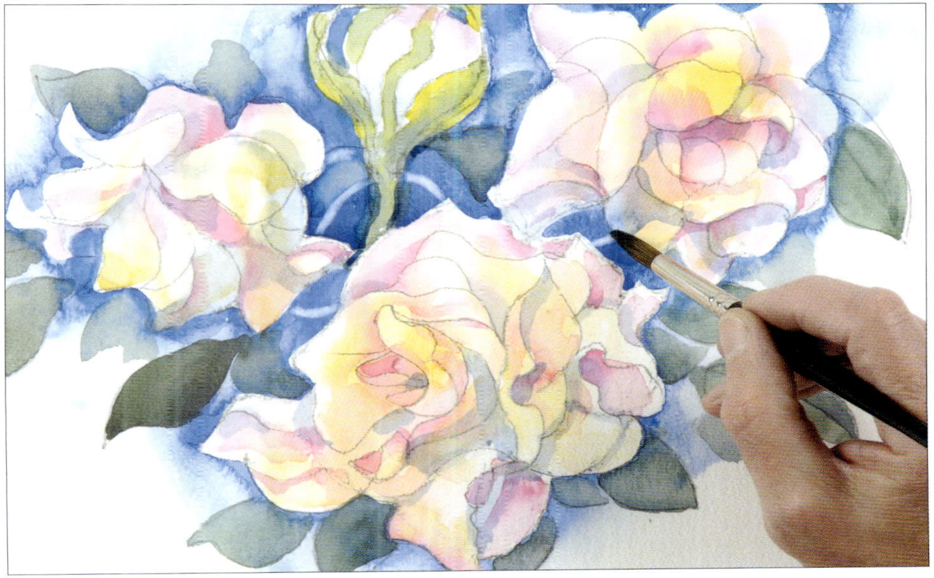

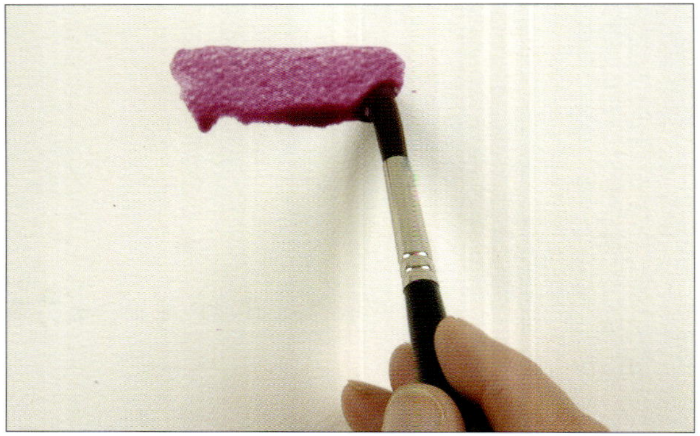

1 A graduated wash moves gradually from dark to light. The technique is particularly effective for painting skies. With your paper tilted at about 20°, apply a wash of paint across the width of the paper, just as you would for a flat wash.

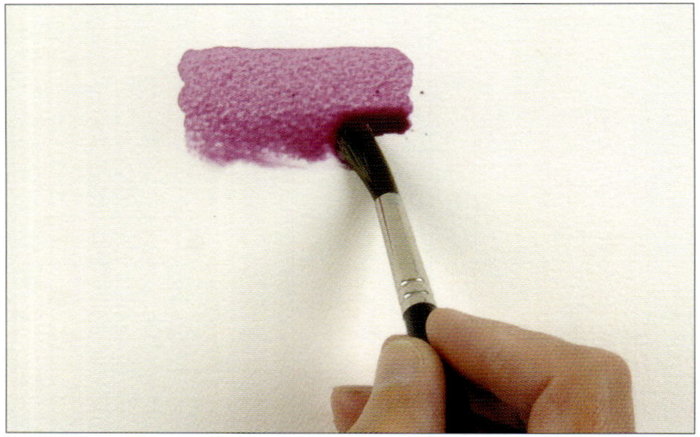

2 Instead of returning your brush to the palette, dip it into clean water. Now paint a second brushstroke across the paper, overlapping the first band along the bottom edge.

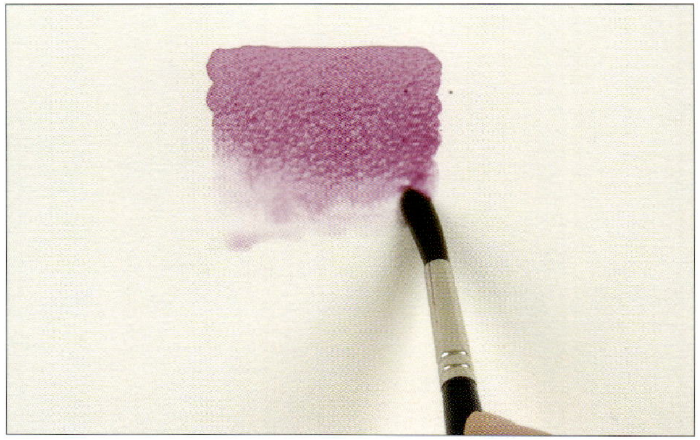

3 Continue the wash by loading your brush with more water and drawing it left to right beneath the previous stroke. Do not worry too much if excess water runs down the paper.

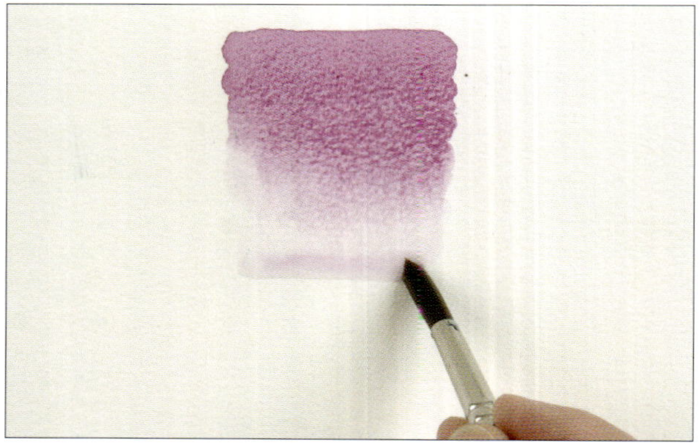

4 If you find there is too much water on the paper, you can dry your brush on a piece of kitchen towel, then just touch the bead of excess paint and the brush will soak it up. Repeat the process if necessary.

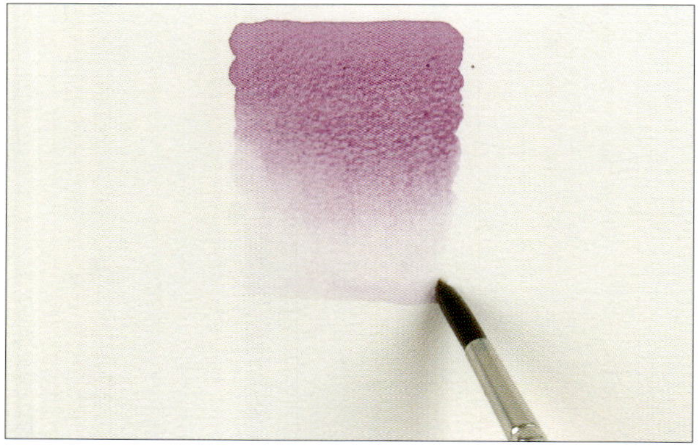

5 Continue to apply brushstrokes, dipping the brush into your water (which will now have picked up some color) until the wash fades to almost no tone.

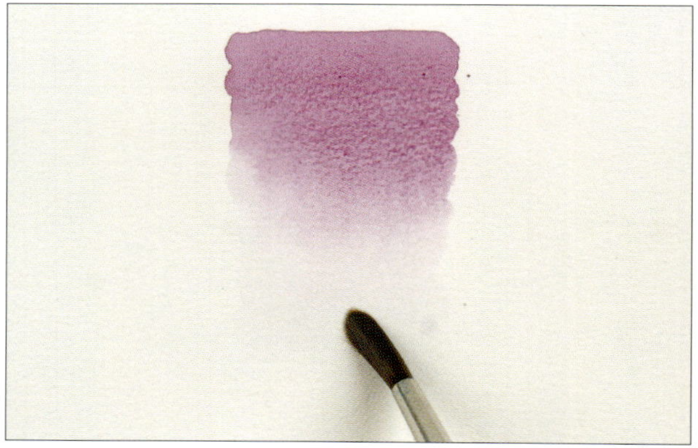

6 Finally, to even up the bottom of your wash, dip your brush in clean water, shake off excess moisture, and run it in a straight line across the bottom edge of your last brushstroke.

**29** Now, still using the point of your brush, add your sap green mix (lemon yellow and ultramarine) into the white lines you've drawn. These stems add to the overall design of the picture. Next put final touches on the flowers with a dilute cadmium yellow mix.

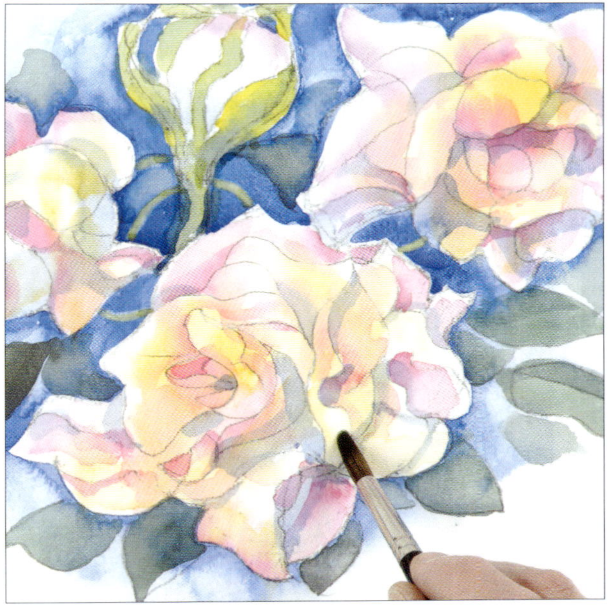

**30** Use the flat brush dipped in water to lighten some of the colors in the flowers. Do not feel you have to add color everywhere; leaving some white paper exposed gives the picture a lively contrast of tones.

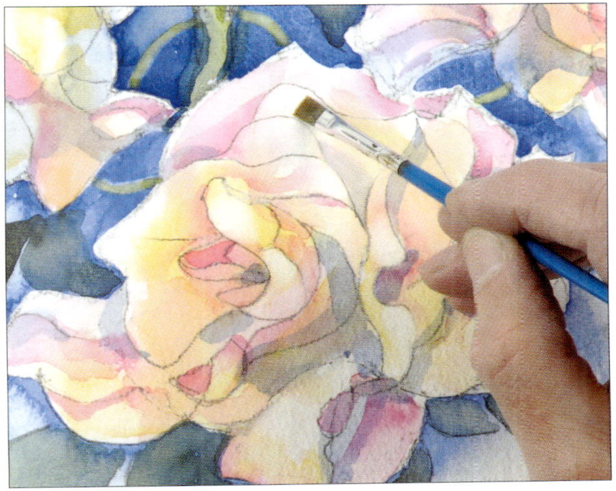

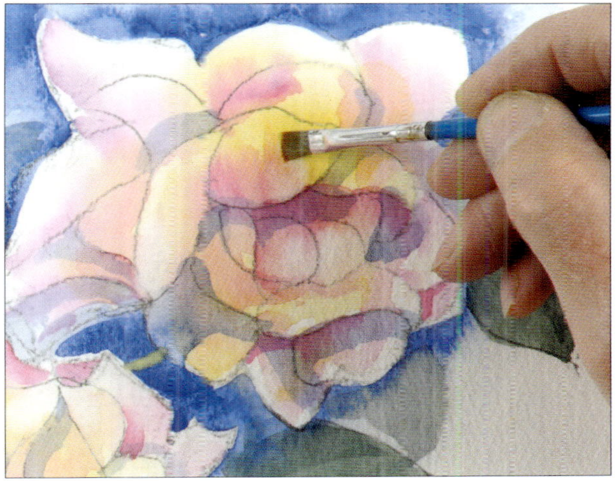

**31** Keep dipping the flat brush in clean water to merge the pink and yellow washes in places. This can create wonderful textures. Work slowly and stop when you see an effect you like.

**32** For the final touch, use the No.3 brush to add another touch of ultramarine blue on the closed flower to denote another hole in the foliage.

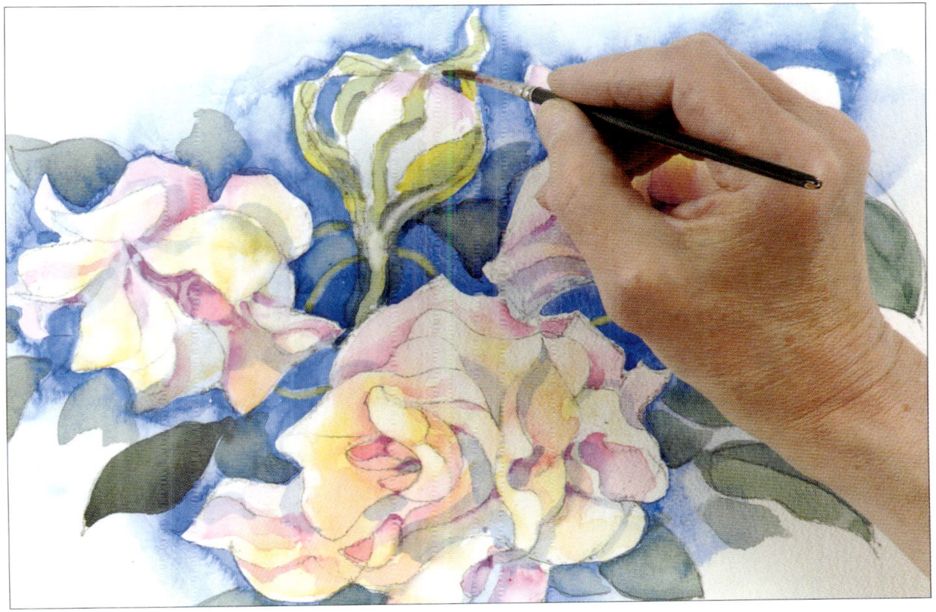

# basic techniques / **flat washes continued**

1 Now try putting a flat wash inside a circle. First, draw a circle with a pencil and compass in the middle of your paper. Then mix up your color and apply the first stroke, curving around the top of the circle. Practice this first curving stroke on spare paper first.

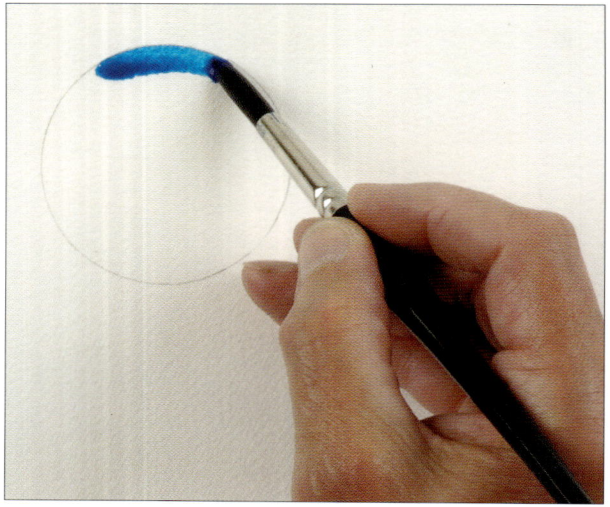

2 After the first stroke, you can use straight horizontal strokes. Remember, the strokes should overlap so you pick up any excess paint from the previous strokes and incorporate it in the new stroke.

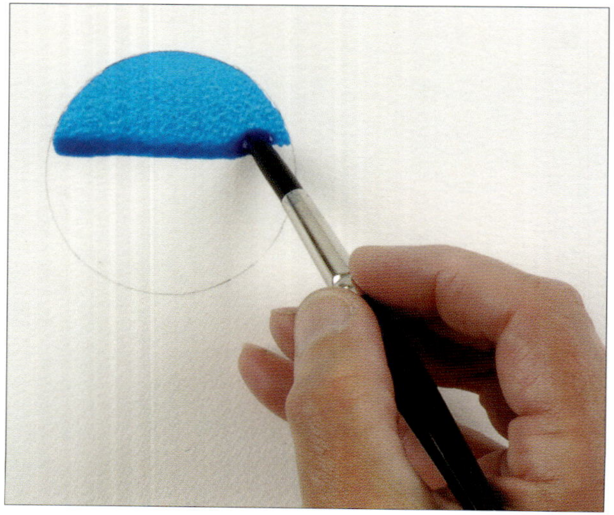

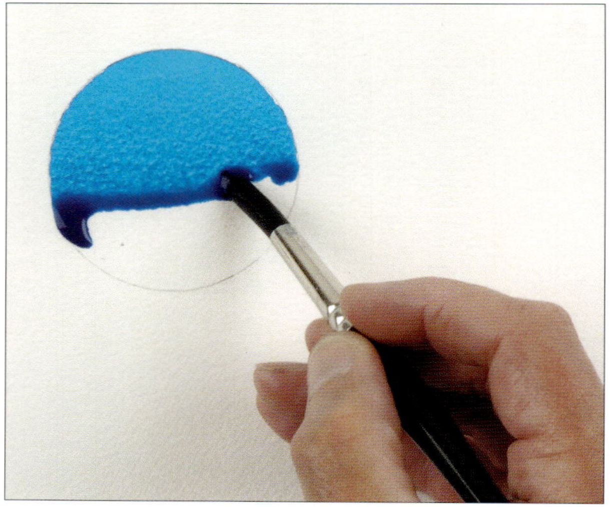

3 Continue working down the circle, using steady, decisive strokes. Tidy up any drips by quickly applying the next stroke. Do not let the paint drip outside the circle. If you find this is a problem, put your drawing board at a less steep angle. Also, try dampening the circle first with clean water.

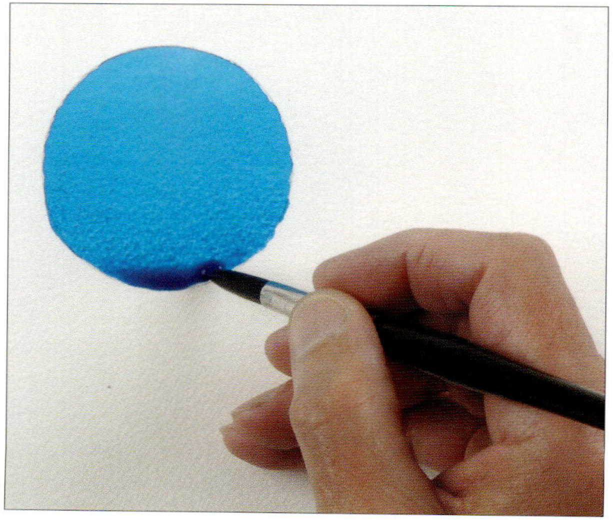

4 Finish the wash with a curved stroke at the bottom of the circle. Clean your brush in water, wipe it on kitchen towel to remove excess moisture, and then use it to remove surplus paint from the last brushstroke.

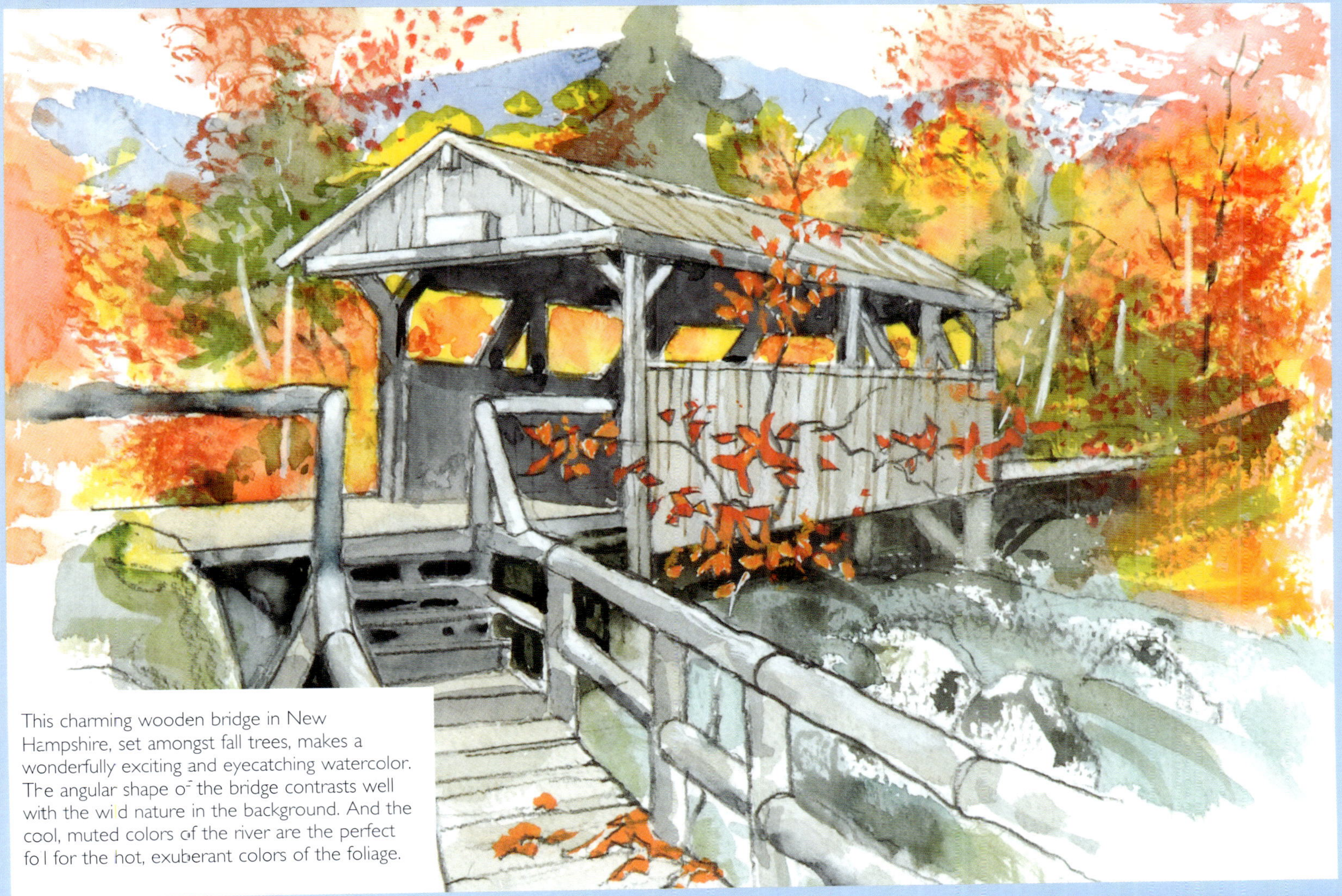

This charming wooden bridge in New Hampshire, set amongst fall trees, makes a wonderfully exciting and eyecatching watercolor. The angular shape of the bridge contrasts well with the wild nature in the background. And the cool, muted colors of the river are the perfect foil for the hot, exuberant colors of the foliage.

**MATERIALS**

**Drawing board**

**Watercolor paper**

**Watercolor palette**

**Watercolors: cobalt blue, violet, lemon yellow, ultramarine blue, neutral tint, Prussian blue, yellow ocher, Hooker's green, phthalo turquoise, raw sienna, cadmium yellow, orange, cadmium red, burnt sienna, white, sepia**

**Brushes: No.10 and No.02**

**Jar of water**

**B pencil**

**Ruler**

**Eraser**

**Sponge**

# basic techniques / **flat washes**

1 Laying a flat wash is an essential watercolor technique—and, with a little practice, it is easy to do. First, mix a large amount of color in your palette and tilt your drawing board slightly toward you. With a fully laden brush, draw a steady stroke across the top of the paper. Due to the tilt of the board, a bead of paint will collect at the bottom of the stroke.

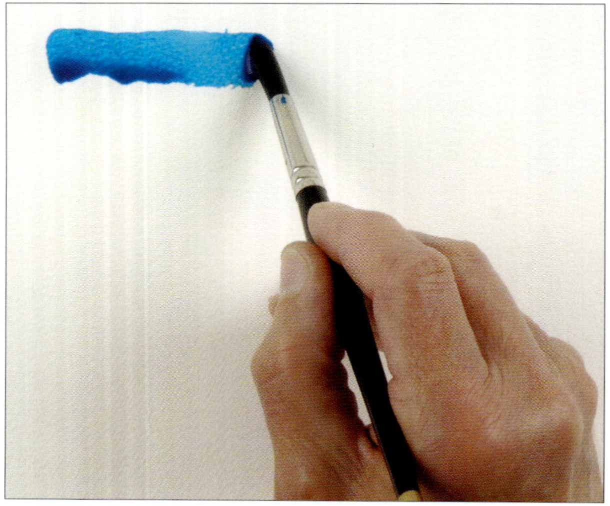

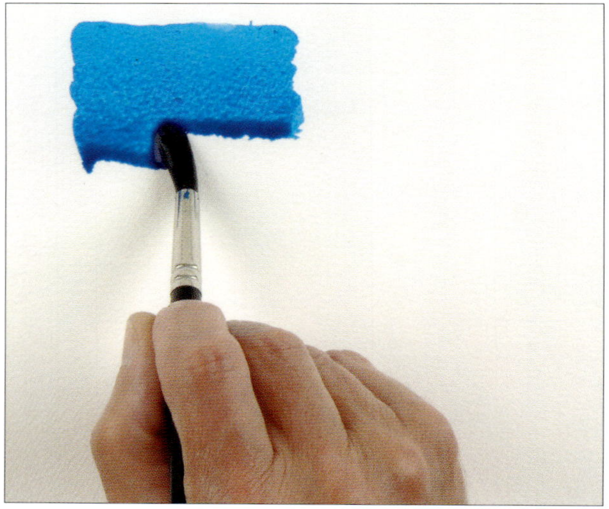

3 Continue working down the paper using horizontal strokes with a fully laden brush. Slightly overlap each stroke so that any excess paint is merged into the new stroke—this is the secret to a uniform, seamless wash.

2 Load the brush with paint again and apply a second stroke under the first. Overlap the strokes slightly so you pick up the bead of paint at the bottom of the first stroke—and always apply the strokes in the same direction, either left to right or vice versa.

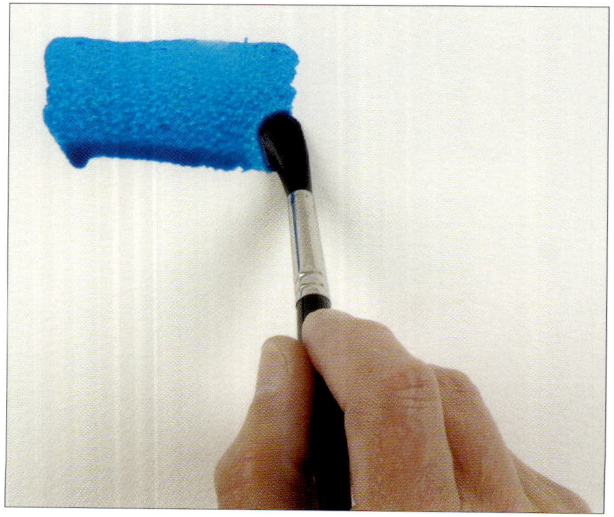

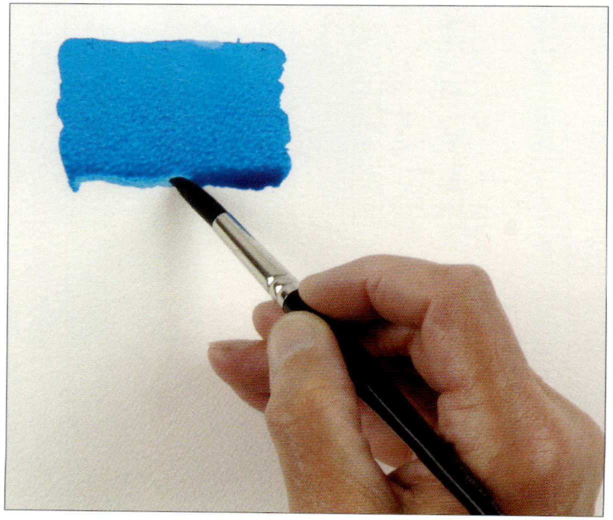

4 To finish, clean your brush in water, dry it on kitchen towel, and then use it to gather up the paint that collects at the bottom of the wash. Leave the wash to dry in its tilted position to avoid the paint flowing back up the paper and creating a 'tidemark.'

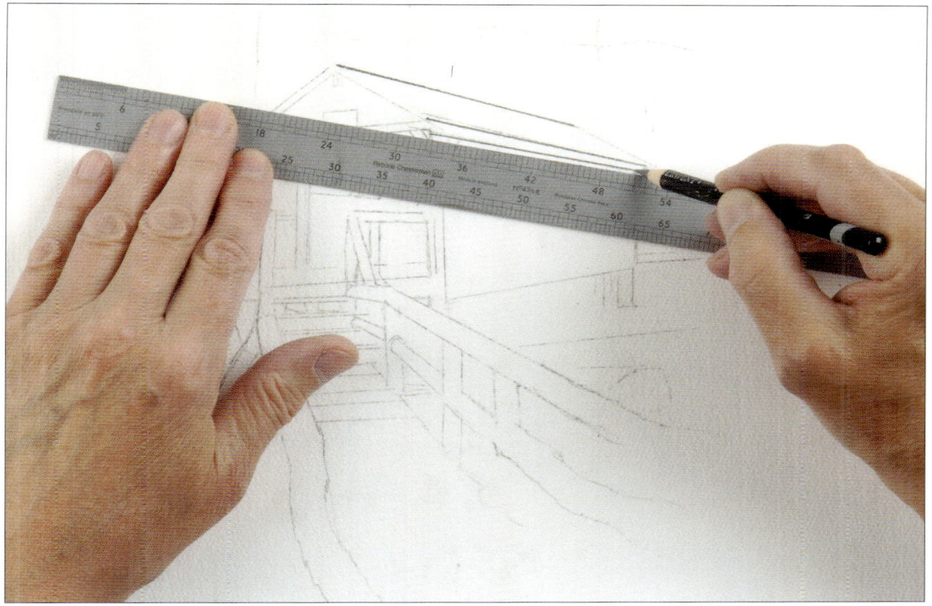

**1** Start by drawing the outlines of the scene with the 2B pencil. You can either trace or copy the image at the beginning of this project. If you are drawing freehand, work lightly at first so you can easily correct any mistakes. Use a ruler to put in the straight edges on the bridge.

**2** Continue drawing the straight lines on the bridge with the ruler. Then draw the openings in the bridge.

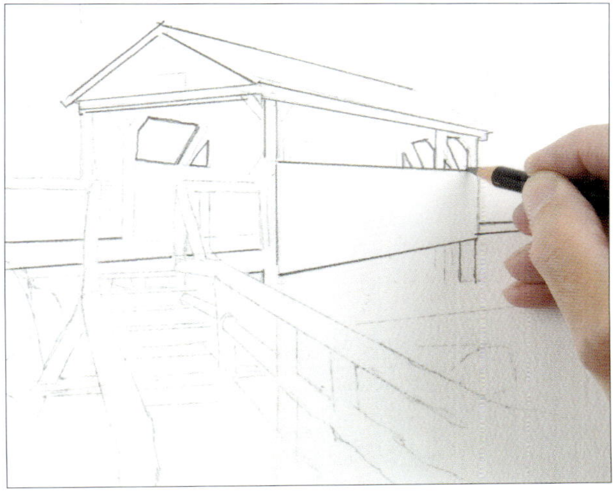

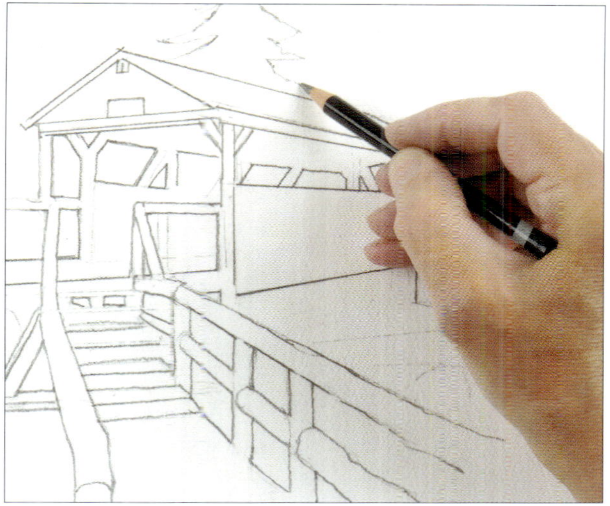

**3** Now draw the footbridge in the foreground. Do not use the ruler here—the bridge is made up of irregular planks and logs, so you want uneven lines. Then start on the outline of the conifer.

**4** Continue drawing the outlines of the trees. Also put in the line that defines the top of the hill behind the trees. Your pencil work can be quite loose here—you can add detail with paint later.

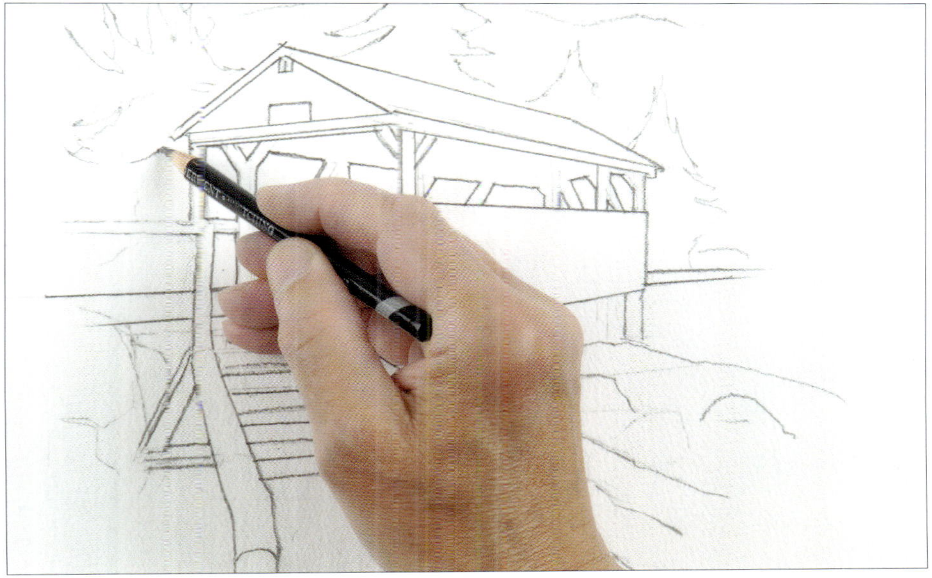

# basic techniques / **controlling the marks you make**

A basic set of brushes is all you need to get started. Round brushes are the most versatile—sizes No.2, No.6, and No.12 should be sufficient. Complete your brush selection with a 1in flat brush to enable you to lay washes in quickly and a rigger brush or No.0 round to register details. In general, the softer the hairs, the more water the brush will hold. However, large, soft brushes are very floppy when wet—and, although they cover large areas, you have much less control over the brushmark. Experiment with different brushes and always practice your mark-making on scrap paper before embarking on a picture.

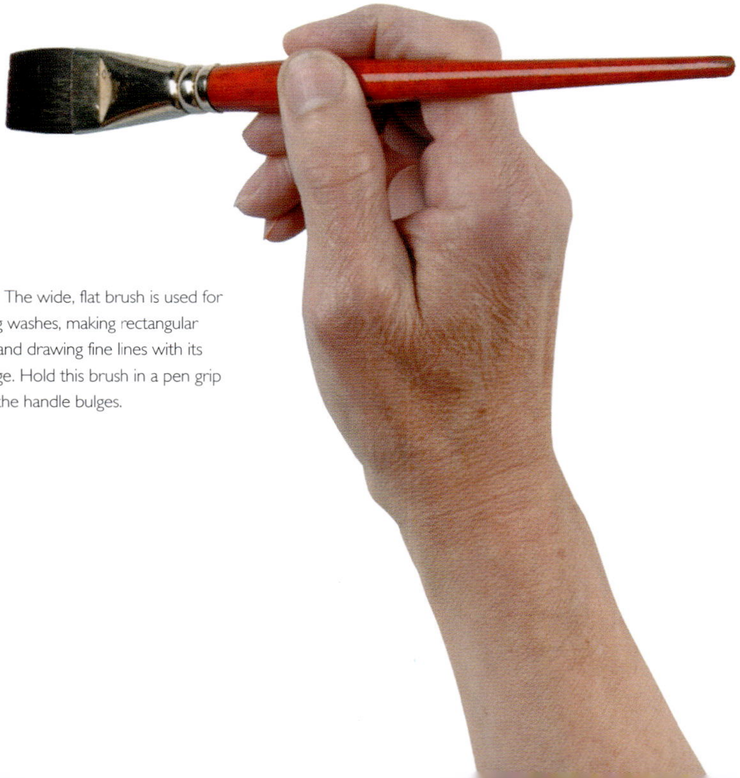

**RIGHT** The wide, flat brush is used for applying washes, making rectangular marks, and drawing fine lines with its thin edge. Hold this brush in a pen grip where the handle bulges.

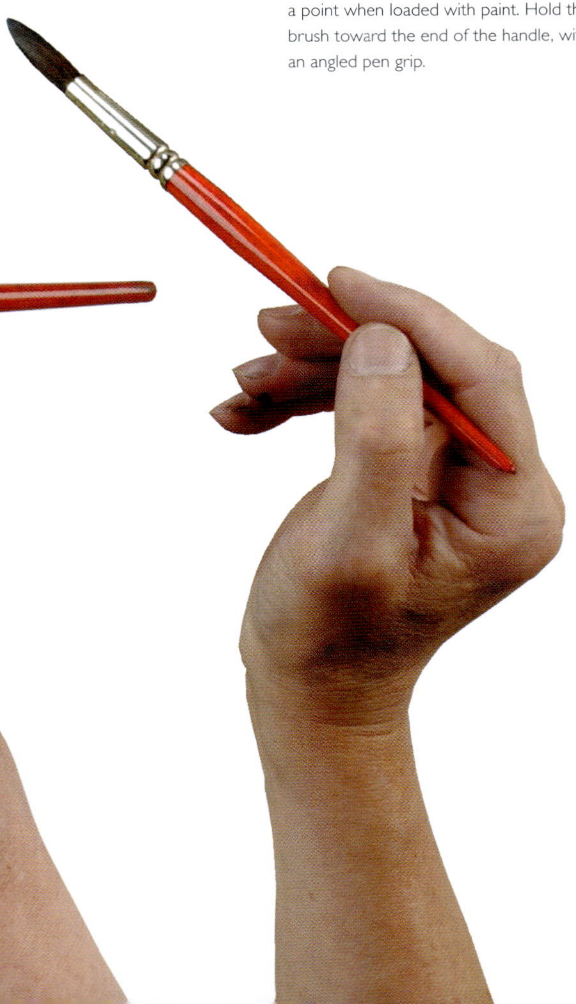

**BELOW** A good round brush will come to a point when loaded with paint. Hold this brush toward the end of the handle, with an angled pen grip.

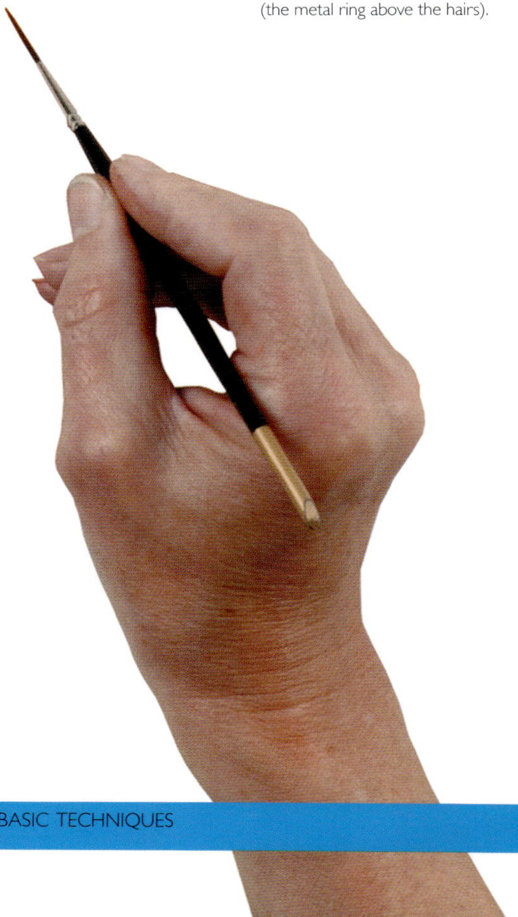

**BELOW** A rigger brush draws exceptionally fine lines. The long hairs carry lots of paint—you will be surprised at how much. Hold this brush as you would a pen, near the ferrule (the metal ring above the hairs).

5 Draw some rocks on the left. Then add a few more planks on the walkway. Make them progressively fainter as you work down the paper. Now mix cobalt blue with violet and apply it, using the No.10 brush, across the distant hills. Keep the brush fairly flat on the paper to attain a broken texture.

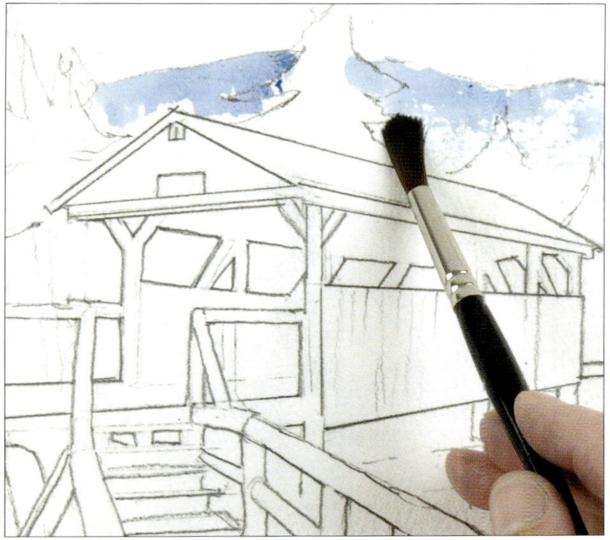

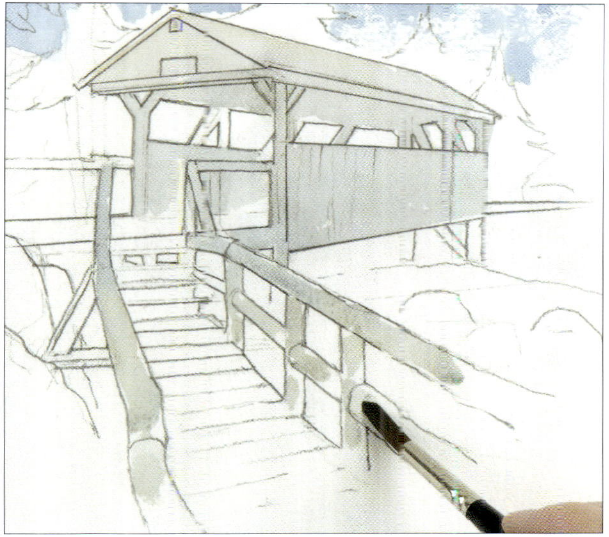

7 Mix neutral tint with Prussian blue to attain a light gray for the timbers of the bridge. Do not worry about going over the pencil lines—the wash will dissolve some of the graphite but there will be enough to see where you are in the composition. Vary the color by adding some yellow ocher to the wash.

6 Make a very weak mix of lemon yellow with a touch of ultramarine blue and add this over the sky area. The aim here is simply to tone down the harsh whiteness of the paper.

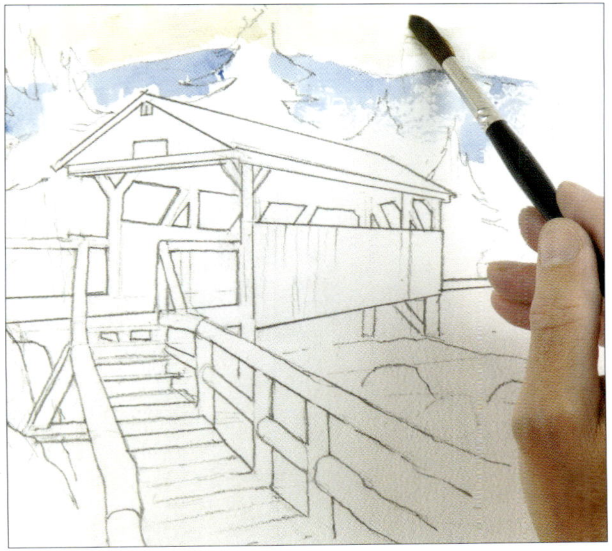

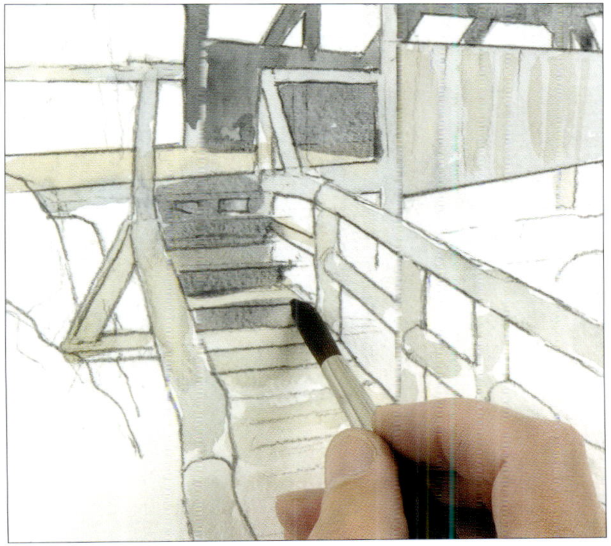

8 Next add more neutral tint and Prussian blue to your mix to create a stronger gray. Apply this to the shadow areas inside the sheltered part of the road bridge and on the steps on the footbridge.

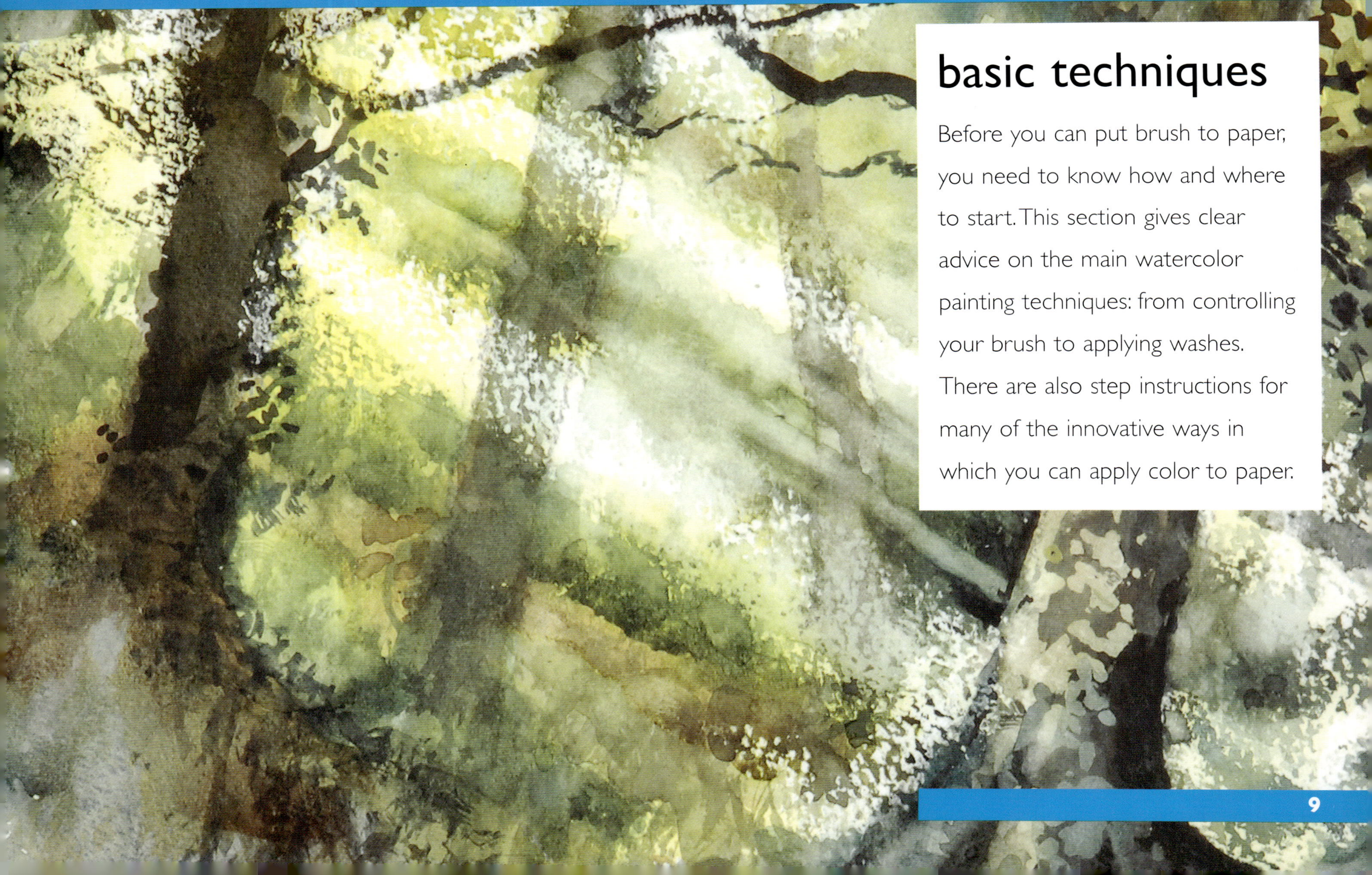

# basic techniques

Before you can put brush to paper, you need to know how and where to start. This section gives clear advice on the main watercolor painting techniques: from controlling your brush to applying washes. There are also step instructions for many of the innovative ways in which you can apply color to paper.

9 Also add your gray shadow tone on the left side of the handrails. This will help bring out their rounded form. Now put in the shadow underneath the bridge with a wash of Hooker's green and touches of your gray mix. Extend the color with the side of the brush over the river to give an impression of rocks, spray and moving water.

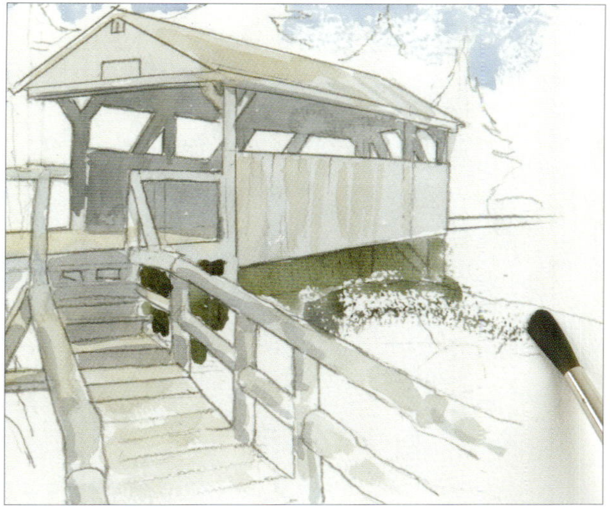

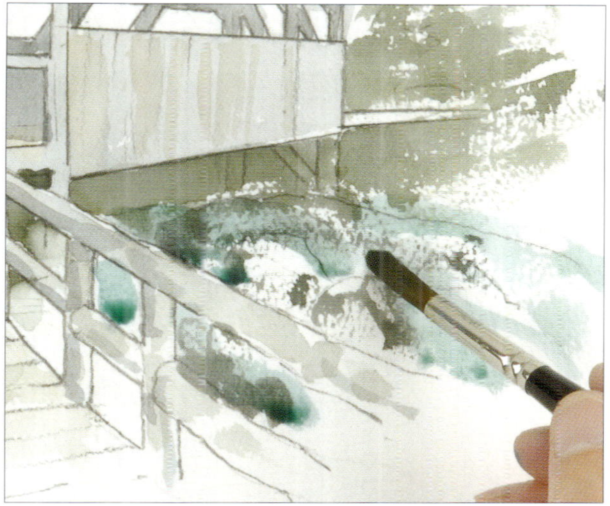

11 Mix phthalo turquoise with a touch of raw sienna for the water. Apply it quickly with loose brushstrokes to create a sense of movement. Leave some white paper showing between the brushstrokes.

12 Use an eraser to clean up any pencil lines that look misplaced or too strong. But keep most of your pencil work, as it adds texture, detail and life to the picture.

10 Continue with the same wash to paint the conifers in the background. Note how the roof of the bridge now leaps forward.

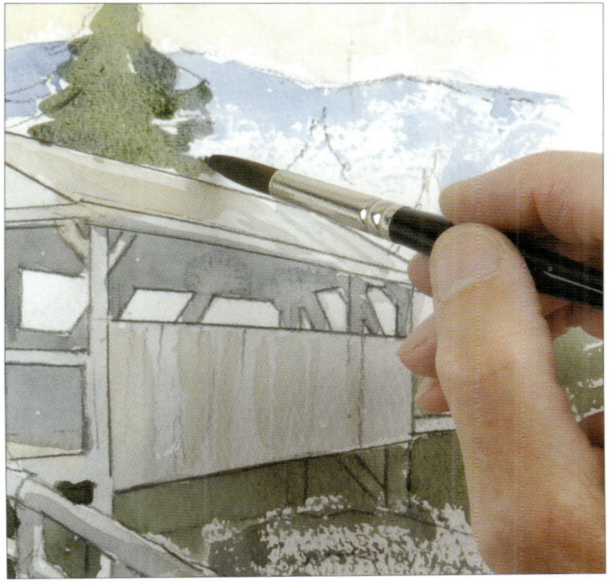

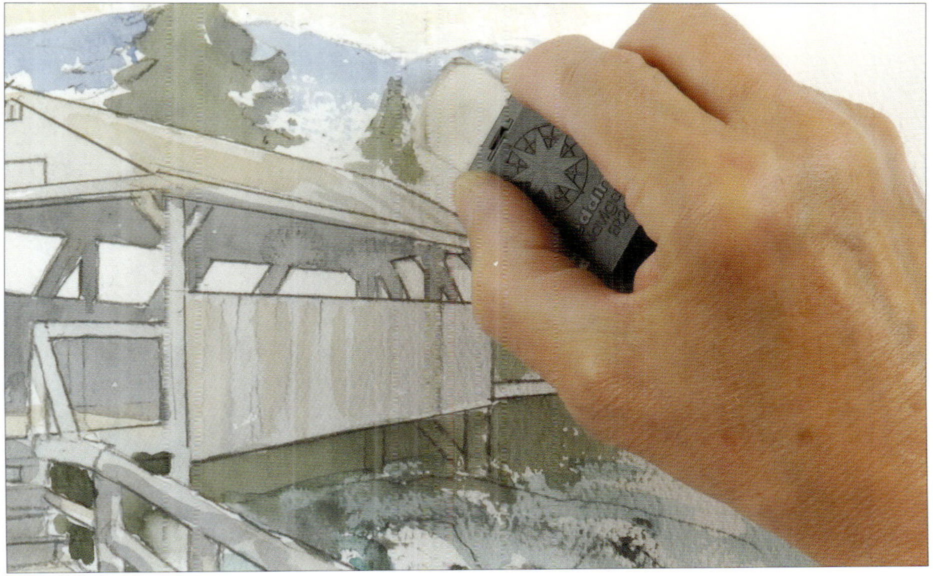

Before painting, you will need to fix your paper to a drawing board or a sheet of plywood. If you are using paper over 140lb (300gsm) in weight, you will not need to stretch the paper unless you intend to use very wet washes of paint. Simply tape or clip the paper on to the board. For lighter papers, stretch the paper, see right. To rinse your brush when changing colors, use a jam jar filled with water or, if working outdoors, a collapsible water pot. Watercolors take time to dry, especially if you are working in cool conditions. Speed up the process with a hair dryer, but be careful not to blow paint across the paper.

Finally, make sure that your workspace is adequately lit—to avoid eyestrain and, importantly, to see colors as they really are. Either sit by a window or use a daylight simulation bulb in a desk lamp—it can be very disheartening to see your work change color in daylight.

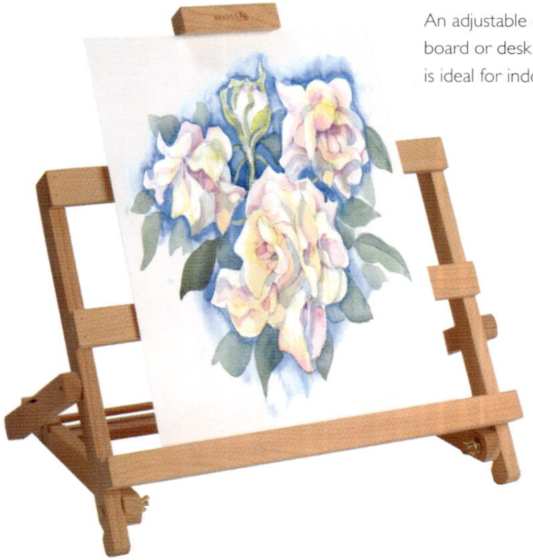

An adjustable drawing board or desk easel (left), is ideal for indoor work.

## STRETCHING WATERCOLOR PAPER

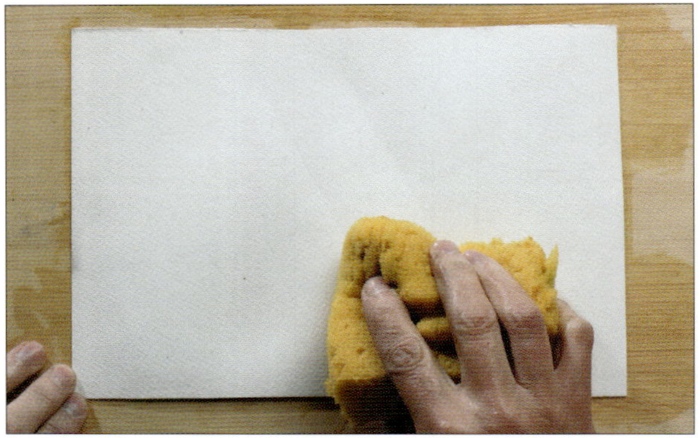

1 Immerse your paper in cold water for a minute. Drain off surplus water. Place the paper on your board and smooth it with your hands. Then dry the edges with a sponge.

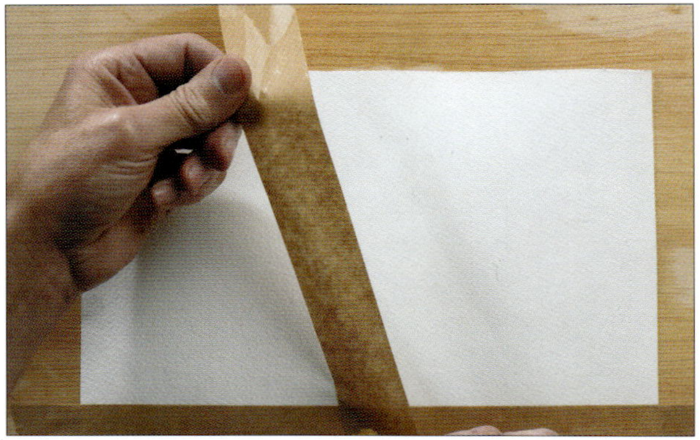

2 Cut four lengths of gummed 2in (50mm) wide brown paper. Moisten one of the long sides with a damp sponge and use it to stick one edge of the paper to the board.

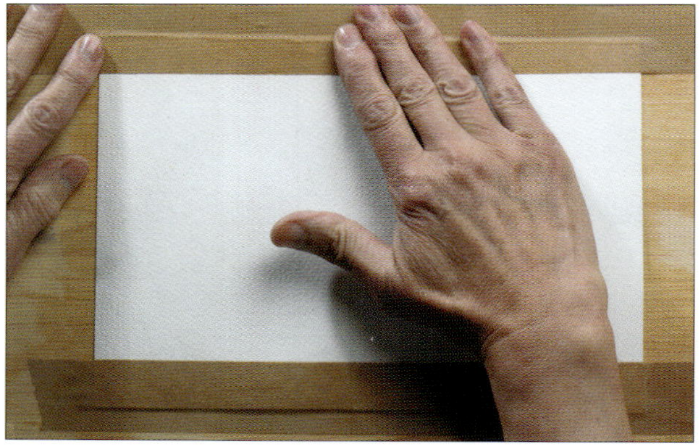

3 Continue to apply the gummed strips to the edges of the paper—make sure half their width is on the board, half on the paper. Use your fingers to flatten the strips down.

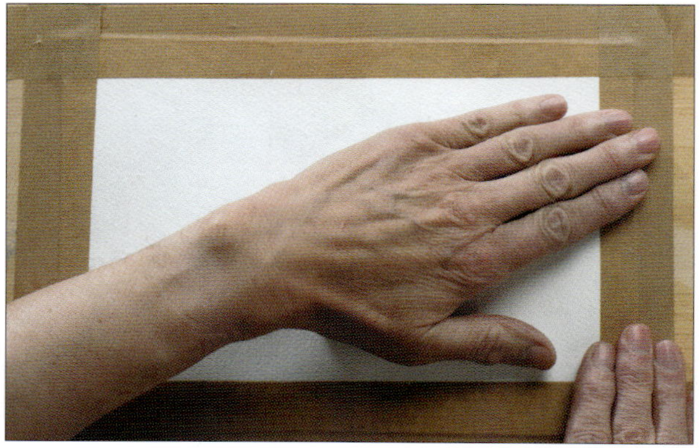

4 Leave the paper to dry naturally, away from direct heat. Do not use the stretched paper until it is dry. Leave the strips in place until you finish the painting and it is dry.

**13** Mix lemon yellow with cadmium yellow to attain a sharp, bright color for the fall leaves. Work the color over the green foliage on the right to create beautiful olive colors.

**14** Continue adding yellow to the background, letting the white paper show through in places. Take the color close to the right and left edges of the paper, but work around the conifers.

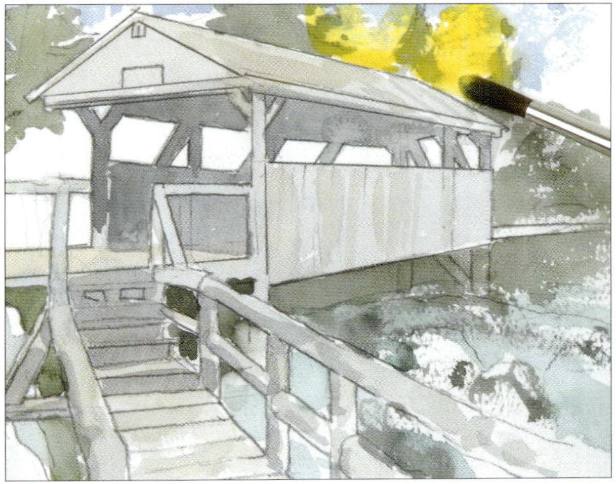

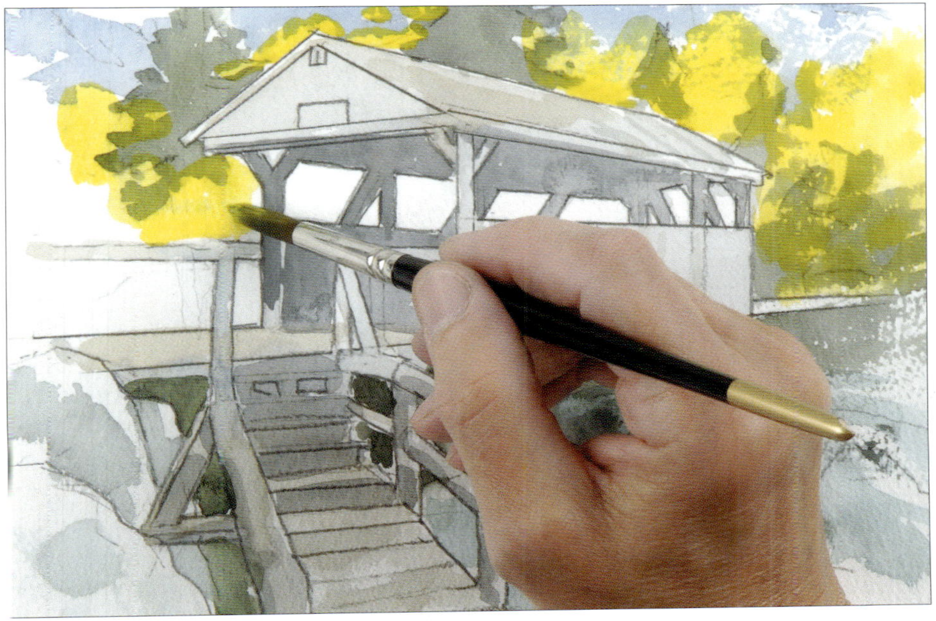

**15** Now mix a wash of orange and drop it into the wet yellow areas. If the yellow areas have dried, rewet them with a brush dipped in water. The orange and yellow will merge on the paper to give a beautiful impression of the range of fall colors.

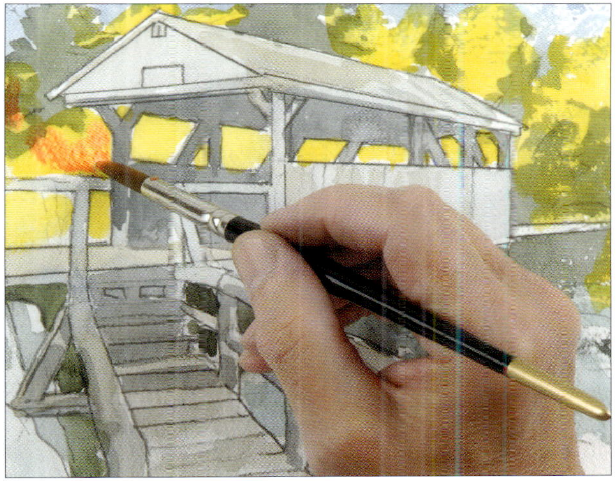

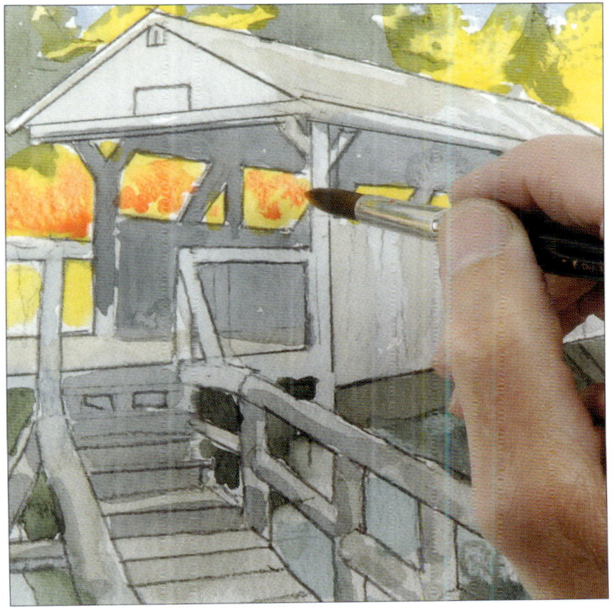

**16** With the point of the brush, carefully add orange in the openings in the bridge. Then continue working the orange across the background.

# materials and equipment / **boards and papers**

Papers designed to hold watercolors, such as the types shown below, generally produce the best results for finished work. They are either machine- or handmade, from wood pulp, cotton, or a mix of the two. Handmade papers, usually consisting of 100 percent cotton, are the most expensive but are rewarding to work on as they have pleasing irregular texture. However, they are usually only obtainable in large sheets.

Do not feel limited to papers specifically made for watercolors. Good-quality white cartridge paper works well, particularly for studies and sketches. Glossy or semi-glossy papers made for printing, such as those found on the backs of calendars, can produce interesting effects. If you see a surface that you think may take watercolor, try putting a few washes on it—you might just be pleasantly surprised by the results.

## paper weights

The thickness of a paper is called its "weight"—it is measured in pounds (the weight of a ream of 500 sheets) or grams per square meter (gsm). Lighter papers (under 140lbs/300gsm) should always be stretched—that is, soaked in water before being taped to a board to prevent buckling (see page 8). Heavier papers can be used in small sheets without stretching, although stretching is recommended for all papers intended for serious work. If you are using lots of wet washes or building up lots of layers of paint, use a heavy paper.

## book sheets or blocks

For outdoor work, you will need a spiral-bound sketchbook that will lie flat. A small sketchbook, about 4 x 6in (10 x 15cm), conveniently fits in a pocket and can be taken out whenever inspiration strikes. Larger sketchbooks, however, allow you to complete more detailed projects, such as landscapes. Alternatively, use 'blocks' of paper, which have glued edges to prevent buckling. Usually these work well, but if too much water is used, the whole block may twist.

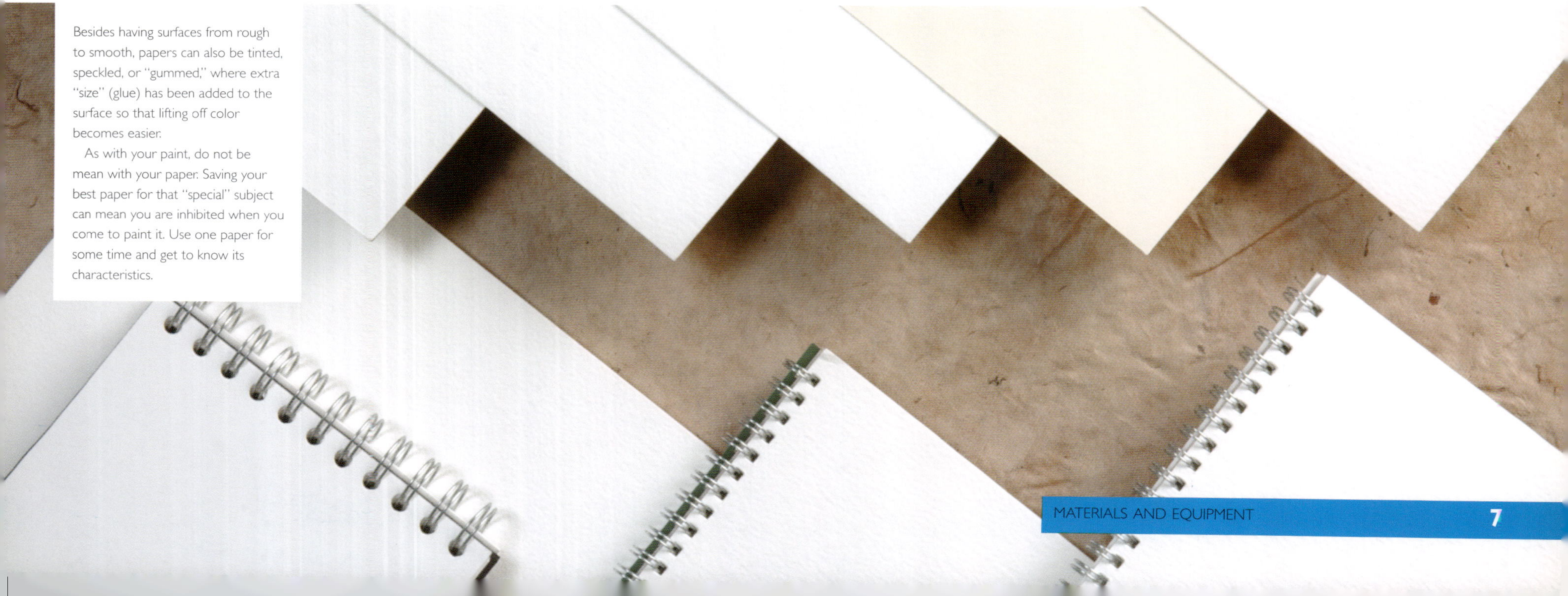

Besides having surfaces from rough to smooth, papers can also be tinted, speckled, or "gummed," where extra "size" (glue) has been added to the surface so that lifting off color becomes easier.

As with your paint, do not be mean with your paper. Saving your best paper for that "special" subject can mean you are inhibited when you come to paint it. Use one paper for some time and get to know its characteristics.

**17** Apply a dry wash of cadmium red with a sponge to render the leaves against the sky. Squeeze the sponge into a ball and dab the color into both dry and wet areas so you attain a variety of crisp and soft marks.

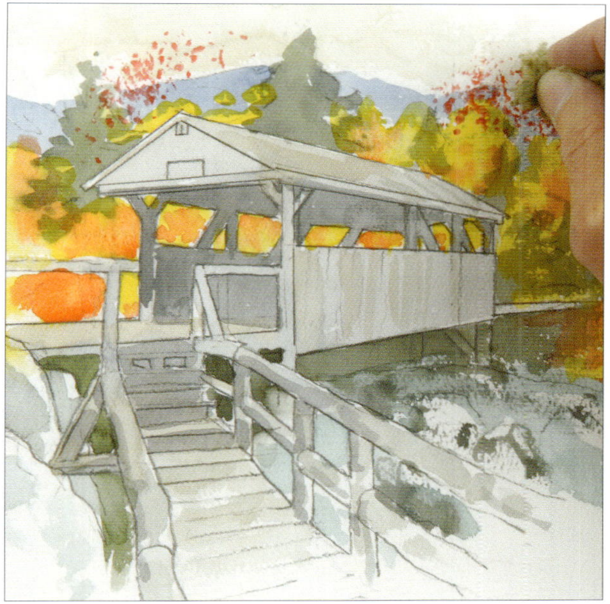

**18** Add some burnt sienna to the cadmium red to attain a darker, but still dry, red. Use the end of the No.10 brush to apply this color on the trees. This will create a stippled effect and give a lively impression of a mass of leaves.

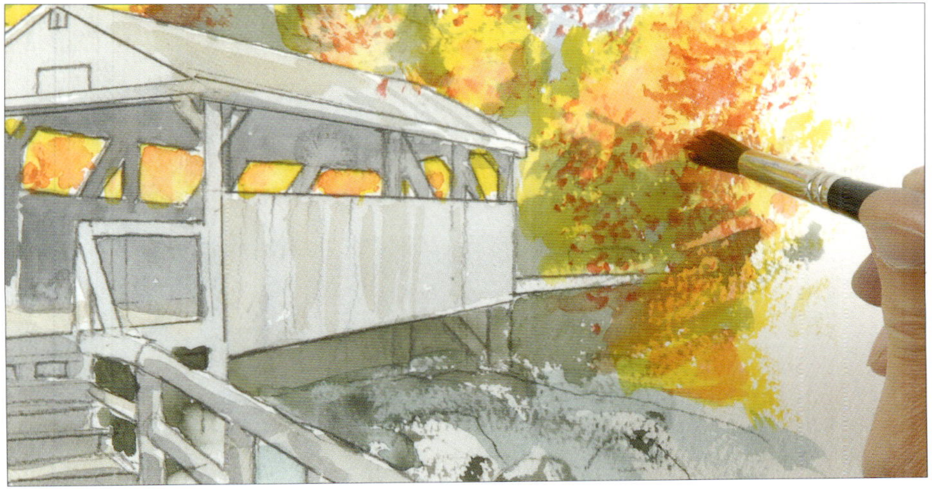

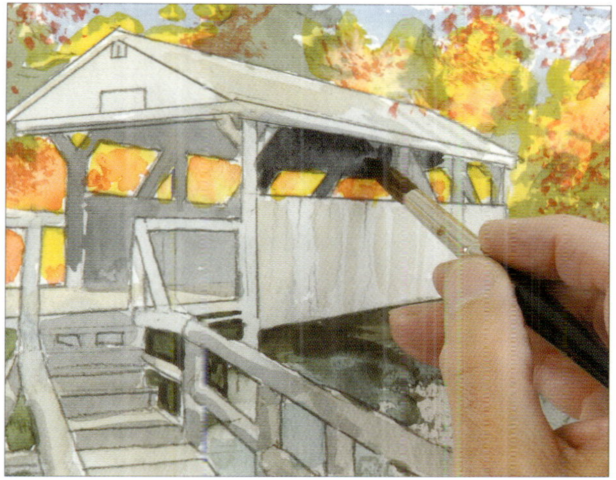

**19** Use a strong mix of neutral tint with a touch of Hooker's green to darken the deepest shadows—under the bridge and under the roof.

**20** With the fine point of the No.10 brush, use your neutral tint and Hooker's green wash to define the gaps in the steps.

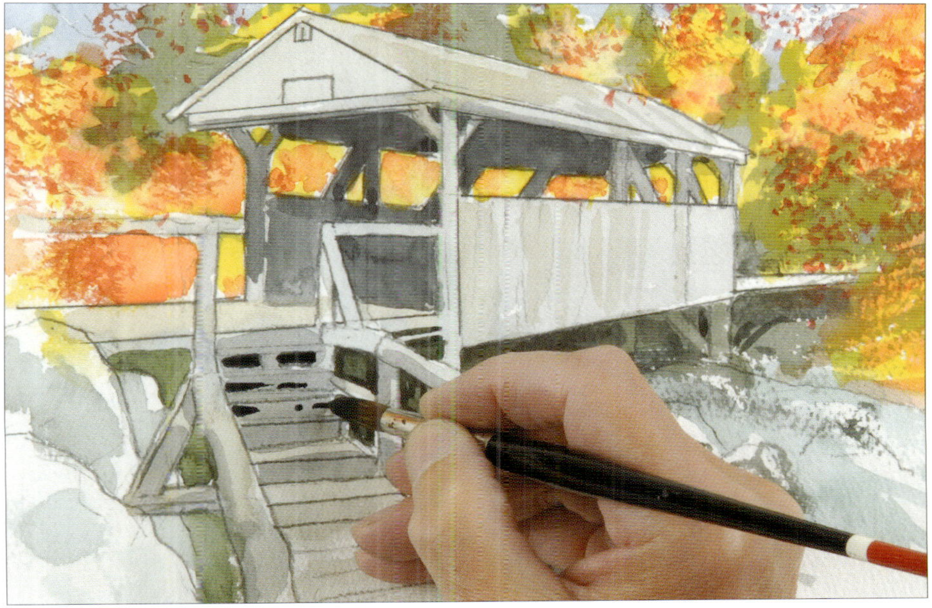

## CARING FOR YOUR BRUSHES

**If you buy a good range of brushes and take care of them as you use them, they should last you a lifetime. Just follow these few tips below:**

**Rinse your brushes in plenty of clean water after painting. From time to time, squeeze a little washing up liquid or rub a small amount soft soap onto your fingers and roll the brush between your forefinger and thumb where the hairs meet the ferrule. This will prevent paint building up under the ferrule, allowing the hairs to return to their proper shape.**

**Don't leave brushes standing in your water jar with the bristles facing down. This will cause the points to curl round and, although they usually straighten after a while, they are difficult to use when the hairs are curved. Don't discard brushes if they lose their point completely—they can be useful as wash brushes.**

**When carrying your brushes prevent the hairs from being damaged by using a brush case, which is simply a cylindrical metal tube with a lid, or you can fix your brushes with elastic bands to a stiff piece of cardboard.**

**If the handle of a favorite brush becomes loose, scratch off the varnish and float the brush in water overnight. With luck, the wood will expand and the handle will tighten again. You may have to repeat this as the wood dries. If this does not work, gently hammer the point of a nail in several places round the neck of the ferrule. This pushes a burr of metal into the wooden handle and sometimes cures the movement.**

No colors can be applied without mixing them first with water, and for this you need a palette. These are plastic or ceramic and come in a variety of shapes and sizes—plastic versions are more suitable for transporting because they are light and less breakable. Larger versions are more useful when mixing lots of paint, or when working with other materials, such as large sponges.

As well as applying color, effects can also be created by 'masking' an area of paper to stop paint reaching it, or removing paint to create highlights. Use masking fluid or a wax candle for masking, and cotton buds for lifting off small areas of paint. For lifting off larger areas, use kitchen towel. You can also work designs into wet paint using the handle of a brush, but to do this add gum arabic to the paint to slow down the drying process.

Use cotton buds on wet paint to lift off color and create lighter spots or highlights. Also use them on larger areas by rolling the bud over the wet wash.

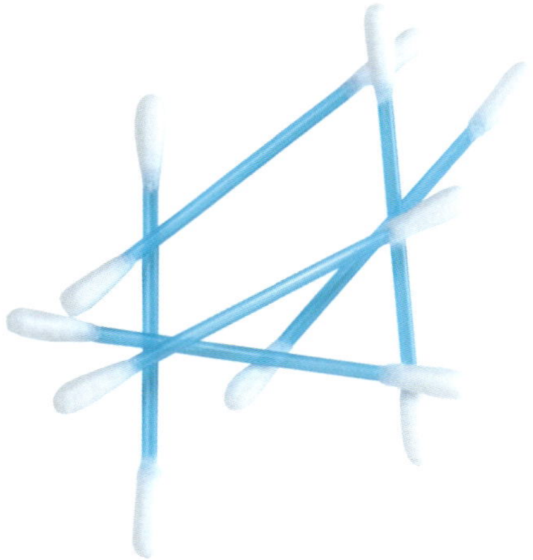

### other accessories

When you want to change your colors, you will need to rinse your brush. A simple jam jar filled with water will do, though a collapsible water pot works best outdoors.

Watercolors take time to dry. This can make applying one wash over another very time consuming. Speed up the process with a hairdryer, but be careful not to blow unwanted paint into other areas of your work.

Last, make sure that your workspace is adequately lit. This will not only avoid eyestrain, but allow you to see colors as they really are. Either sit by a window, or use a daylight simulation bulb in a desk lamp—it can be very disheartening to see your work change color in 'real' light.

The range of palettes is enormous, both in ceramic and plastic. The ceramic versions are heavier and more prone to breakage but have the advantage that they do not stain—the plastic ones eventually retain some color in their surface.

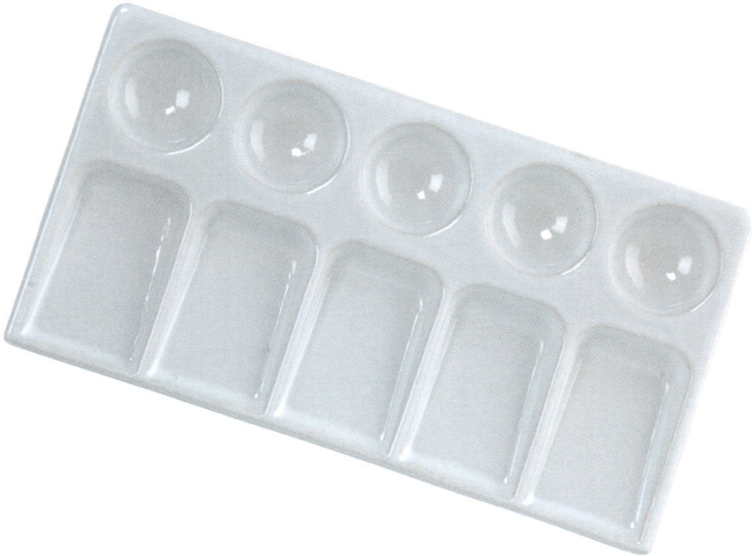

**21** Now add some branches with the 2B pencil. The curling branches will contrast with the straight sides of the bridge and enliven the plain side of the shelter. Try to let the pencil line taper off toward the end of each branch.

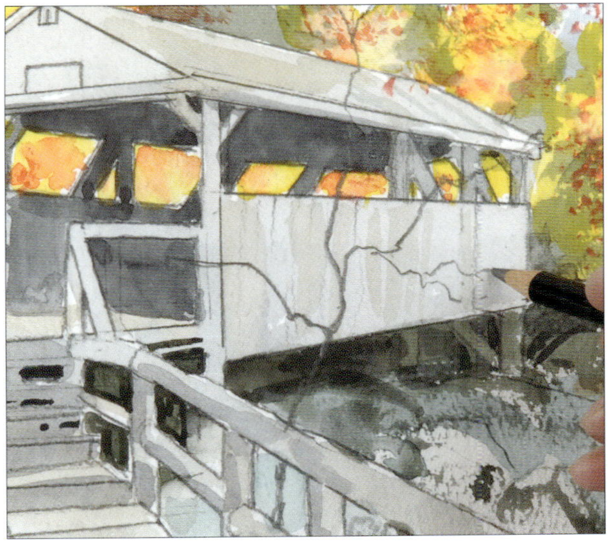

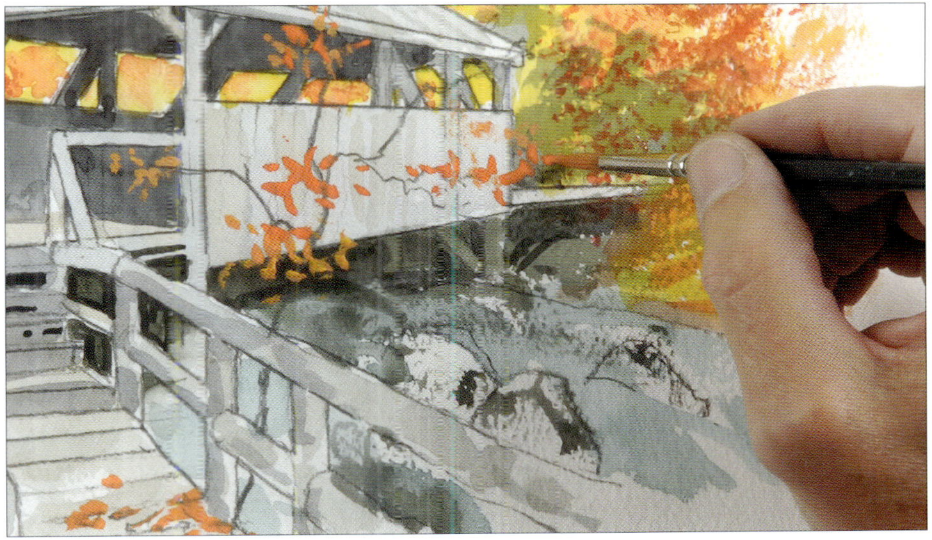

**22** Now add some foliage on the branches using the No.2 brush and a dry mix of orange and a touch of white. The white makes the paint opaque so it stands out against the gray tones. Be careful, though, if you add too much white you will get pink, not orange.

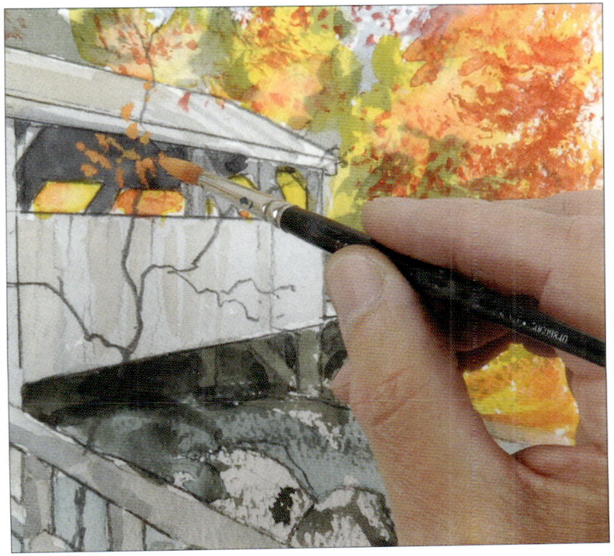

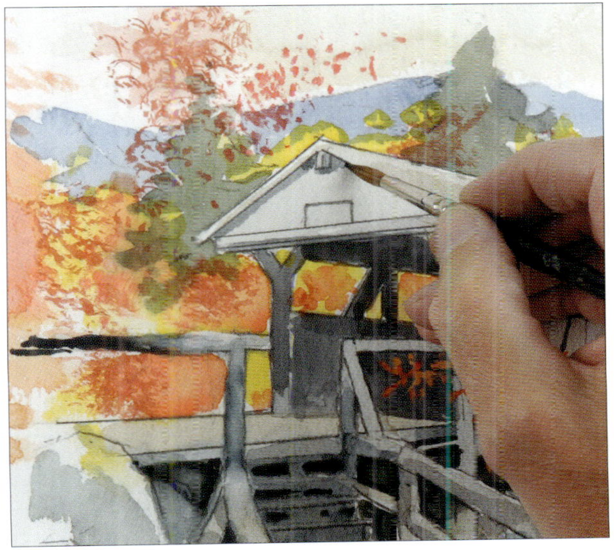

**23** Continue adding leaves along the length of the branch. Simply dab on each leaf with the point of the No.2 brush.

**24** Now with your neutral mix, add the cast shadows under the overhanging eaves. These shadows are telling; they help the viewer perceive the three-dimensional form of the bridge, rather than flat shapes of tone and color.

# materials and equipment / **brushes and sponges**

Over the centuries, almost every kind of hair, bristle, and fiber has been used to make brushes. However, it is generally recognized that the tail hair of the sable (a member of the weasel family) is the best for watercolor brushes. These hairs are fine but tough, designed by nature to stand abrasion on rocks and ice. The Kolinsky variety is regarded as the very best. Unsurprisingly, sable brushes are expensive.

Synthetic fibers are the main alternative to sable and have now reached a very high standard, but there are some important differences. Synthetic fibers (or 'filaments') are made by stretching nylon fibers to breaking point while they are still viscous. This means that the tips of the fibers are the weakest parts, making them inclined to wear out. By contrast, sable is toughest and most resilient at the tip. Also, being hair, it has a scaly surface, which helps the brush to hold more liquid. The advantage of synthetic brushes is their comparatively low price. For this reason, only consider buying two small sable brushes to start.

There are three main types of brush, all named after their shapes—round or pointed (a general-use brush), flat (usually a large brush for washes), and 'mop' (a large, round brush, again for washes). Brush sizes are usually denoted by a measurement or by a number. Large wash brushes, designed to apply lots of color quickly to paper, are often measured in inches, such as ¼in or 1in. Smaller brushes are often numbered, with size 14 being among the largest and size 0 among the smallest. A small, flat hog hair brush, more usually associated with oil painting, is handy for scrubbing out color.

Brushes are not the only way to apply color to the page. Natural sponge is a great way to create "accidental" patterns, and is especially useful for creating free, detailed areas of foliage, which could not be created by painting individual leaves. Have a few different sizes ready—larger sponges create different textures than smaller ones.

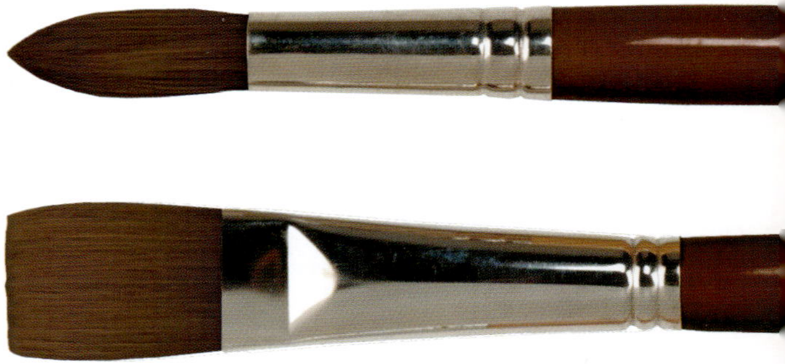

**ABOVE** In addition to your choice of two round brushes, select a large, round "mop" brush (top) and two large, flat brushes (bottom). All are used for washes.

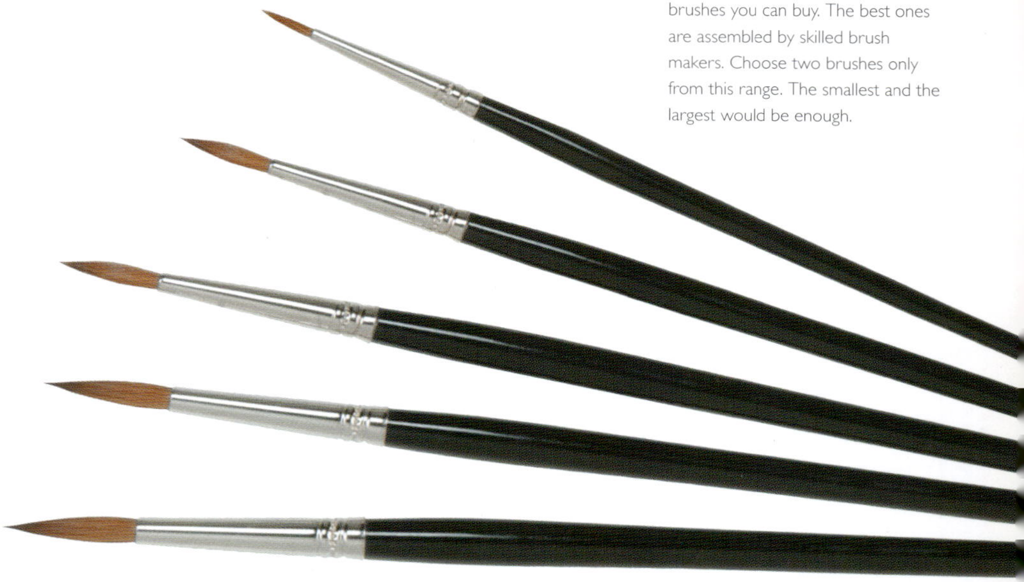

**BELOW** Pointed sables are the finest brushes you can buy. The best ones are assembled by skilled brush makers. Choose two brushes only from this range. The smallest and the largest would be enough.

**BELOW** Flat, hog hair brushes like the ones on the left are very useful. These brushes are not used for applying watercolors, but for scrubbing out areas where the paint is too dark. Use a synthetic brush for this purpose.

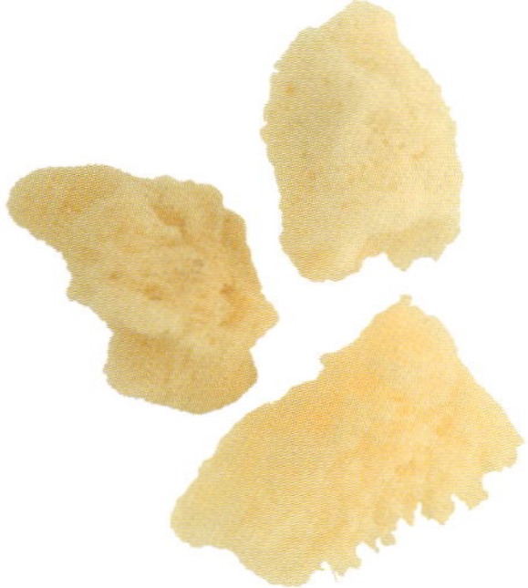

**LEFT** Natural sponges are best for making accidental textures on your work, such as leaves on trees. Larger sponges have coarser textures than smaller ones, so try to have several different sizes to produce several different results.

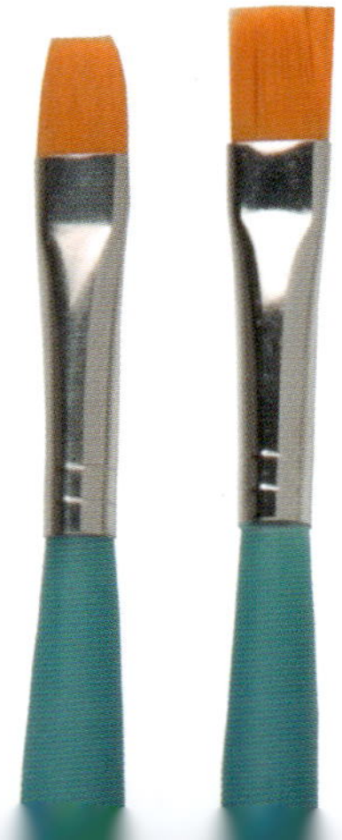

25 Add cast shadows under—and to the right of—the sign on the front of the roof. Now dampen the No.10 brush and soften any harsh edges in the background foliage.

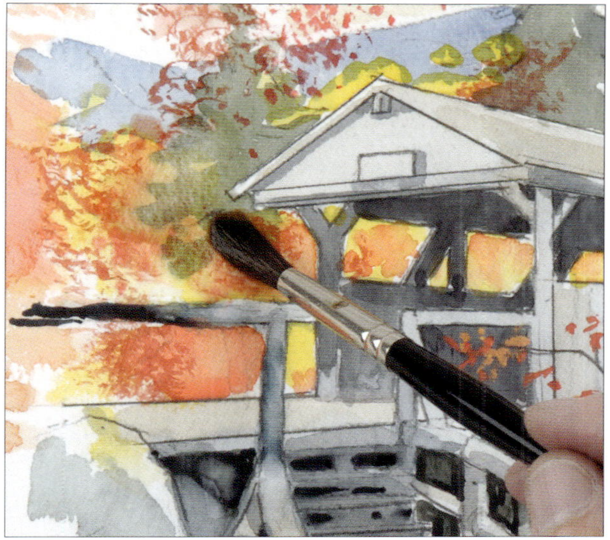

26 Build up the warm color and weathered texture of the roof using a weak wash of sepia and the No.2 brush. Also use the sepia wash to vary the color on the road and footbridge.

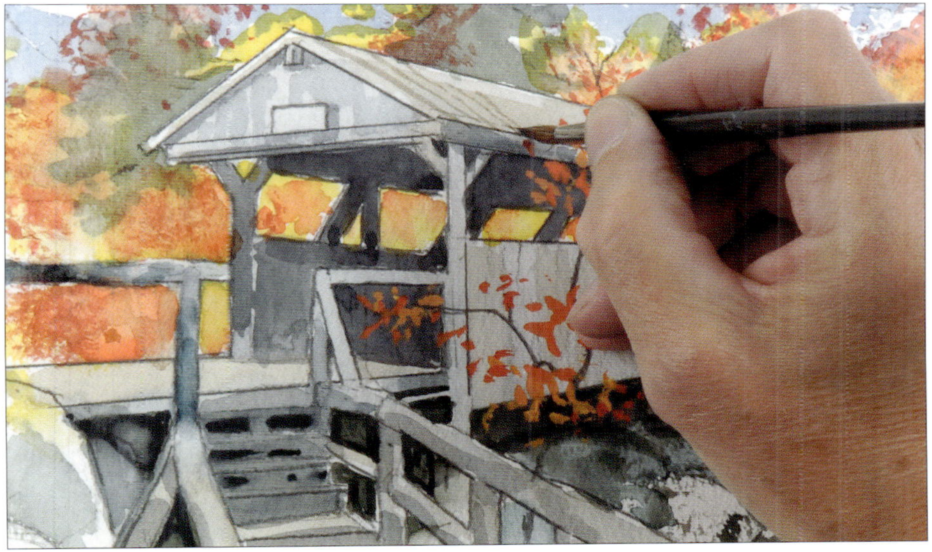

27 To give an impression of pale tree trunks, dampen the tip of the No.2 brush and lift out paint with long, thin brushstrokes. Also put in one or two silver birch trunks with white and some darker trunks with neutral tint and raw sienna. Try to "lose" and "find" each brushstroke so each trunk looks as if it is partly concealed by foliage.

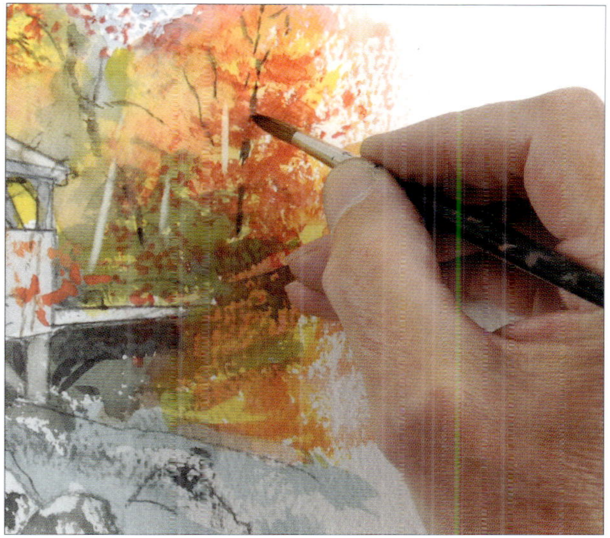

28 Use the 2B pencil to strengthen the outlines of the railings. This will help lead the eye into the painting. Also outline some of the leaves on the branch. Finally, use the orange and white mix to add a few leaves on the footbridge.

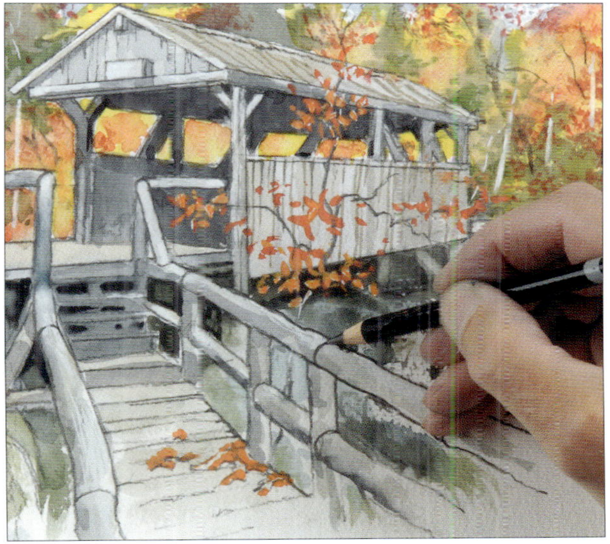

# materials and equipment / **paints**

One of the great attractions of watercolor painting is that the materials required are very simple. Buy a brush, a small selection of colors, a palette, and some paper and you are ready—all you need to do is add water! You can work almost anywhere with watercolors and have great fun experimenting with different combinations of brushes, paints, and paper.

## watercolors in pans

Watercolors are available in pans and tubes. Pans consist of small plastic trays into which paint has been squeezed and dried—the pigment dissolves when touched with a wet brush. You can buy half pans or larger whole pans, both of which slot into tailor-made boxes. Pans are convenient—the color is instantly visible and if you keep the pans in a box they are always in the same position. They are also economical as you only take a little paint at a time. However, it can be difficult to produce large amounts of paint quickly for large pictures. If this presents a problem, use whole pans and a wide, flat brush.

## watercolors in tubes

The paint in tubes is the same as in pans but is mixed with gum arabic and glycerine to make it liquid. Most manufacturers sell the same color range in both tubes and pans. Tubes give a large amount of color quickly, which is ideal when you have large areas of paper to cover. If you squeeze out more paint than you need on your palette, you can often use it at your next painting session. However, you cannot see the true color of the paint until you open the tube, and you have to remove and replace lids, which can interrupt your work flow.

## paint boxes

Most paint manufacturers produce box sets, from pocket-sized versions with pan colors (right/below) to large studio sets containing both pans and tubes. Boxes often work out less expensive than buying colors separately and the selections contained in them are usually sensible. If your favorite color is missing, you can easily insert it in place of one you use less often. If you intend to sketch outdoors, look for a box that has a handy thumbhole or a ring underneath.

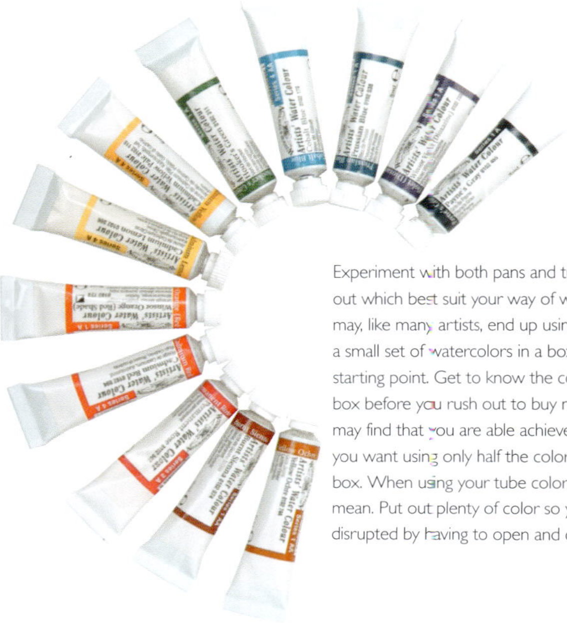

Experiment with both pans and tubes to find out which best suit your way of working. You may, like many artists, end up using both. Buying a small set of watercolors in a box is good starting point. Get to know the colors in the box before you rush out to buy new ones. You may find that you are able achieve the results you want using only half the colors in your first box. When using your tube colors, do not be mean. Put out plenty of color so you are not disrupted by having to open and close tubes.

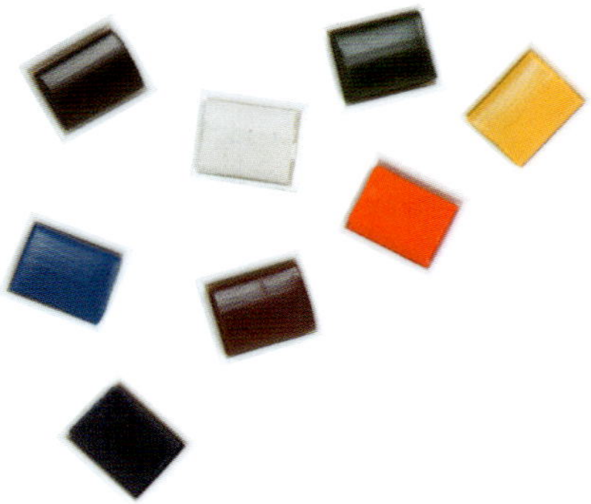

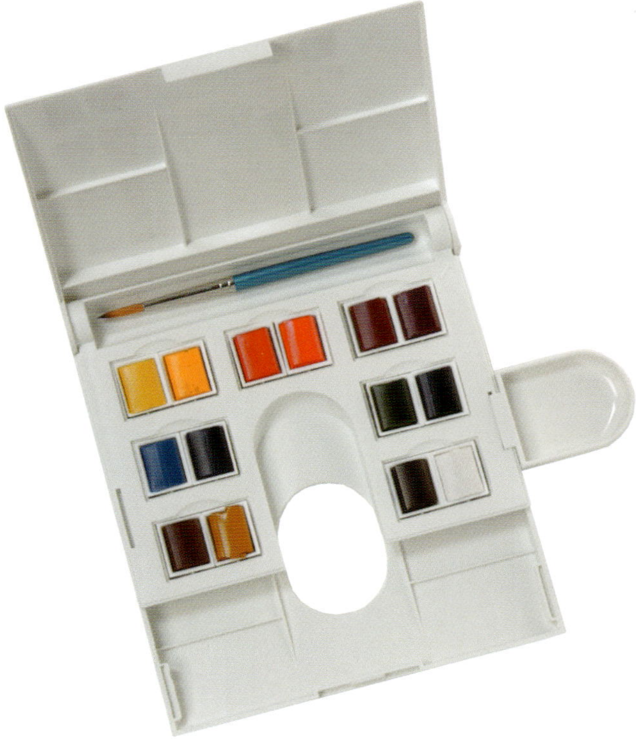

# Summary of projects

## PROJECT 1: BREAKING WAVES

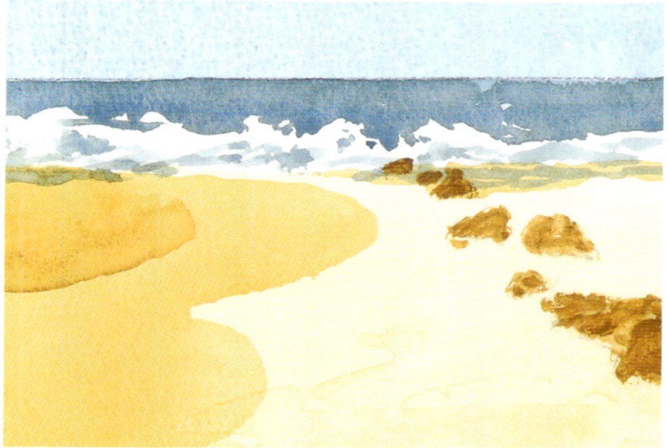

### MATERIALS

- Drawing board, Watercolor paper
- Watercolor palette
- Watercolors: cerulean blue, ultramarine blue, viridian, Payne's gray, raw sienna, and raw umber
- No.10 round brush, Jar of water
- HB pencil, Ruler, Eraser
- Kitchen towel, Tracing paper

The bright painting style in this project perfectly captures a summer's day at the beach. Between the sunny yellows of the sand and the bold blue of the sea, the waves crash on the shore. Find out how to create lively waves like this by leaving areas of the watercolor paper unpainted.

## PROJECT 2: STILL-LIFE WITH GOURDS

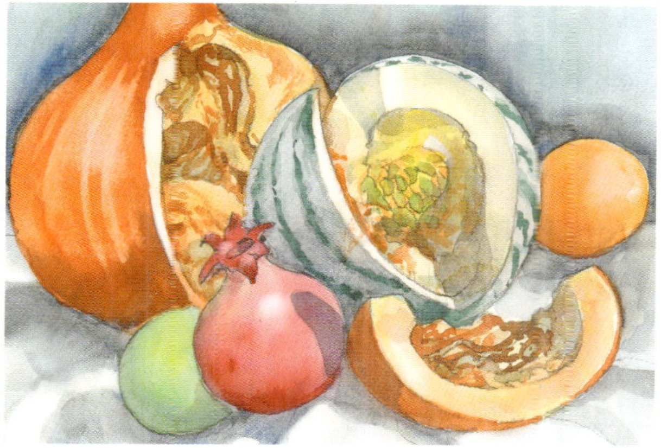

### MATERIALS

- Drawing board, Thick watercolor paper
- Watercolor palette
- Watercolors: ultramarine blue, burnt sienna, cadmium yellow, lemon yellow, cadmium orange, cadmium red, yellow ocher, neutral tint, viridian
- Brushes: No.12 round, 1-inch flat, Jar of water
- 2B pencil, Eraser, Kitchen towel

This vibrant still-life is full of exciting contrasts. The bold colors of the fruit leap forward against the subtle shadows in the tablecloth and the smooth, rounded forms work well against the detailed texture of the flesh and pips. This project shows you how to create a pleasing a composition, alive with vivid hues and intricate pencil work.

## PROJECT 3: WOODLAND SUN

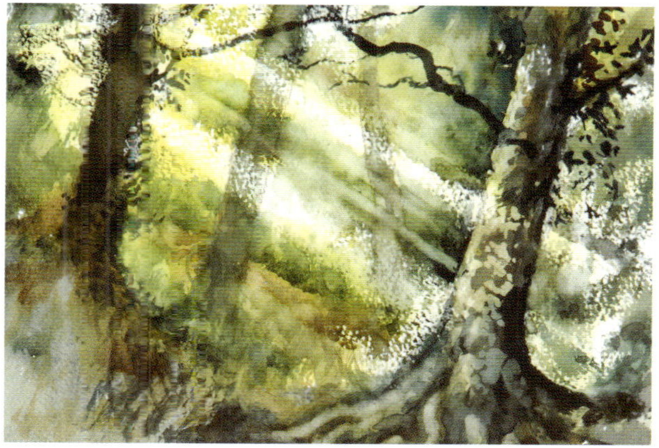

### MATERIALS

- Drawing board, Thick rough or semi-rough watercolor paper
- Watercolor palette
- Watercolors: cadmium yellow light, ultramarine blue, viridian, burnt sienna
- Brushes: No. 8, No. 12, No. 1, Jar of water
- 2B pencil, White candle, Craft knife

To capture a scene like this, try to paint in a free, uninhibited manner. Don't fuss over details. Instead let one color run into another and apply the paint quickly in pleasing patterns. Remember, leaves and branches move in the breeze, so the shadows and highlights constantly shift and the background comes in and out of view. Painting in a loose style will imitate this effect and, more importantly, add life to your painting.

# introduction

What the great artists showed is that successful watercolor painting often depends as much on the effects created by your color choice as on composition, which is where an understanding of how color works comes in.

Look at the color wheel (right) to see how colors are grouped. For each picture you paint, you will need a watercolor to represent each of the primary colors so that by mixing them, you can obtain all the secondary colors. The primary colors you choose should be determined by the scene you wish to paint. For example, if you are painting cool clear skies and distant hills, choose cobalt blue to represent blue in the color wheel; permanent rose to represent red; and cadmium lemon to represent yellow. All three colors are cool, enabling you to maintain a consistently cool palette—no clashing 'hot' colors will appear. Likewise, when painting a warm scene, use a warm blue, red, and yellow for your primaries. This idea, along with using complementary colors, which appear opposite each other on the color wheel and produce harmonious contrasts, will help you keep your colors balanced.

A good exercise is to make your own color wheels for warm and cool colors. Draw several circles 4in (10cm) in diameter and divide each circle into six pie slices. Paint your three primaries in alternate slices and then mix them: red with yellow for orange, blue with yellow for green, and blue with red for purple. Place these secondary colors in between the primaries and you will see exactly which ones work out well for your picture. Keep this worksheet as a reference palette.

**taking style cues**

Look at all artists' work, old and new, for ideas and inspiration. Research as many examples as you can, learning each artist's methods and techniques. This does not mean that you should try to produce exact copies of their work, but by your review you will develop your own knowledge and taste.

This book goes hand-in-hand with your own research by providing a wealth of instruction on just what can be achieved with watercolors. Highly accessible, practical, and instructional, what you will gain from it in technical skill will give you the competence that leads to confidence. It is this confidence that will enable you to express your thoughts in paint—it is easy to forget in the struggle to master materials that the real aim of painting is the expression of ourselves. Good technique and practical skill make this expression easier.

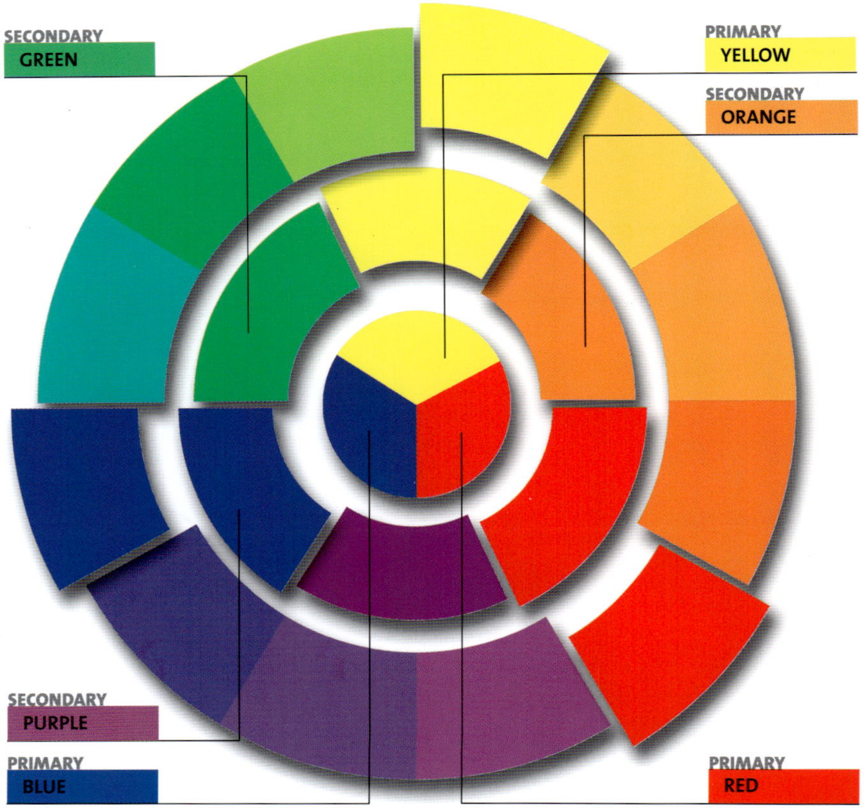


The color wheel is a great reference for artists. The three colors in the center are the primary colors. Primary colors are the ones that cannot be obtained by mixing other colors together. The middle ring shows the colors that are created when you mix two of the primaries. Red and yellow make orange; blue and yellow make green; blue and red make purple. These are called secondary colors, and show the colors you can expect to create when you mix primary watercolors in your palette. All colors can, in theory, be created by mixing varying amounts of the primaries. The outer ring breaks down the secondary colors further into 12 shades.

## PROJECT 4: RIVER BOATS

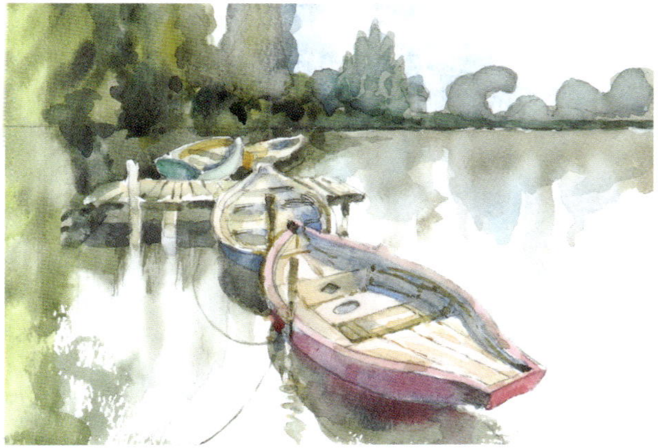

### MATERIALS

Drawing board, Watercolor paper

Watercolor palette

Watercolors: ultramarine blue, viridian, burnt sienna, Payne's gray, permanent rose, cadmium yellow

Brushes: No.10 round, rigger brush, Jar of water

HB pencil, Ruler, Eraser

Tracing paper

This scene has a wonderful sense of stillness and tranquillity. The brightly colored boats lead the eye into the calm of a river, where a light mist hovers above the gently moving water. Discover how to create this impression of stillness by using a wet-in-wet technique to paint both the water and the trees beyond.

## PROJECT 5: STILL-LIFE WITH ROSES

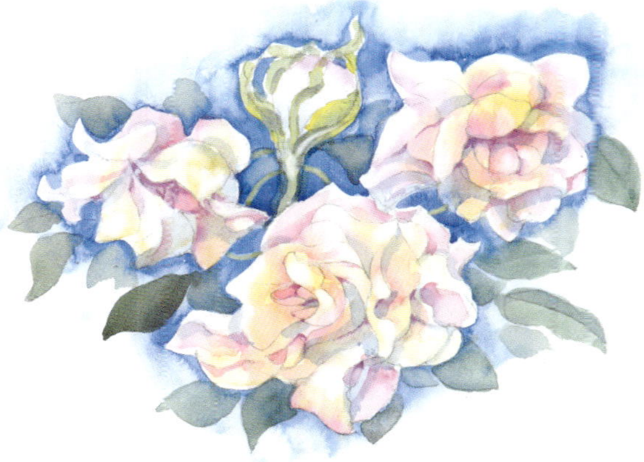

### MATERIALS

Drawing board, Thick watercolor paper

Watercolor palette

Watercolors: cadmium yellow, permanent rose, ultramarine blue, lemon yellow, viridian, burnt sienna

Brushes: No.12 and No.3 round and No.5 flat

Jar of water

B pencil, Eraser

This painting has a wonderfully exciting visual rhythm—the eye is kept on the move by the gracefully curving petals and leaves of the open flowers, while the closed rose provides an important focal point in the center of the composition. Although the picture looks complicated, it's really quite easy to paint. Do not worry about capturing the shape of each petal perfectly. Instead try to render the series of colors and tones that each petal is composed of.

## PROJECT 6: VERMONT FOOTBRIDGE

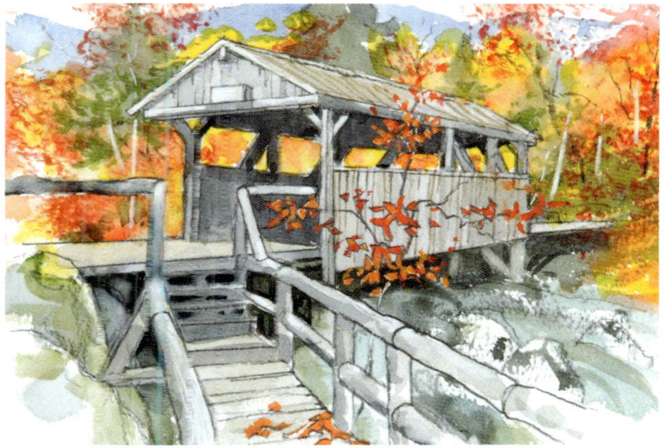

### MATERIALS

Drawing board, Watercolor paper

Watercolor palette

Watercolors: cobalt blue, violet, lemon yellow, ultramarine blue, neutral tint, Prussian blue, yellow ocher, Hooker's green, phthalo turquoise, raw sienna, cadmium yellow, orange, cadmium red, burnt sienna, white, sepia

Brushes: No.10 and No.02, Jar of water

B pencil, Ruler, Eraser, Sponge

The footbridge and the river in this scene lead the eye onto a charming old road bridge and a vibrant range of fall colors. Find out how to capture such fall splendor using a variety of easy-to-learn techniques—including working the paint wet-in-wet, applying paint with a sponge, and stippling with the end of the brush.

Published in the United States in 2010
by Tangent Publications
an imprint of
The Axis Media Group
8c Accommodation Road
London NW11 8ED

www.axispublishing.co.uk

Creative Director: Siân Keogh
Editor: Matthew Rake
Designer: Sean Keogh
Production: Bili Books



ISBN: 978-1-904707-87-5

9 8 7 6 5 4 3 2 1

Printed and bound in China

# contents

**John Barber** is a professional artist whose work has been published by many leading publishers worldwide. His interest in art and design have led to diverse commissions, including model-making for film and TV, sculpture, and stained-glass design, in addition to painting. He has lectured widely on Turner and Rembrandt, and regularly teaches painting courses in Suffolk, England.

# PAINTING WITH WATERCOLOR

JOHN BARBER

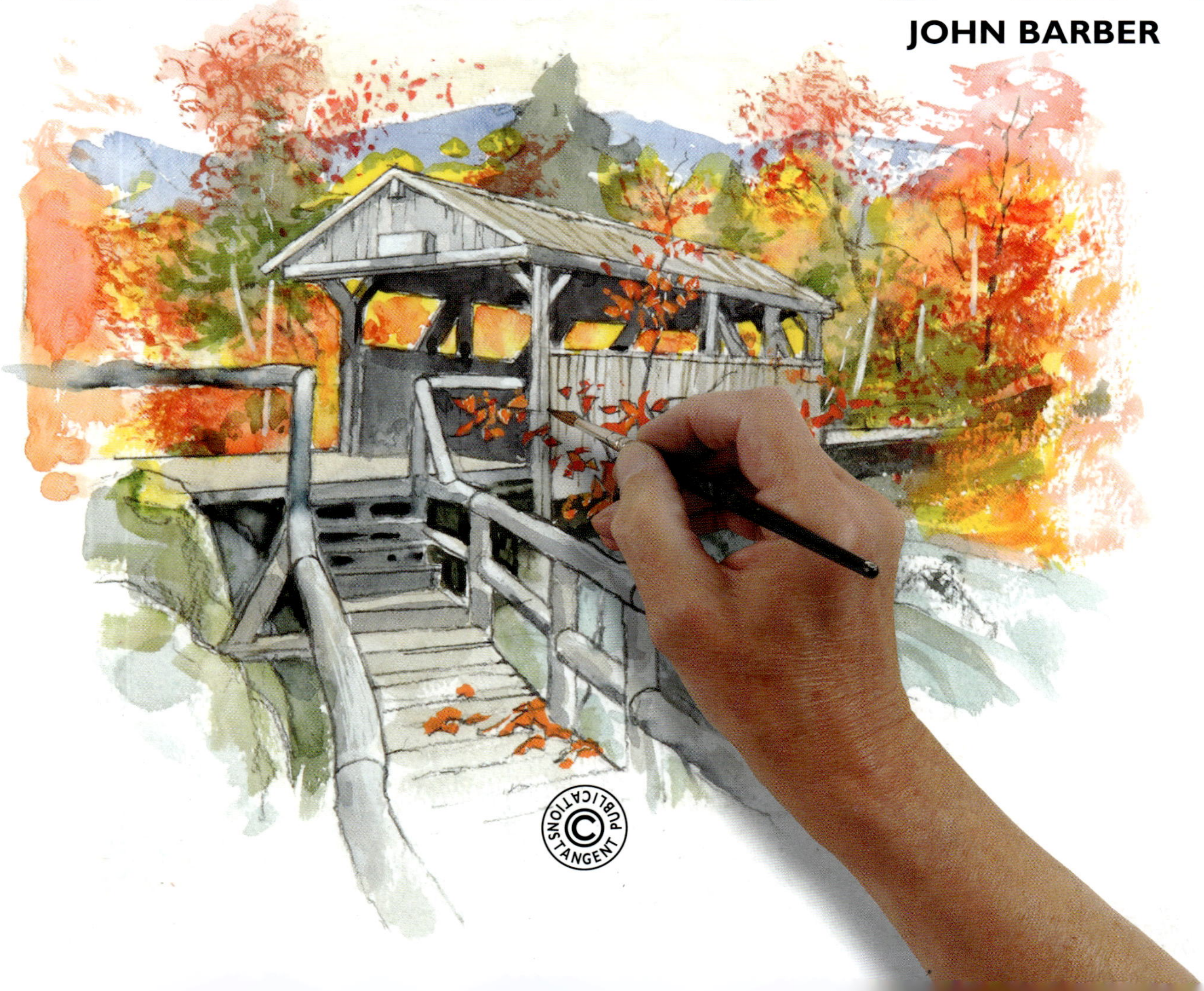

TANGENT PUBLICATIONS